Practical Newspaper Reporting

Titles in the series

Series editor: F.W. Hodgson

Broadcast Journalism   Andrew Boyd
The Computerized Newspaper   Paul Williams
Creative Newspaper Design   Vic Giles and F.W. Hodgson
Freelance Journalist   Christopher Dobson
Journalism Workbook   Brendan Hennessy and F.W. Hodgson
A Journalist's Guide to Sources   David Spark
Law and the Media   Tom Crone
Magazine Journalism Today   Anthony Davis
Modern Newspaper Practice   F.W. Hodgson
Newspaper Language   Nicholas Bagnall
Picture Editing   Tom Ang
Practical Newspaper Reporting   Geoffrey Harris and David Spark
Practical Photojournalism   Martin Keene
Printing: A Guide to Systems and Their Uses   W.R. Durrant
Subediting   F.W. Hodgson
Writing Feature Articles   Brendan Hennessy

Practical Newspaper Reporting

Third edition

Geoffrey Harris and David Spark

Edited, with additional material, by F. W. Hodgson

Focal Press

Focal Press
An imprint of Butterworth-Heinemann
Linacre House, Jordan Hill, Oxford OX2 8DP
225 Wildwood Avenue, Woburn MA 01801-2041
A division of Reed Educational and Professional Publishing Ltd

℞ A member of the Reed Elsevier plc group

OXFORD   AUCKLAND   BOSTON
JOHANNESBURG   MELBOURNE   NEW DELHI

First published 1966
Second edition 1993
Reprinted 1994, 1996
Third edition 1997
Reprinted 1998, 2000
Transferred to digital printing 2001

© Geoffrey Harris, F. W. Hodgson, David Spark 1993

British Library Cataloguing in Publication Data
Harris, Geoffrey
    Practical Newspaper Reporting
    1. Reporters and reporting
    I. Title   II. Spark, David   III. Hodgson, F. W.
    070.4

Library of Congress Cataloguing in Publication Data
A catalogue record for this book is available from the Library of Congress

ISBN 0 240 51511 0

For information on all Focal Press publications
visit our website at www.focalpress.com

Printed in Great Britain by Antony Rowe Ltd, Eastbourne

CONTENTS

List of illustrations   ix

Acknowledgements   xi

1   What is news?   **1**
Assessing news value – Good news and bad – Readership –
News ideas

2   Gathering the news   **7**
The news room – Calls and contacts – Tip-offs – Reading
newspapers – Chasing the facts – Tools of the job –
Taking notes – Making inquiries – Dealing with people –
Being fair – Being thorough – Who to ask and where to look

3   Picture ideas   **21**
Working with a photographer – What makes a picture? –
Colour

4   District reporting   **26**
What makes a reporter – Local geography – Beyond your
district – Getting to grips – Nursing your contacts –
Organizations – People in the know – The local angle –
Diary jobs

5   Interviewing   **37**
Preparation – Background – Establishing confidence –
Reluctant people – Using your notebook – Let them talk –
The bell that rings – Coaxing answers – Checking back –

Telephone interviews – Controversial interviews – Finding
the hidden story – The second interview – Where interviews
can fail – Attempts to vet copy

6 News writing   **53**
Where to begin – What is new? – Starting with a quote –
Opening sentence – Stick to the facts – Simple and precise –
Grabbing the reader – Order of facts – Explanations –
Helping the reader – Changing subjects – Handling
quotations – The right length – Facts and figures – Entering
your text – Presentation – When time is short – Read it
through – Complaints – Good taste – A note on short reports

7 Newspaper language   **77**
The problem with codes – Sentence length – The right word –
Correct English – Words and idioms – Slang and contractions –
Technical language – Foreign words – Double meanings –
The right word order – Variety and rhythm – Numbers –
Political correctness – Loaded words – Worn phrases –
References

8 Reporting the courts   **92**
1 Court structure – Magistrates' courts – Crown courts – High
Court – County courts – Coroners' courts – Consistory courts –
Courts-martial – Tribunals and inquiries – **2 How to write up
court cases** – Notes – Who, where and what? – Court feature
articles – **3 Privilege** – **4 Restrictions on reporting** –
Committals for trial, remand hearings and adjournments –
Contempt of court – Crime and accident stories – Young
offenders courts – Family proceedings – Divorce courts –
Rape and indecency – Code of Practice – **5 The probation
service** – **6 The police** – Useful telephone numbers

9 Reporting local government   **124**
The local councillor – Council meetings – Writing it up – The
council officer – Radical change – The stories to look for

10 Politics   **134**
Independents – Electioneering – Election procedure – Party
organization

11 Business and industry   **145**
Knowing the firms – Trades councils – Disputes – Shop

stewards – The employers – Company publications –
Employment and industry services – Winning their confidence

12 Reporting religions   155
Weddings – Priests and ministers – Islam – Hinduism and
Sikhism – Judaism – References – Useful telephone numbers

13 Some thoughts on sportswriting   165
Going to a match – Writing your report – Words and
openings – Colour and variety – Vocabulary – Midweek
sportswriting – Sporting reference books

14 Summarizing   177
The short report – The long report – Balance sheets

15 Feature writing   183
Finding ideas – Illustrations – Interviews – Behind the facts –
Comment – Good beginnings – Building the text – Some
writing tips – A note on leaders

16 Arts reviewing   192
Shaping your review – Amateur theatre – Professional theatre
– Theatre: basic background – Drama festivals – Music –
Singing – Pop, folk and jazz – Films – Television – Books

17 Newspaper structure   211
Who does what – Copy input – What happens to your
story – Page production – Press and post-press – Conclusion

18 Looking things up   219
The arts – Aviation – The Bible – The churches – English
language – Geography – History – Industry and companies –
Local government – Local information – National affairs and
information – Parliament – People – Press and radio – The
services – Sport – World affairs

19 A note on ethics   224
Press complaints – Accountability – Informants – People in
the news – Journalists and their readers – Further reading

20 Careers in journalism   230
The NCTJ – In-house training – NVQs – Journalism degrees –
Other courses

Appendix 1   Investigative reporting   235

Appendix 2   Code of Practice for the Press   239

Index   245

ILLUSTRATIONS

Figure 2.1 The computerized news room with its bank of VDUs –   8
a busy corner of the editorial floor at *The Northern Echo's* office

Figure 3.1 What makes a picture? In this example the cleverly   24
caught expression on the face of former Foreign Secretary
Douglas Hurd livens up a political occasion. It was taken by
Hull Daily Mail photographer Richard Walker using a long
telephoto lens near 10 Downing Street, and it won for him a
Merit Award in the Fuji European Press Awards. Richard
also won the £1000 BT award in the NCTJ National Certificate
examination

Figure 5.1 Pictures and interviews play their part in the   51
presentation of an important news story – an example from *The
Independent*

Figure 6.1 Another edition deadline approaches – a reporter keys   72
in a court story in the news room at the *Manchester Evening News*

Figure 13.1 How a good picture can enhance a sporting occasion –   168
another award-winning effort from young *Hull Daily Mail*
photographer Richard Walker showing how the Great Britain
Rugby League team celebrated a try against Australia at
Manchester

Figure 17.1 Who does what? This chain-of-command diagram   212
shows the set-up in the editorial and advertising departments of
an average sized newspaper

Figure 17.2 Where the stories come from – the news room as the   213
heart of the news-gathering operation

Figure 17.3 A sub-editor calls up a story – note the extra row of   215
command and function keys at the top of this editing keyboard

Figure 17.4 The cut-and-paste method – a compositor makes up   217
a page using typeset bromides of stories. Note the page layout
and rolls of stick-on tape rules

ACKNOWLEDGEMENTS

I am indebted to the editor of *The Northern Echo* for permission to use the picture on page 8; the editor of the *Hull Daily Mail* and photographer Richard Walker for pictures on pages 24 and 168; the editor of the *Manchester Evening News* for the picture on page 72 and to News Group Newspapers for the use of the two photographs on pages 215 and 217. I am grateful to Keith Hall, former Chief Executive of the National Council for the Training of Journalists, and to Rob Selwood, his successor, for allowing me to take up their time with my questions. Once again I have been delighted to work with Geoffrey Harris and David Spark on bringing out this third edition of their classic work.

F. W. Hodgson
Editor
Butterworth-Heinemann Media Series

1 WHAT IS NEWS?

Suppose you had the task of planning a newspaper and you had before you ten reports which began in the following ways:

1 The Prime Minister has announced the appointment of a new body to regulate company takeovers.
2 Fifteen people have been killed in a battle in Congo.
3 Bournemouth used 500 million cubic feet of gas last year.
4 Maureen Johnson, aged 17, was sitting in her bath when she heard a hammering on the door. 'What's up?' she shouted. 'The house is on fire,' came the reply.
5 The chief executive's exit has hit Toad shares.
6 The Mayor said yesterday that the Government's new housing policy might or might not be good for the town.
7 The chairman of the Finance Committee and a 21-year-old shopgirl have disappeared from their homes. Both have left letters to say they have gone together to Biarritz.
8 A 50-year-old home carer will meet the Duke of Edinburgh during his visit to Blanktown next week.
9 Three memorable goals enabled Blanktown United to reach the semi-final of the FA Cup last night.
10 Five hundred of the world's highest-paid scientists have gathered in Oxford to discuss elementary particles.

How would you assess the news value of these reports? Which would you use and which would you reject?

This is really, of course, an editor's or chief sub-editor's task, but a reporter should also be able to recognize what is news for the newspaper; to spot which aspects of an assignment are the ones to be given prominence in writing the story; to understand why a particular job is being covered.

What is it that makes an event or a set of facts news – and what is it about one news idea that gives it a better rating than another? How do you assess news value?

Let us look again at the stories given above. You will notice, when you start to sort them, that a lot depends on the type and readership of the paper you work for. If yours is a country weekly you would reject the Congo story and stress the local football club's success, the chairman's elopement and the home carer story. Unless your weekly was very staid you would find a prominent position, too, for Maureen Johnson's interrupted bath. A proportion of the non-football readers would identify with the Cup success, and many would go for the human interest in the elopement, the home carer and the bathtime story.

If you worked on a regional or national quality morning paper your choice would be different. You would give prominence to the Government's plan to regulate takeover bids. It is an important move. You would get in a paragraph or two about the battle in Congo, or several paragraphs if you were writing for a well-informed readership. If the battle were part of a well-reported crisis you might give it a much bigger show.

A national tabloid might run the elopement story, particularly if it could get a picture of the girl. It might, on a slack day, use a few paragraphs on an inside page of Maureen Johnson's bath, but the home carer's story would not rate sufficient interest outside the local area.

A provincial morning or evening paper would use these three reports prominently if they were within its circulation area. If they were not, the elopement story and maybe the bath story could be given space on a page of national news.

The Oxford elementary particles debate would probably be given coverage in the more upmarket national papers and those circulating in Oxford – and perhaps Cambridge. The Bournemouth gas report would rate a few paragraphs only in the Bournemouth paper.

The views of the Mayor would not arouse much enthusiasm among readers unless the story turned out to be more interesting than its opening. The Toad shares story was featured on several City pages. It could intrigue national papers. What on earth are Toad shares?

Assessing news value

What can we learn from this exercise? Two important things:

1 It is fairly easy to define what news is.
2 It is less easy to assess its value. Why? Because we are talking about two different things.

All ten of the stories we have looked at passed muster as news because it was the first time the information they contained was being put before the reader; they were saying something new. If what any of them was saying was not new then the story would not have been a news story, for newness is an essential quality of news.

The *Shorter Oxford Dictionary* has a useful definition for news: 'Tidings; new information of recent events; new occurrences as a subject of report or talk.'

The term 'information' is important because it is the information or knowledge of an event rather than the event itself that news is concerned with. The event might already be known to the reader but not the new information that is being presented. A single event can go on generating news in this way for days and even weeks. A secret marriage can become news years afterwards because information about it has come to light.

Many writers in trying to define what news is have got bogged down in the qualities that news stories contain. 'News is people,' says Harold Evans, former editor of *The Times*. Well, it frequently does involve people; but it can also concern legislation or an archaeological discovery, or all sorts of things.

News should be surprising; it should be dramatic; it should, said an American editor, make people say 'Gee whizz!' All useful qualities if we can find them – and editors are crying out for such qualities in their papers' stories – but a story can still be news even if it lacks them.

The crux of the matter is that to merit its place in a newspaper news should not only be news in an absolute sense of being new; it should also be the sort of news that the readers of the paper are likely to want to read – and there is an almost infinite variety of newspapers and readerships. A story's news value is the value it has to the newspaper printing it. This is why such variable answers were possible to the questions we asked about the ten examples at the beginning of this chapter.

Good news and bad

Some critics complain that newspapers prefer printing bad news to good because it sells more copies. It begs the question: what is bad news? In some developing countries, governments who want the news all to be good say that newspapers should be guided in what they print by the interests of national development. The more confident – and more courageous – journalists refuse to be bound by their government's view of the national interest. The result is that in such countries police raids and sedition charges are rife.

In Britain just about any news, good or bad by whatever yardstick one wants to apply, can get into newspapers if the context is right. One good news story regularly covered is the economic success of the Far East and of Far Eastern companies investing in Britain. Because of this a bad-news story – an anti-government strike in Korea – got a lot of coverage. It showed Korea's success to be shakier than we thought.

This backs up the finding of former BBC man John Venables (*What is News?*, Elm Publications 1993) on good and bad news that bad news is published because it is disturbing. People read newspapers to find out what may be threatening them in the big world outside. It helps to forearm them. Another ex-BBC man, John Wilson, wrote in *Understanding Journalism* (Routledge) that bad news was simply more memorable than good. We all remember our hairier and most embarrassing moments.

In a democracy the readers are the ultimate arbiters of the sort of news they want to read. If a newspaper's news content is not right for them they don't buy it. There is plenty of choice. Newspapers are the forum in which all manner of news, opinions and people compete for hearing.

Readership

In Britain there are many sorts of newspapers: tabloid dailies for readers who want to be entertained as well as informed; quality dailies with a mostly better-educated, often professional readership; specialist papers such as the *Financial Times* and the *Angling Times*; town evening papers serving big conurbations; country weeklies spreading across counties. Some papers specialize in foreign and world news. There is *The Guardian* with its big following among teachers and academics; the *Daily Mail* with its strong women's readership; papers with pronounced political leanings – some dedicated to particular parties, or even religions, and a variety of civic newspapers and free newspapers serving the interests of advertisers.

Among this wide choice it is possible to suggest a few general principles. The most important – as has been explained – is that news values for any newspaper depend upon the readers, and upon the editor's concept of what the readers will want to read and can be persuaded to read.

With general newspapers, and certainly most provincial dailies, evenings and weeklies on which journalists are likely to start their careers, it is worth assuming that a large segment of the readers, male and female, will not have had higher education. Another useful assumption is that the primary interest of readers in buying the local paper will probably be in people and the doings of people. Television interviews encourage viewers in this tendency to see every issue in personal terms. Although committees and plans and statistics are the fodder of local news and are vital channels of information, it is often the personal story which catches the reader's eye – the story of Maureen Johnson's bath or the eloping chairman.

Readers are interested in how the news affects them and their children, but they are also interested in how it affects other people. Many readily identify with people in trouble; they are intrigued by those involved in controversy, with people at the centre of great events. For instance, they might not normally want to read anything about Congo, but if a great crisis came upon the people there and was graphically described then their interest could be aroused.

News ideas

Here are some more general principles:

- In pursuing news ideas a good test is: could it appear just as well in tomorrow's papers as today's? If it can wait till tomorrow then it should give place to an idea which must be done today. Good ideas that are not pursued at once can be overtaken by events – or by a rival paper. But beware here: you may feel that an idea that seems fruitless will have to yield to one in which the facts are more certain; yet occasionally you might get an exclusive story by pursuing facts that are hard to obtain.
- Whatever the story you pursue and present to your paper, not only must it be new; it must have the best and most complete facts you can obtain and you must be able to vouch for their accuracy.
- Unexpectedness is a useful news quality. Big fires and robberies are unexpected and they concern people – two top qualities.
- Do not give an exaggerated importance to 'latest news'. Your newspaper will be happy to get in aspects of a story which are too late for its rivals. But this journalistic one-upmanship can be lost on the reader who might find what was said or done earlier more interesting or important. A story can still be worth using even if it has appeared in another paper. If the story is of interest to your paper, your readers may want to see your version – as long as it is your version in your words.
- The newness of news is enhanced if it is also the disclosure of a secret. 'A newspaper lives by disclosure,' wrote a famous editor of *The Times*, John Thaddeus Delane, after a great row with the government of the day. William Randolph Hearst spoke similarly: 'News is something which someone wants suppressed. All the rest is advertising.'
- As for importance; while this should be relative to a newspaper's readership there are events, such as the announcement of a general

election or the outbreak of war, which take precedence because they are important moments in history. Part of a journalist's task is to arouse readers' interest in things which he or she judges to be important. The position and space that stories occupy in a newspaper are reflections of a quality judgement of their importance within the pages.

In examining the techniques of newspaper reporting the model taken for the purposes of this book will be that of an average British provincial newspaper – a town evening or weekly serving a community with a wide cross-section of area and edition news plus supporting features and sport. There will be many references, however, to journalism in the wider field.

The chapters that follow will look closely at the routine of news gathering, at the variety of assignments likely to be covered by a young reporter, the use of contacts and inquiries, the handling of human interest stories, techniques of interviewing and fact checking and legal restraints on reporting.

They will also give guidance on news writing, and will examine specialisms such as the coverage of courts and councils, industrial and sports reporting and the arts.

2 GATHERING THE NEWS

Every day reporters go looking for news. Newspaper columns have a relentless appetite for it; no sooner are they filled than the process starts all over again. Round the clock. Day after day. Week after week.

News can be found anywhere in a newspaper's circulation area – and occasionally outside of it – anywhere where anything worthy of remark is happening. But it has to be organized, pursued, checked and written up in a way that makes it readable and attractive to the readers. It requires particular skills.

The news room

The heart of the news-gathering operation is the news room. Here the news editor (or chief reporter) presides over the news desk, compiling the diary of jobs, briefing reporters, monitoring the day's (or week's) coverage, checking the finished stories, liaising with the photographers, answering queries, signing expenses and briefing the editor and chief sub-editor on the progress of the operation.

Technology has changed the face of the news room of old. The reporters still have their desks there but in place of the bedlam of typewriters and telephones there is the faint hum of computer terminals, with their near-silent keyboards, and the twinkle of telephone console lights. Instead of piling up paper, news stories scroll across the VDU screens as reporters bend over their terminals.

It is a change more apparent than real. Apart from the shift to on-screen writing, the reporter's role has altered less than any other in the computerized newspaper industry. News gathering and news writing remain as they always were, the heart of a newspaper's purpose.

The news editor, who has invariably been a senior reporter, briefs reporters in varying detail on the requirements and expected length of

Figure 2.1 *The computerized news room with its bank of VDUs – a busy corner of the editorial floor at the* Northern Echo's *office*

stories to be covered from such information as is known. Many of the stories will be diary jobs – i.e. jobs entered in advance in the news-room diary. Under this heading come courts, councils, committees, tribunals, inquests, political speeches, weddings, meetings, arts events, sporting fixtures and opening ceremonies. Though the existence of the event is known in advance, what actually happens or is said or done on the day provides the news.

There are also the unexpected events – deaths, accidents, fires, robberies, strikes, weather stories, crashes, sinkings, and occasionally the odd fight or elopement. A third category of news jobs could be put together from tip-offs – i.e. information reaching the office or a reporter from contacts about potential news. Such stories might concern a variety of human situations and achievements, tales of heroism or of unfair or shady dealing. Tip-offs often provide a newspaper's more spectacular and exclusive stories. There is a fourth category of news jobs – ideas that stem from reading the papers or watching TV or simply from personal observation.

Some material for a newspaper's stories – which are still referred to as copy – can be gathered on the telephone, and a good deal of checking and preparation can be done in the news room and the office library, where cuttings of stories are filed and reference books kept. For most reporters, however, work means being out of the office ... in fact, being where the news is happening.

The news editor will expect check calls to be made by reporters from the job so that progress can be noted and briefings updated; and also that copy deadlines be kept. Reporters, even new ones, quickly become aware of these things. They will learn from experience that, no matter how well they have written a story, if it misses the edition they are in trouble. They will learn also that there is not just one deadline, but a deadline for each edition of the paper and sometimes special deadlines for particular pages.

Calls and contacts

Every newspaper employs some system of regular calls, either personal or by telephone, on known or likely news sources; for example, on the police, fire officers, hospitals, council officials, MPs, undertakers and secretaries of organizations. Parliamentary journalists check what questions have been put down for answer by ministers or attend press briefings.

Whatever your newspaper, make your network of calls as wide as time allows; apart from your attendance at courts, councils and public meetings, this might be your only contact with some important sources of original news. Since many calls will be in vain there is a limit to the time worth spending on some of them, but they should nevertheless be made courteously, whether on the phone or personally.

They are better made in person if possible. Always give your name and newspaper. Do not just say, 'Is there anything for us?' Try to give your informant a bit of help. Busy people are often hard put to remember things that happened only a few hours before.

Some weekly papers rely heavily on calls for their village and small-town items, and would be the poorer without this sort of information.

At police stations make sure the officer you speak to is authorized to give information. At sub-stations where a sergeant is in charge it is unfair to press a constable for information when the sergeant is out. At town offices be sure to call on the CID (Criminal Investigation Department) as well as on the uniformed police.

Chief constables are normally in touch with editors concerning arrangements for press inquiries. If you are not told about something you might have been told about, tell your editor. (See police section, pages 121–3.)

Calls on ministers of religion and secretaries of organizations often turn up more information about what is going to happen than what has happened. Make a note of these things.

Beyond routine calls you need contacts. These are people you see perhaps only occasionally but who are useful for information if news blows up in their direction. It may be the secretary of a trade union or voluntary organization, a director of a company, a village sub-postmistress, a garage proprietor on a lonely road.

As you do your job you will encounter people who you will recognize as potential contacts for the future. Note their names and telephone numbers. Get yourself a notebook, indexed if possible, or divided alphabetically to take names, addresses and telephone numbers as your contacts build up. It will become your most valuable asset as a reporter. When news occurs if you have the right name and number in your contact book it can save you numerous telephone calls, half an hour of time and a great deal of nervous energy.

Newspapers and reporters are well placed if they can persuade their readers and contacts that they have a part in the paper. You want people to approach you, not wait for you to approach them. A keen reader can be the source of many a story or picture.

Tip-offs

Your daily round is a source of spin-off news as well as contacts. While you are working on one news story the germ of another might appear. Perhaps at a music recital the secretary tells you that the music society is having to close for lack of support. Or in court a youth is accused of taking away a motor cycle; it is the fifth time the same machine has been taken. What has the owner to say?

Council meetings are full of unanswered questions that crop up in debate. Note any likely line of inquiry, any pearl of information dropped into the discussion.

Never spurn the person who approaches you, even if you are busy and you get a message that someone is at the front counter wanting to see you. It may be a crank (there are a few about). It may be an angry person wanting a correction, or someone with an interesting grievance; but it may also be someone with a piece of news no reporter has yet come across – perhaps the biggest story of the week.

Reading newspapers

You do not always have to depend for news ideas on other people. You can cultivate your own powers of observation. Why does that building strike you as strange? When did that notice appear? Was it known they had started work on the new factory? What is going on at this level-crossing?

A source of news ideas other than diary jobs can be the news programmes of radio and television – often a passing mention of something that is going vitally to affect your area. You must read your own newspaper, too, to know what topics are of current interest, to follow its tone and style, and to find ideas for more news.

Here are some random items from an edition of the *Lancaster Guardian*.

> Some Lancaster market traders are set to quit their stalls at the end of the financial year.

Who is leaving? What do they sell? What has gone wrong for them? Are there problems with the market and for the market?

> At Quernmore School, Year Five and Six children were set a project to look into the draft district plan and they came up with plenty of their own ideas.

What are these ideas? What the children had to say about greenfield and brownfield sites could be more interesting than the comments of adults.

> More than eighty people have answered Lancashire County Council's plea for school crossing patrol recruits.

Who are these budding lollipop men and women? A local group with their lollipops could make a picture.

Advertisements and readers' letters are rich sources of stories. A *Lancaster Guardian* letter complained about local petrol prices compared with Blackpool's, another about people shooting on the local marshes at 7 a.m. at weekends. Who's shooting? Do other people complain?

Advertisements included planning applications to build a distribution depot and demolish shops, and one from the Environment Agency seeking nominations for the regional fisheries advisory committee. Anglers in the area would be interested to know if anyone local was appointed.

Craven District Council invited business ratepayers to a meeting to discuss its budget. This could be worth attending. The Yorkshire Dales Millennium Trust advertised for finance officers. What else is it doing with its £8 million? The trust is based well away from any sizable town so its plans may not be regularly covered in the press.

Finally, Business Link was advertising seminars for young companies. Here was a chance to meet new business people.

If you get news from advertisements, check that it has not already been reported on. Decisions on local authority advertisements, for instance, could have appeared in the council minutes.

Besides your own paper, take time to glance at any others you can lay hands on, including the nationals. Here's what you should be looking for:

1   Ideas for stories or future diary dates.
2   Local stories reported elsewhere that your paper has missed and may warrant follow-ups.
3   Ideas for pictures.
4   National news that may have local echoes – i.e. expeditions that may involve local people, marketing news in City and business columns that could affect local trade, national sports items with local connections.

Other things to look at: letters to the editor, diary columns, showbusiness items, news in brief, sporting briefs, job advertisements, wills, obituaries; academic, church and other appointments; news of industrial orders and technological developments (especially in the *Financial Times*).

Almost every pamphlet and piece of paper that comes into the office is worth a glance. Even parish magazine items can contain the germ of an interesting news story. And do not forget to comb council minutes, especially the more obscure and cryptic references. Minute R 371–8 may conceal an issue that is dynamite.

Chasing the facts

Given an assignment by your news editor or chief reporter, it is then down to you to produce the story. But remember that however accurate, fair and well written your account, its success will hinge on your perseverance in getting the facts. If you are unsure of your briefing ask questions before you leave the office. Be sure you know what is expected of you. Give yourself time to check reference books. Above all, check the library for any filed cuttings that relate to your assignment. Using the cuttings files should be second nature to a reporter. They can show if your story really is new, and can fill you in with previous references to the subject or to those involved.

Nothing is more damning than for a sub-editor to have to go back to the reporter and say: 'This is all old. It's been written about before. Haven't you read the cuttings?'

At the same time do not take too long on the preliminaries. The informant you need to see may be leaving in an hour's time. Remember also the time it will take you to get from A to B. You might have three locations to visit. If you have a set time to meet someone, arrive a few minutes early rather than late.

Tools of the job

Don't forget your notebook – and mark the date and a reference on it so you can turn back your notes in three months' time after someone has queried your account. For shorthand note-taking (you should by now have learnt, or be learning, shorthand) you need a couple of sharp soft-leaded B or 2B pencils with you. Ballpoint pens can be used but they are less useful for shorthand outlines and won't write if you are leaning against a wall or if it is raining.

Always dress suitably; reserve your casual clothes for off-duty times. Jeans, leather jackets and roll-top sweaters are not adequate for most engagements, and these may vary considerably even in the course of a day. People will have more confidence in you and your paper if you are properly dressed.

Taking notes

You may be attending a meeting or a court hearing or a dinner at which your main task is to watch and listen to what goes on. Check with an official afterwards if there is anything you do not understand. Ask the person for the names of speakers you do not know; check the spelling.

At meetings, keep an ear open for an unusual or interesting point of view, or for decisions of interest to your paper. If it is a provincial weekly it will want at least a few sentences from each speaker. One quoted at length does not make up for four or five not quoted at all. Your report should reflect the various points of view.

You will not need too many notes to wade through afterwards, but you will want a verbatim note of every important statement you intend to quote. To keep down your notes, ignore the preliminaries, the platitudes and the funny stories (unless they are good enough to retell in the gossip column). Try to edit long-winded explanations as you go.

Stay to the end if at all possible. It is galling to see an account of an event in a rival paper based on some dramatic incident that occurred five minutes after you left. Out of courtesy, try to explain to the secretary if you have to leave to attend another function or prepare your story for its deadline.

If a speaker refers to some published body of facts, check the reference afterwards. If a speaker is replying to something someone has said, check that the other person is being quoted correctly. If a speaker makes an attack on someone not present, give the other person a chance of reply. Reports of damaging statements without an opportunity for the other person to reply are a common source of grievance against newspapers.

Watch out for the unexpected. When an accused person was cleared of a charge at a Newcastle court he was carried away shoulder-high by the crowd. Any reporter who assumed the acquittal was the end of the story missed the most vivid part of it.

Making inquiries

If your job is to make inquiries rather than attend a function, the cuttings library should be your first port of call. But do not accept that a cutting from your own newspaper is necessarily accurate. Match it against others – and look for mistakes that are copied from cuttings to stories which then become cuttings again.

Examine carefully the information you have. If necessary, go and talk personally to the main person named.

A builder has built a group of houses of an unusual kind. They are centrally heated, have small courtyards instead of gardens, have a garage each and also a parking space. These spaces are behind the house; a footpath, not a road, runs along the front. You ask why the builder decided to build houses of this kind, who designed them, what are the aims of the design, why the idea of courtyards, and so on.

More important, you want to know what they cost and what the people living in them think about them. Always try to see how the subject you are inquiring into affects people.

Dealing with people

Try to persuade people you interview to let you use their names and addresses. Anonymous quotes from 'a passer-by' carry little conviction. The readers might suspect you of inventing them.

The danger in seeking personal views and statements is that you may cause embarrassment or be considered intrusive. The Code of Conduct of the National Union of Journalists reads: 'In obtaining news or pictures, reporters and press photographers should do nothing that will cause pain or humiliation to innocent, bereaved or otherwise distressed persons.'

Courtesy is the best policy. Explain what you are about. Do not ask questions in an aggressive or demanding manner. If your presence is unwelcome, leave. Never go to the house as the bringer of bad tidings. Let the police call first. Be patient and sympathetic with people.

If you are dealing with people against whom allegations have been made you will need to be tougher. Point out that it is in their interest to make a comment rather than let a one-sided story go into the paper.

You will find that every person you talk to puts a situation in a slightly different light. Here you must rely on your judgement of what you have been told to make your account as balanced and accurate as possible. The basic facts of a situation often seem like a nut kernel covered in shell upon shell. The reporter's task is to peel the shells away to get at the truth.

Make your interviews in person if you can. People much prefer to talk to someone they can see in front of them rather than at the end of a telephone. Going to see your informants helps you to get to know them, which might be useful in the future. It makes it easier to listen and to seize opportunities for further questions on the spot. But do make a proper appointment if there is time.

If you cannot get to the person you want to talk to, think of someone else who might help. Try to avoid being put off with promises of answers tomorrow or next week. Also, if you can, avoid confidences in case they get into print and cause embarrassment. If you are given a confidence be sure to keep it. Off-the-record information can be a waste of time at the moment but it often stores well for the future.

If people try to persuade you to keep your story out of the paper tell them you will pass on their request to the editor. Do not make any promises. Put your questions to them just the same. Do not be fobbed off by being asked to talk to someone else. The other person may be unavailable on the day.

Being fair

If your inquiry concerns local government affairs and is controversial rather than routine try the chairman of the appropriate council committee rather than the chief officer concerned – the chairman of the education committee rather than the chief education officer.

With a controversy, be sure to get on to people on both sides of the argument. If anyone is reluctant, point out how damaging a one-sided report could be. Getting both sides is your safeguard against the inaccuracy of prejudiced informants. One-sided stories can also be damaging and legally dangerous.

Similarly, when you are writing about a report or document containing allegations or criticism about people, try to give them a chance to make their reply.

Being thorough

You cannot be too thorough. You need to answer all the questions the reader will ask and all the questions you will ask yourself when you come to write your report. The person you spoke to: what is his name, occupation and full address? This Mr Jones of Smiths Ltd: is he chairman, chargehand or what? And what are Smiths Ltd? Old established? Canners of beans, employers of 500 or was it 800? This 'recent' event: was it last week, last year? This fatal accident: where did it occur?

Do not be content merely to record opinions. Get people to give the facts on which they base them. In a strike, for instance, what the two sides say about each other matters less than the facts of the situation that caused the strike. You need these facts. It is curious how the hard facts of a dispute get lost in the shouting.

There are other points of detail that may not be necessary but which will give added life and reality to your story: the feel of the place where an event happened, the colour of a suit ... Get all the facts you can when you can. There is no substitute for them. You can always prune down; it is hard to add on facts when you have left the scene and the people have all gone home, and you have not taken a note.

Who to ask and where to look

Here is an alphabetic list of possible informants and useful documents for checking information. Don't forget that a local university will have experts on a wide range of subjects. It may publish a list.

Accidents: Local police, ambulance station, hospitals, county police press office, doctors, eyewitnesses (but beware of accepting allegations as fact), firms owning vehicles involved (speak to manager), local office of Automobile Association or Royal Automobile Club, railway public relations officers, airport manager, Royal Society for the Prevention of Accidents, *Annual Abstract of Statistics* (in town reference library) which gives national figures for all types of accidents.

Air: Airport managers, operating companies, tour operators, travel companies, aircraft building and leasing firms, Department of Transport, *Jane's All the World's Aircraft*.

Animals and birds: Local inspector Royal Society for Prevention of Cruelty to Animals, local officer Royal Society for Protection of Birds, police. County council's animal welfare inspector (cattle).

Architecture: Owners or proposers of buildings, council architect, local architects, civic society, conservation society, county or district planning officer.

Army: Public relations officers at divisional headquarters and major camps, press office Ministry of Defence, regimental depots (especially for history).

Arts: Librarians, art gallery and museum curators, secretaries of arts/music societies, arts departments at colleges, theatre managers, town or county arts and drama organizers, education officer or director, festival organizers.

Betting and gaming: Bookmakers, club managers and secretaries, local council (for regulations), Acts of Parliament in public reference library.

Buses: Company managers, traffic commissioners (for licensing matters), local councils, consumer organizations.

Cars: Automobile Association and Royal Automobile Club, garages and dealers, police.

Children's welfare: Education officer or director, school medical officer, director of social services, chairman social services committee (for children in care), inspector National Society for Prevention of Cruelty to Children, local secretary or organizer National Society for Mentally Handicapped Children (Mencap), local health authority.

Churches: Clergy, ministers, bishops and their secretaries or chaplains, superintendents and district chairmen (Methodists) (See Chapter 12).

Elections: Council press office (size of electorate, number and names of nominated candidates), party agents and local secretaries, regional agents, *Whitaker's Almanack* (for Parliamentary election details).

Electricity: Electricity-generating companies, power station managers, regional electricity companies, consumer bodies.

Evening classes: Colleges of further education, adult education officer, local secretary Workers' Educational Association, area colleges; Birkbeck College, London University (for evening degree courses); university boards of extra-mural studies.

Exports: Regional press office for the Department of Trade and Industry, export companies, manufacturers' associations.

Farming: County or local secretary National Farmers' Union, ADAS (advisory service).

Fishing (inland): Angling club secretary, Environmental Agency regional office.

Food inspection: Chief environmental health inspector, Meat Hygiene Service.

Food poisoning: District director of public health, director of testing laboratory; food safety team.

Footpaths: Council or county surveyor, clerk to parish council, county planning officer, local secretary Ramblers' Association, secretary archeological or history society, residents or landowners concerned.

Gas: Company press office, area managers.

Handicapped people's welfare: Director of social services, Women's Royal Voluntary Service organizer, Training and Enterprise Council, careers officer; local secretary Scope, Mencap, Muscular Dystrophy Group, groups for physically handicapped, schools of the Shaftesbury Society, homes of the Cheshire Foundation.

Hospitals: Press officer of hospital trusts, hospital telephonists (inquiries concerning casualties admitted), local health authority, community health council.

Houses: Local estate agents, surveyors and (for prices), housing associations, building society bulletins, council housing department, housing manager, chairman housing committee, Citizens' Advice Bureau, chief environmental health inspector, the Census (figures on houses without baths), council press office (improvement grants), council architect, engineer and surveyor, local builders, property developers.

Industrial development: Council chief executive, district and county planning officers, regional press office for Department of Trade and Industry, chairman of development committee or planning committee, regional and local development organizations, manufacturers' and trade associations.

Industrial firms: Company press officers, managers and managing directors (do not rely on information from people who do not have the authority to give it), *Stock Exchange Year Book*, Chamber of Commerce.

Industrial smoke: District director of public health, chief environmental health inspector, Environmental Agency regional office, firms concerned.

Industry and trade: Secretary Chamber of Commerce, regional press office Department of Trade and Industry, individual firms, town halls.

Local government problems: Council chief executive, council press officer.

Medicine: Doctors, local secretary British Medical Association, local family health services authority (complaints).

Mental health: Director of social services, local health authority, medical superintendent or consultant at psychiatric hospital, local secretary Mencap and Mind.

National Parks: Park planning committee, county planning officer, Countryside Commission, local secretary Ramblers' Association, Youth

Hostels Association, Council for the Preservation of Rural England, landowners, chief executives of local councils.

Old people's welfare: Director of social services, Women's Royal Voluntary Service, secretaries of senior citizens' clubs, clergy, ministers of religion, Age Concern.

Planning: County or city planning officer, council surveyors and engineers, chairman of planning committee, secretary civic societies and civic trusts, county surveyor (roads and traffic), Friends of the Earth, Council for the Protection of Rural England.

Playgrounds and playing fields: Council press officer, parish council clerk, local or county secretary National Playing Fields Association, secretary county's Community Service Council.

Post: Head postmaster for the area (usually in nearest large town).

Railways: Company public relations officers will be willing to help; for a quick answer approach a stationmaster, district manager or workshop manager (but see Chapter 11).

Rivers: Regional press office of Environmental Agency.

Road transport: British Road Services, local or regional secretary Road Hauliers' Association and Freight Transport Associations, independent hauliers, *Annual Abstract of Statistics* or *Monthly Digest of Statistics* (in reference libraries).

Roads and bridges: District engineer, county surveyor, local office Automobile Association or Royal Automobile Club, regional office of Highways Agency.

Royal Air Force: Station adjutant or press liaison officer, Ministry of Defence.

Royal Navy: Press liaison officers at naval establishments, Ministry of Defence.

Schools: Chief education officer, chairman of education committee, divisional education officer (in counties), school heads, local secretaries National Union of Teachers and National Association of Schoolmasters/Union of Women Teachers.

Scientific matters: heads of departments at universities and colleges of further education.

Shipping: Shipowners and lines, local office of Shipping Federation (employers), local representative of Chamber of Shipping, local offices of National Union of Seamen.

Shops: Secretary of Chamber of Trade, secretary Union of Shop, Distributive and Allied Workers, store and shop managers.

Street lighting: Engineer to district council, clerk to parish council, police.

Taxes: Local inspectors do not usually talk to the press, but will give you leaflets; you might have to write to or telephone the Press Office, Inland Revenue, North-West Wing, Bush House, Aldwych, London WC2B 4PPP (tel: 0171–438–7356; fax: 0171–438–7541).

Television: ITV companies' public relations officers; BBC has press officers in London, Belfast, Birmingham, Bristol, Cardiff, Glasgow, Leeds, Manchester and Newcastle upon Tyne.

Trade unions: Local contacts vital here for reporters – trade union representatives can be hard to find; most sizable unions have regional offices but there may be only a clerk on duty.

Unemployment figures: Regional office of Central Office of Information, offices of Department of Education and Employment, *Employment Gazette* (your local library will have one).

Universities: Press officer, heads of departments.

Vandalism: Police, council press officer, parks superintendent, chairman of council's housing and parks committees.

Water: Water company press officer.

Weather: Meteorological Office; geography department at university or polytechnic.

Youth employment: Careers officer for town or district, Training and Enterprise Council.

Youth organizations: Local youth organizer, county youth organizer, chief education officer or director of education, local secretaries Scouts, Guides, Boys' Brigade, etc., secretary county youth clubs association, youth chaplains and other clergy, secretary of local standing conference of youth organizations.

3 PICTURE IDEAS

Reporters should think in pictures as well as in words. This is not just to help them describe what they see; it is to provide picture ideas for the photographers of their newspaper.

Pictures give a newspaper page much of its initial impact and help in the page design. The news page can be passably well filled if its reporters follow a fairly set routine day by day; but photographers cannot take the same pictures day after day if their pictures are to be more than wasted space.

What makes a good news picture? It needs to grasp the essence of the news. It needs people in it, and the people, wherever possible, should be its major interest. Even if they are not, you still need people to give life and scale. Inanimate objects – buildings, oil storage tanks, museum pieces – usually make poor news pictures on their own.

The best people are children, for they can be relied on to be natural. They do not have the strong desire of older children and adults to look as much like an inanimate object as possible when photographed. The people in a good news picture should look as if they are living. They should not just stand there: they should be in action. It should not be 'John Smith with the house he built' but 'John Smith putting the finishing touches to the house he built'.

Broadly speaking, newspaper pictures fall into two classes:

1 Those which are interesting in their own right and which will attract the reader's attention regardless of what they are about. A picture of a pretty girl, for instance, is a pleasure merely to look at without reading the caption which says: 'Janet B— who has won a scholarship to the Royal Academy of Dramatic Art. . . .' Or a small child with a wonderful expression as he receives a gift from a store's Santa Claus. It is not really news that John Smith, aged four, had a present bought for him; the picture gets in on its own merits with only a slight breath

of topicality. Photographers are always on the look out for well-known people doing something mundane: tying a shoe-lace, shopping in a supermarket, eating a hamburger.

2   Pictures that will illustrate a story and make it more vivid, sometimes regardless of the intrinsic merit of the photograph itself. A picture of a man looking at a crack in a wall, for example, cannot be very exciting nor, by itself, likely to hold a reader's attention. But if it illustrates a story about cracks which have appeared in the walls of houses six months after they were built, it assumes a fresh importance. Readers turn from the story to the picture (the reverse of Class 1) and the situation is made clearer in their minds.

The photographer's dream, of course, is a picture which is both Class 1 and Class 2. Instead of the small boy with Santa Claus mentioned above, it is a picture of a bedraggled little girl sitting on the grass clutching a doll, crying her eyes out after a train smash. This is the sort of picture both appealing in its own right and illustrating a story better than words could. Some pictures are so memorable that they become icons, the definitive expression of an important event, such as the young Chinese student trying to arrest the advance of the tanks in Tiananmen Square.

Reporters must be on the look-out for both these main types of picture, keeping clear in their minds the purpose for which the photographer will be sent on the assignment if he or she is to go unaccompanied. This particularly applies to the Class 2 pictures where the picture-subject may not be obvious to someone (e.g. a photographer) who does not know the news story behind it. If you are not going with the photographer, make sure that whoever does the briefing has sufficient facts to be certain that the picture will tie up with the story.

It also helps if you can supply details which will make it easier for your office to arrange to get the picture – e.g. the best time and place for your subject to be photographed, and the telephone number in case the photographic staff want to vary either of them. Remember to ask for this kind of detail at the same time as you are getting your story.

Working with a photographer

If you have to accompany a photographer, teamwork can ease the job for both of you, particularly on jobs which cover a big area and/or involve a lot of people (e.g. a county show, a big fire). If you obtain details about a subject, pass them on to the photographer for the caption to save asking for them afresh. If the photographer, in taking a picture purely for its visual appeal, stumbles across a story or something that contributes to the story, make sure this is passed on to you so that you can follow up the lead.

Do not work entirely independently of one another. A reporter can also help in certain circumstances by controlling passers-by or inquisitive children. He or she can save time for both reporter and photographer by being prepared to stipulate exactly what and who is to be photographed if the picture is to tie up with the story. The best picture often requires the assembling of a group of people: children with a headmistress who is leaving; workpeople celebrating a big new order.

What makes a picture?

Always, on every job you go on, ask yourself: 'Will this make a picture?' or 'Is this story complete without a picture?' There is a constant demand for picture subjects and when you have acquired an eye for pictures your recommendations will frequently be acted upon.

Some subjects are dubious because they look extremely drab in the newspaper. The oil storage tank, mentioned earlier, may be the pride and joy of a local engineering firm but it is a poor subject for photographs because it has no visual appeal. It could really be linked only with a story about residents who object to it spoiling the view, the picture thus in effect saying: 'This is how the view is spoiled.' Derelict sites are often tempting from a news point of view ('This is where the new concert hall will be built') but the picture itself will be dreary.

Other subjects may be dubious because of technical difficulties: an express train speeding through a station at night is impossible to photograph except with the most elaborate equipment. Your photographer(s) may not possess the necessary lens to take a life-size picture of the Roman coin dug up in a garden.

Flashlight pictures rarely reproduce as well as those taken by natural or available light (e.g. normal room lighting) because the flash tends to kill the shadows which provide moulding and relief for a face or scene. Photographers can use a 'bounced' flash technique if there is anything to bounce the flash off, but if there is not (e.g. in a large hall) it has to be the more customary and less satisfactory frontal flash. The point of mentioning this is that if you are able to choose between fixing up a picture at (say) 3 p.m. in soft autumn sunlight, outdoors, or the same picture at 8 p.m. indoors with flash, then choose 3 p.m. The picture will have a better chance of good reproduction.

Flashes also tend to darken the background because they carry only a limited distance. Therefore a group of dignitaries in evening dress – black clothing against a black background – will, at worst, appear as a

Figure 3.1 *What makes a picture? In this example the cleverly caught expression on the face of former Foreign Secretary Douglas Hurd livens up a political occasion. It was taken by* Hull Daily Mail *photographer Richard Walker using a long telephoto lens near 10 Downing Street, and it won for him a Merit Award in the Fuji European Press Awards. Richard also won the £1000 BT award in the NCTJ National Certificate examination*

group of featureless white faces and white shirtfronts hanging in black space.

Look out for opportunities for pictures that have a natural attractiveness for the bulk of the readership: animals, particularly young animals; babies and young children.

Some areas of the country offer fine views and some newspapers are glad to use them. A section of landscape, even in town, can sometimes provide a picture which will summarize weather or season. A reporter on the move can often spot the possibility of a picture like this.

Many newspapers will want some action in their seasonal pictures. Here again reporters can be helpful if they can suggest where the photographers can find pictures of, say, children gleefully sleigh riding, or pretty girls basking in unexpected spring sunshine in their lunch-hour.

The tradition of group pictures is dying hard. The reasoning behind these face-packed halftones is that everyone in the picture will want to buy a copy of the paper and possibly, too, a copy of the photographic print – a source of income for many local newspapers.

This reasoning is not invariably sound. Many of the people in the picture may be buying the paper already and the number of extra copies sold could be negligible. Against this is the likelihood that only a fraction of the readership will be interested in a particular group photograph and that the bulk of them find it an uninteresting waste of space. A small gain may have been made at the expense of boring the majority of readers. Many newspapers have abandoned this type of picture, though they still take some extra group pictures at an event – in addition to the pictures intended for publication – for public sale.

A few group pictures can have an intrinsic interest even for the outsider: a retiring headmaster, for instance, in the midst of a huge group of children gathered informally around him, symbolic of all the children he has known in his career. This kind of picture can work only when it is given generous space and the reproduction is good.

Colour

The shift to web-offset presses for newspaper printing has made the use of colour easier and cheaper. As a result, more and more newspapers are using full-colour illustrations.

The mistake some make is in imagining that a great variety of colours in a single picture is what is most effective. In fact, the colours tend to cancel one another out or to give a comic-paper effect. A single splotch of bright colour against a more sombre background is more effective and more striking to the eye.

In view of the higher cost of colour than of black and white for reproduction purposes, it is likely that decisions about suitable subjects will be taken at a fairly high level. Nevertheless, reporters on today's newspaper will be expected to look out for colour subjects, and they will be popular for suggesting something less obvious than the flowers in the park.

4 DISTRICT REPORTING

Reporting, to most young journalists and especially those under training, means working at one of the many hundreds of morning, evening or weekly papers published around the country, either from the paper's main office or from branch offices covering a 'district'.

Different newspapers mean different things when they refer to 'district reporting'. In one office all the staff might operate from a central reporters' room, each travelling out into a particular geographical area and returning to the reporters' room to input copy. Another newspaper may operate sub-offices some distance from head office, with perhaps just a junior reporter there as the editorial representative, or a junior under a senior reporter. In another variation, a district reporter may live in a district and write copy at home, inputting into the office system from a work station.

But whatever your office means by 'district reporting' the objective is clear: to wring as much news out of the geographical area you are covering as is possible.

The difference between being a district reporter and being one of a staff covering diary jobs from head office is that in a district you are, to a large extent, responsible for finding your own news stories as well as covering them. This calls for an added resourcefulness, especially in a thin week with every available possibility needed to be followed up.

One aspect of a district reporter's life is that the output is easily measurable, especially where a newspaper changes or 'slips' a page or pages for a certain district and must have an adequate amount of news from that district, that week, to be able to do so. The sub-editors can instantly perceive when news from a district is falling below normal in volume. So can the readers.

Conversely, the subs can also see just as quickly that a district reporter is turning out more than average and, provided the copy is good, such a reporter can be regarded as a valuable standby when copy from other districts is scarce.

The district is a place where the junior reporter can shine. It is probably the first opportunity for sorting the sheep from the goats, the born newsgatherers from those less fortunate.

A junior who can squeeze a constant flow of good stories out of an unpromising district either possesses, or has developed, qualities of initiative, resourcefulness, ingenuity and independent news judgement which will be valuable in his or her later career. It could eventually give a reporter a great advantage in know-how over reporters who never had the chance to cover a district: never had the inestimable opportunity to slog round in the winter rain, chasing receding stories. . . .

What makes a reporter?

Some reporters in this situation might take the attitude that they will get paid the same whether they bring in a lot of stories or a few. They content themselves with covering diary jobs and little more. They do little that an intelligent shorthand typist could not do.

The difference between a bright shorthand typist and a true reporter is that a reporter can:

1 Search intelligently for news stories.
2 Recognize them.
3 Follow their course until there's enough material for the newspaper's need.
4 Present the story in a way that makes people want to read it through until the end.

You can learn mechanics of reporting under today's training programmes, but whether you become a good reporter or not depends on whether you have this eye for news. The district is the place where this ability can be honed, and the techniques you learn there can be applied on a star assignment when your name has become a household word.

It may be that your newspaper is hampered some days by lack of space and that again and again the good 'district' stories you write are cut down or even thrown away.

Do not despair.

Most newspaper readers, in the weeklies field especially, are regular readers who buy the paper because they know roughly what they are going to find in it. While they have to be considered (and considered very carefully) from a circulation point of view, paradoxically it is really the other people in your district in whom your newspaper's circulation department is most interested: the people who do not take the paper at all.

Generally, the diary jobs will look after the people who already take the newspaper. It is the unexpected off-diary story which might make someone buy a copy of the paper who does not usually buy one.

Local geography

Surprisingly, some district reporters are not sure of the exact geographical limits of their district. One often finds, for example, that they do not know whether a certain road is in their district or not. First thing, then, is to study maps. Get to know the boundaries of your district and, so far as they are marked, the things within it which are yours.

Ordnance Survey maps and street directions can be valuable sources of information about a district to which you are newly assigned. In most districts there are corners where reporters have seldom penetrated. You must cultivate a curiosity about them (curiosity is a primary quality of a good district reporter).

Perhaps in some remote corner of your district an Ordnance Survey map marks 'Gravel pits'. You should know them. If you do not, resolve to go and look at them when you get a chance. Perhaps all you will see is a rather sordid landscape. But you may see children playing on disused and water-filled areas.

Would the thought occur to you that this could be dangerous? Would you find out where they live, go to see their mothers, and ask them if they are happy about having unfenced lakes within a child's reach of their houses?

Would you be surprised if the mothers said they were indeed anxious about it and were trying to take the matter up with the local council?

Would you be able to create a story out of this (not forgetting to suggest a picture of the children dabbling in the water)?

Or perhaps someone is fishing there and knows the old, old story about some legendary carp of incredible size said to inhabit the water. . . .

Or the gravel diggers have been finding odd-shaped bones. Or have struck oil. . . .

Fanciful? Hardly. It is from this kind of long shot that some good stories originate. So study the map, poke about in the quiet corners of your district. They may not be so quiet as you thought. At worst, they can provide some photographable scenery which eventually will come in handy for the first-sign-of-spring picture many weeklies like.

Here is a general note. The writer went down an incongruously rural-looking lane in an industrial district he once covered, having noticed it on a map. At the end of the lane he found a whole family living in a chicken incubator (a tiny heated shed) due to the housing shortage at the time.

Naturally, they achieved fame in the next issue of the newspaper and the story and pictures led to them getting a council house.

Not an earth-shaking story but quite an acceptable run-of-the-mill one for a weekly.

Beyond your district

Even if you feel you know the district's topography and all its organizations and official bodies there may be others outside its boundaries which nevertheless exert an influence on it.

Here is a simple example. A school half a mile over the borders of your district may take a large number of students from within your district. This is frequently true of big schools, technical colleges, art schools, and so on. The technical college, for instance, may be miles from your area but its top scholarship may be won by a student from your district – which might make a story.

Another example: an outlying corner of the district may have developed fairly quickly and the police station covering that neighbourhood may be outside the bounds of your district. If another district reporter has it covered, well and good, but the police station might be outside the newspaper's coverage area altogether, and in that case it is up to you to call on it in pursuit of the news from that neighbourhood in your district. This principle also applies to fire stations, which are tending to be spaced further and further apart.

Hospitals which serve patients from your area may be outside your district. Obviously, contact with such hospitals will help your coverage of your district.

And where do the people from your district go when they want to see a football match? They may support the strictly local team, but many may prefer to travel some miles to see a team of better standard outside the newspaper's coverage area. It is up to you to add interest to your district's news by making sure your paper has something about this team's games. Draw it to the attention of your superior.

Getting to grips

You are now over the preliminaries and are becoming familiar with the district and getting to know what bodies exert an influence on it. Now comes the brunt of it: getting yourself installed to such an extent that hardly anything can happen in your district without your knowing about it.

An important point: in making inquiries it is better, unless you know the people pretty well, to talk face to face though, of course, the telephone is the only method of making your calls in an emergency or if your time is limited.

You must have a host of close contacts in all walks of life and all parts of the district. These are the people who can give you your main stories other than routine diary events.

They may or may not be connected with some sort of organization. If they are, try to bear in mind that, first and foremost, they are your contacts and only secondarily the representatives of organizations.

The local scout leader may want to talk about a fairly routine scout camp but your visit may result in a slightly better story than that. Let us imagine he suddenly recalls that one of his lads is going to attend an international scouting event in America. You could interview the boy, find out what he thinks about his trip, fix up a photograph. This story will interest a larger proportion of your readership, not because they are interested in scouting but because they want to know about a boy of 15 who suddenly gets a trip to New York. Perhaps one in five of your readers will be interested – a considerable improvement on the perhaps one in 120 for a routine story about a scout camp.

If you visit your contact rather than telephone, and if you can cultivate his or her acquaintance sufficiently, it is unlikely that the visit will end without some general conversation: 'Did you hear that So-and-so, the grocer on the corner, won £6000 on an accumulator bet and is going to Bermuda for a holiday?' And you have another little story.

Or you notice that your contact's children are at home although it is not holiday time. You comment on it and it turns out that parents in the neighbourhood are staging a one-day 'strike' as a protest against the condition of the road to the school entrance. The school would be unlikely to ring up and tell you about it; the local council almost certainly would not. Thus can a news situation first become known.

It would need developing, of course: interviews with the appropriate people, probably a picture or two, but it is a good story because it will interest a larger number of your newspaper's readers.

Nursing your contacts

If each contact gives you a first-class story once a year, make 52 contacts and you will (arithmetically) have a good story every week ... Obviously, it will not work out so simply but the principle is clear.

Make sure that any new contact knows exactly who you are and where you can be reached. When you go into a new district, give out visiting cards right and left (which your office will print for you). There is nothing more disastrous than to have a new contact ring an opposition paper with a good story under the impression that you represent that paper.

Try to regard the little pars and domestic-interest items as an excuse for going to see somebody rather than as an end in themselves. There may be people, of course, for whom you do not need an excuse, who are naturally talkative perhaps because of their occupation, such as a licensee or a barber or a café proprietor. Quite a proportion of such people like to give you 'something for your paper', possibly for their own self-satisfaction but, in any case, to your advantage.

The fact that your paper has been covering an area for a hundred years does not mean that every possible source inside the district is being tapped. You can invariably add new ones.

Organizations

Some areas may have comprehensive lists of organizations, perhaps in a guidebook, perhaps at the town hall or council offices. It is up to you at least to know of the organizations in your district.

Some you may learn about at meetings. For instance, at a trades council you might hear some trade union branches mentioned which are new to you. The trades council secretary, who should be a firm contact, would probably give you a list of member branches. Some of these may yield useful stories – for example, the national secretary of a union coming to speak to the local branch at a time when there is tension in the air for that particular union.

Your own paper can be a guide. Regularly read through the classified advertisements. You might find that a firm you have never heard of in your district is advertising for staff for a special project; that a social group is advertising for premises; that a sports club not on your list is advertising for players. Find out about these organizations, and now or later invent an excuse to make yourself known to them.

Reading the classifieds, too, can often yield the little gem of a story: someone advertising a live python for sale, or a collection of war relics collected at great personal risk. You can never assume that the advertising department passes these on to editorial.

Read the opposition newspaper too (if you have one) and make sure it is not getting stories from organizations in your district with which you have no contact.

A sector of local life that can be overlooked is the federation type of organization. It can be forgotten because it is somewhat diffuse, not easy to see; for example, a federation of Women's Institutes in your district, or a grouping of residents' associations or horticultural societies or football referees or young farmers' clubs. A newspaper may often have contact with the individual members of such a federation but not with the federation itself.

Political parties have a fairly complex structure which can yield new contacts: the divisional or constituency party, ward parties, council 'groups', women's sections, youth sections at each level, and so on in each of the major parties. Though relations at the top between your newspaper and the political parties may be handled by a senior or even the editor, there is plenty that can be gleaned by a young junior at district level.

Some of your district organizations will be more active than others, and frequent calls upon representatives of the less active organizations would be a waste of time.

This does not mean that they should be forgotten, or left to send in their own news items. All your calls should be divided into classifications of frequency of calling, ranging perhaps from a daily call at the police station down to once a month or even once a quarter for groups which meet at those intervals. The point is that when their representatives do have something exciting they will know you as the person to ring up.

One contact often overlooked is the local councillor. If your district contains a parish or district council of its own, you have a good selection from which to choose. Alternatively, your district may send a representative or representatives to a council which meets outside your district; and if it does you should be getting to know these people. They will be able to tell you in fine detail what the council is proposing to do in your district.

In addition to this direct news, a local councillor usually knows a great deal of what is going on in the neighbourhood apart from council matters.

Councillors, by the nature of their work, have a good local knowledge and can often help you with queries, giving background information to a particular story even if their answer itself is not for publication.

As a beginner in journalism, you are not yet covering meetings of the local council, but the council minutes, which are regularly published, may nevertheless give you some clues to stories of interest to your district which have been missed through lack of local knowledge by a senior journalist at head office.

Schools are a good source of local news. Each has its own domestic events: sports days, speech day, harvest festival, outings, holidays overseas, teachers retiring, etc. They are also great exchanges for news and gossip brought to the school by the children. Some of it reaches the teachers or headmaster, who may pass it on to you if you are a regular caller: such as the boy whose mother has just had triplets to bring the number of her family up to twelve boys in all.

Churches are an obvious choice for contacts. Factories make a good call, on the principle that people are interested in whatever affects their pocket. If a local firm goes in for a new product its workpeople are going to be interested to read about it because it may mean more overtime or better security of employment. Shopkeepers and others who depend on the factory's workpeople for their trade will be equally interested.

A very large factory can be a town in itself, with a great range of social activities and sports leagues. These have a restricted interest for your readership but may be worth covering for the bigger stories that might emerge.

The larger firm will also issue an annual report and may include you on its mailing list. This can give your district readership some interesting facts about the firm's trading year and its prospects.

If you have one or more large factories in your district it is worth keeping an eye on the financial pages of the national papers. It can happen that a fierce battle might be raging in the City concerning the shares of a local firm, the outcome of which will vitally affect local people.

In this respect it is as well to know who controls a local factory. It may be part of a large financial organization which is making headlines on the Stock Exchange although your local factory is not mentioned by name.

Friendly relations both with the unions in a factory and with the management are worth cultivating. Unfortunately, strikes happen. When they do, both sides tend to clam up, but if they have been dealing with you for some time, and know they can trust you, they may speak to you and no one else.

People in the know

There is a category of people in any district who know what is going on but who have no official position. Such a person may be a farmer, a cinema manager, a garage proprietor, a licensee, or a housewife. You will come across them sooner or later and it is up to you to cultivate them. Sometimes they will give news in exchange for other news, and you will come to know their preferences. The garage proprietor, for instance, may be interested in developments in local sport which have not yet been published.

If you are alert and perceptive, even a walk around will repay you. Look at notice boards, or the showcases in which postcard advertisements are displayed. Watch out for incongruities: why, for instance, should that little house be showing a poster for a national embroidery exhibition in London? It may turn out that the grannie in the house has a national name for embroidery and has done it since she was seven.

In a small community a newsagent is often worth calling on. He stands to make a profit from the number of newspapers he sells: the larger the number, the larger the profit. Newsagents will often give you news items culled from customers' chat, particularly if you call regularly, because they know the stories could increase the sales in their neighbourhood.

Bodies which look after old people can often come up with human stories – Age Concern or the WRVS, for instance. Evening classes can be fertile ground: a class of women, for example, learning subjects such as car maintenance or plumbing, or husbands in a cookery class.

Once you have made contact, keep an indexed notebook with names, addresses and telephone numbers, and keep it up to date in case you need someone in a hurry.

The local angle

Time and again you will have to follow up the local application of a national story even if you have not been put down in the diary for it. Government budgets are always worth looking at in detail for this kind of local repercussion; sometimes a budget can cut a town's staple trade away from under it.

Various kinds of magazine can also provide you with minor news stories if you read them with an alert mind. Very often, in a line or two, a parish magazine will contain the germ of a little story: an annual charity which has been distributing to 'the needy' for 200 years is being suspended this year because of the lack of any needy. Properly followed up, this could make a useful local story which, although not especially hard news, might nevertheless be an interesting reflection of how times have changed.

Other magazines and bulletins worth reading for news angles may be issued by residents' associations, political parties, associations for the afflicted or disabled, hospital leagues of friends, factories (staff magazines), Rotary clubs and chambers of trade. Few will contain items which are stories in their own right but many will have items which lend themselves to follow-ups.

Diary jobs

Diary jobs (i.e. of known forthcoming events) are still one of the most valuable sources of news in a district, and their exploitation depends almost entirely on the alertness of the reporter.

Let us assume that you are assigned to a routine diary job such as the annual meeting of a horticultural society with the usual review of the year, election of officers, and so on. Before the meeting gets under way it is announced that the vice-chairman will preside because the chairman is abroad. If you were not a district reporter you could merely include this in your report and, broadly speaking, your duty would be done.

But as a district reporter you have got to recognize this as a story opportunity, not a story in itself but the opportunity to get one later. So, after the meeting, you ask the secretary why the chairman is abroad, and where is he?

The chances are that it will be some sort of routine trip – a winter holiday in Switzerland or a business trip to Brussels. But there is one chance in ten that the trip is an unusual one: perhaps the chairman has won a top award in his occupation which entitles him to three months' study in Chicago; or he is a botanist and has gone on a six-month trip up the Amazon to collect orchids; or he has decided to drive overland to Hong Kong. Your inquiry has paid off, one way or another. You can either see his family and get a story about the trip while it is in progress or wait until the chairman comes back and interview him then. Or both.

Another example, also from real life, was the occasion when a young reporter was at a council meeting in his district at which the chairman announced, with regret, the resignation of the chairman of the housing committee, due to ill health. He proceeded to pay tribute to the work and character of the retiring councillor.

A reporter sent from head office could have been excused if he had accepted this at face value, put it in his report, and left it at that. But it was a district reporter who was covering the meeting and he instantly recalled that earlier in the week he had seen the housing committee chairman about another matter, and the chairman had seemed in good enough health then. This gave the council chairman's statement a strange ring.

As it happened, the weekly paper concerned wanted this council meeting report the same night for publication the next day. Despite the urgency, the reporter decided to go to see the housing committee chairman when the meeting finished, which was about 11.30 p.m. When he got to the man's house, the wife said her husband was out and would be back after midnight.

About an hour later the chairman came walking down the road to his home. The reporter met him – they were, of course, friendly already since the chairman was one of the reporter's district contacts – and the reporter put to him the council chairman's statement about 'ill-health'.

'I've never felt better in my life,' said the committee chairman. 'Come inside and I'll tell you all about it.'

It turned out there had been a great row inside the council's controlling party about the vital question of housing which was of major importance in the district. The council chairman's statement about 'ill health' was a cover-up. The committee chairman was quite prepared to spill the beans that he had resigned because of disagreement over housing policy, and to give chapter and verse of what the disagreement had been about.

This made the local paper's lead story. It had sprung, if you remember, from the little red light that had flickered in the district reporter's mind when the phrase 'because of ill health' had been used. Two other papers which had sent head office reporters to the meeting completely missed this story.

This chapter has tried to show the difference between what is needed by a reporter sent on a specific assignment by a main office and a district reporter given *carte blanche* in a geographical area.

A district reporter who tells head office 'There's nothing happening in my district this week' is confessing failure. Something is always happening but you have got to know how to find it. In doing so, you will gain an invaluable, hard-won knowhow of where news is likely to come from, and what news is. It is hard work – but a great experience.

5 INTERVIEWING

The newspaper interview in general use is a twentieth-century invention which has grown from a daring novelty to a basic part of reporting technique. Much of the information a reporter obtains comes from interviewing, though he or she has the option of using it in differing ways: attributing it directly to the informant; writing it as information coming from the newspaper; combining it with the results of other interviews and other stories; or storing it in mind as background information on a general subject. There is also the big set-piece interview for a feature article or profile. Interviews with well-known people are popular.

The use of shorthand has had a great deal to do with the importance of interviewing, for the ability to record speech as it is spoken not only assists detailed, accurate reporting but also adds immediacy and vividness. Fast, confident shorthand is an immense asset. In these days of on-the-spot radio and television coverage, a newspaper reader is often in a position to compare the interviewee's actual words with what a newspaper claims he or she said. The difference in a word or phrase can be more easily spotted and will always weaken a reader's faith if the printed version is incorrect.

Tape recorders can be used to verify accuracy but as recording instruments alone, even though miniaturized, they can frighten an interviewee into silence unless the operator is really experienced. Listening to a recording takes as long as the interview it records.

Preparation

Some of the most important aspects of an interview take place beforehand. The selection of interviewee may be done for you by your office, either by a diary marking or verbally. If the choice is yours, make sure of two things: Is the interviewee likely to know what he or she is talking about (ask yourself this question for the sake of your newspaper)? Is the information you want within his or her jurisdiction (ask yourself this for the sake of the interviewee)?

Limitless trouble can be caused by approaching the wrong individual. You may interview the gatekeeper at a factory and come away with a fraction of the full story. The gatekeeper later gets a reprimand for not passing you on to an executive. No one is satisfied.

For every normal purpose the request for an interview must be made to the right person: the headmaster of the school and not the school-keeper, the clerk of the council and not the person on the town-hall switchboard, the owner of the shop and not one of the counter-hands. In the normal way you must at least make the attempt to adhere to the principle of working from the top downwards. In many organizations there is an established channel for press inquiries which should always be tried first, if not solely.

Timing your approach is also vital. In most cases an interviewee is giving you something which is of commercial value if it is going to help sell your newspaper – only where people want free publicity are you giving the interviewee anything. It follows that, where possible, you must ask for your gift at a reasonable time.

People who receive you cordially at 10 a.m. will not be so cordial if you rouse them by telephone at 3 a.m. It is also a matter of courtesy, where circumstances permit, to make an appointment. This is not always possible but where it is it is a mistake to omit it. Asking for an appointment is more highly thought of than most reporters realize, and it has the practical advantage that it can save you calling for an unexpected interview and finding the person is away or too busy.

Background

Having established the right person and the right time, consider whether you have established the topic of the interview. This may be a simple human experience for which no particular background knowledge is required: someone reaching the age of a hundred, a woman expecting her fourth set of twins, someone who has been the victim of a robbery.

But it may be something more complicated: a row over the running of a hospital for instance. If you are to ask intelligent and rewarding questions it is essential you know something about the way the hospital is administered. A sudden strike at a factory: do you know the definition of an unofficial strike? Would strikers get strike pay? Who would have called them out?

Knowing something in advance can save you making a fool of yourself and undermining your interviewee's confidence. You also have to think not just of the subject but of the story. The subject itself may not be new. What is the story that makes the subject worth returning to? An interview should have a clear purpose of producing some news.

Before setting out find what you can of the person or subject from the office library or cuttings files. Or ask a senior colleague. It is a good idea to think of some likely questions before the interview, perhaps even on the way to it if time is short. The obvious questions will occur to you anyway; likely ones could concern side issues or contingent matters. Some reporters jot down questions in their notebooks beforehand but it is better, when you become more adept, to memorize them.

Do not be afraid to ask simple questions even if they make you appear ignorant. Simple questions attract simple answers. They can also have the advantage of testing assumptions.

Establishing confidence

Upon arrival your immediate objective is to establish the interviewee's confidence in you. You must appear to be the sort of person who can be trusted with information, able to get it down right and present it sensibly.

Do not arrive inappropriately or shabbily dressed. Many people will feel that erratic dress presages erratic reporting. You do not go as an individual but as a representative of the newspaper. 'Casuals' are fine at a sporting event or on holiday but in formal circumstances they can affront.

In most interviews you must pay attention to the normal courtesies. If you walk straight up to people in the street and start asking questions, they will stand it only for so long. A self-introduction is essential, usually some formula such as 'Good morning – I am from the *Blankshire Times*, etc. . . .' You should also make clear your purpose.

Indoors, with a stranger, do not sit until you are invited to, do not smoke without asking (and offering), do not lounge, do not interrupt the interviewee's work more than you can help.

You must make a quick assessment of your interviewee to decide the approach. This is important. Flippancy might establish you with a soldier out on an exercise but it is unlikely to be popular when you approach the brigadier. Some journalists have a natural ease with strangers. With a complete stranger a neutral approach is best, not familiar, not patronizing, not servile, always courteous. If you are nervous, never be afraid that your nervousness is showing; it is understandable if you are approaching a stranger and implies a certain amount of deference, which never does any harm.

After you have opened the conversation by identifying yourself, get to the point. If the interviewee forestalls you with small-talk about the weather you must play along, but the key phrase 'I have come to see you about...' must come early. So state the purpose of the interview clearly. The interviewee's response is an important clue to how you are going to get along.

The person may answer brusquely, 'Oh you have, have you?' Now you know you will have to watch your step. Or you may get that unexpected reply, 'Why? Who said anything about ...?' – implying that it has never happened, or that it is nothing to do with them, or that you are misinformed. This is a not uncommon gambit to throw you off. Never give a literal answer such as 'Mr Jones told me, etc....' The interviewee may decide to give Mr Jones a piece of his mind next time they meet, and say nothing further to you.

The rude answer is exceptional. It is also surprising how many people will readily consent to an interview which may bare their private or business lives. Usually the answer to your statement 'I have come to see you about ...' will be 'Oh, yes ... come inside ... what can I tell you?' The odds are on your side.

Reluctant people

Between the rude answer and the cordial welcome is the guarded reception. Often it is from an expert who does not particularly want to talk to journalists and is not confident of your ability to understand him over the phone. You may do better face to face. Sometimes it is from someone who will eventually consent to an interview so long as it is off the record or is not attributed to them by name. Usually they make this condition clear near the start of the interview.

Always consent to it at that stage. As the interview progresses, and you show yourself to be apparently trustworthy and sensible, they may well relent. If they do not, you can always ask them later if they are still of the same mind or whether a certain fact or sentence can be regarded as 'on the record' and the remainder left 'off'.

Once in a while, you will have to stipulate that unless the interview is on the record, or attributed, you would rather not conduct it at all. You may still part friends, and in this rather rare case it is worth asking, 'Can I quote you as saying you have "No comment"?' This is a poor substitute for a meaty interview but, even so, a 'No comment' can be quite revealing in the circumstances, indicating that the interviewee has a reason for not talking, or that it is not considered reasonable to connect his or her name with the event.

It occasionally happens that an interviewee will readily talk to you but at the end of the interview adds, 'Of course, this has all been off the record, you understand'. The interviewee has caught you on the hop here because you cannot go ahead and publish the information as if nothing has been said. You may try to talk the subject out of it – some people like to be coaxed. But really if you had the slightest suspicion that this might happen, you should have asked perhaps more than once during the interview, 'I take it we can use this?' or any similar question expecting the answer 'Yes'.

But above all, when you have agreed to the off-the-record interview or to the withholding of the name, you must stick to the bargain. There is hardly a worse journalistic crime than breaking an undertaking, and neither the interviewee nor your editor will forgive you.

More difficult are the people who are averse to being interviewed at all and who will tolerate you only as long as you do not upset them. Here the first approach is to be absolutely correct (announcing who you are, why you are there, etc.). If interviewees can find enough fault with this they will evade being interviewed at all.

Very often, if you are building up several interviews for a composite story, the difficult person might become approachable if you point out that you already have some viewpoints on the subject and would like theirs too. On other occasions it is justifiable to say that you already have some information but would like their confirmation so that a balanced report gets into the paper. Quite often this prompts the hitherto difficult person to say, 'No, it is not like that,' and they will then launch into a full account as they see it.

Others refuse because of false modesty. They want to be coaxed into talking – a rather tedious type but if you play the game their way they will usually talk in the end.

Ultimately, you will come across the person who will just not be interviewed and on whom all your wiles are wasted. If a blank refusal is rudely phrased, or accompanied by some scathing comment, it is a cardinal rule not to be drawn. Never answer rudeness with rudeness. Report the rudeness when you get back to the office and leave any further steps to others who may be in a position to hit back more powerfully than you, if hitting back is necessary.

You might have to recognize that, deservedly or undeservedly, the person you are trying to interview can be fired, or even jailed in some countries, for talking to the press. Nicholas Ridley lost his ministerial job in Mrs Thatcher's government after expressing his views on Germany to a journalist over lunch. In 1996 a research council fired its head of communication because of her direct and honest reply to a *Sunday Times* question. A scientist with a Swiss company lost his job when a newspaper article drew his bosses' attention to his innovative work. They decided they were not interested in pursuing it.

Using your notebook

The correct point at which to produce a notebook will vary from subject to subject, ranging from public relations officers who hope they are going to be quoted from their very first words onwards to persons who are so shy that you do not produce your notebook at all. In the latter case, jot down the main points as soon after the interview as you can manage. In fact, never omit to make notes after the interview even if you could not do so while it was in progress; if you have no notes you have no defence if the interviewee denies everything.

As a general rule, it is a good idea to let the subject talk a little and take out your notebook when something interesting is said, with perhaps a comment such as 'I'll make a note of that'. This implies that it is so interesting you dare not trust it to memory alone. The subject will be flattered, and you have got your notebook working.

Let them talk

One of the commonest faults in interviewing is failing to let the interviewees tell their story – assuming that they are not reluctant to do so. It is a fault to start jumping in with questions before interviewees show any sign of drying up. Let them tell the story as far as possible without your help. Look for quotes which will give life to your story.

The best way to do this is merely to ask 'Can you tell me what happened?' or 'Can you tell me anything about it?' Many reporters fail to do this, and start asking questions so early that they tend to bottle up the person's own account.

Once your interviewee has started talking, do not halt the flow with any questions except those necessary to keep the main drift of the story clear in your mind. Do not at this stage ask questions about minor details.

If the interviewee is a stranger, keep your personal reactions to the minimum during this initial stage unless the person expresses things in such a way as to show they want a reaction (amusement, horror, surprise). Only when the person appears to have run out of information should you come in with questions.

First, go back for the details. Constantly refer to the note you have made of the person's account. It is here that intelligent use of shorthand and a notebook will score every time over the reporter who believes it can be carried in the head.

Now you can roam around the main theme of the story, asking those questions which may or may not produce something interesting – questions you may have thought up before the interview. By this time you will know whether they are still applicable or not, whether they should be forgotten or rephrased.

Try to get exact answers. When was 'recently'? What were the 'one or two difficulties'? How many was 'several'? Who were 'the people who helped'? Make sure, too, that you are quite clear about the exact meaning of any answer you are given. Ask for an explanation if necessary. Don't make false assumptions – for instance that what happens once happens all the time.

Interviewing is like a lucky dip – you dip in with a question and you never know whether it is going to bring up a prize or not. But, as with a lucky dip, the more dips you take, the more likely you are to get some prizes.

Never forget to ask: 'How/why did all this come about?' The past can throw light on the present and may suggest a further avenue of questioning. Then, too, always ask 'What will happen now?' (i.e. in the future).

Just because an answer comes late in the interview it does not mean it is only a minor fact. Most people do not have the same news sense as a journalist and something that seems unimportant to an interviewee, hardly worth mentioning, is often the best and most important part of the story.

The bell that rings

There are as many different kinds of interview as there are news stories, and it is obviously impossible to lay down what questions should and should not be asked at each one. Nevertheless, guidance can be given to the type of answer which should excite your interest and your further questioning – the type of bell that sometimes rings, or should ring, in your mind as an indication that here is something to go into your story.

Take as an example the following run-of-the-mill story. Assume you are told by the police or the fire service that there has been a fire at such-and-such an address occupied by Mr So-and-so: time of outbreak 11.30 p.m.; cause unknown; no personal injury; one fire appliance attended; damage to furniture and fittings in downstairs front room. Nothing much on the face of it, but you go and see the householder the next morning.

You find him in. Remember that the householder is likely to be distraught. Allow for this. You find him reasonably co-operative and you get down to business with the time-honoured, 'Can you tell me what happened?'

He answers (the numbers refer to points which will be discussed later):

'I was asleep (1) upstairs (2) last night (3) and everything was quiet when there was a knocking at the front door that woke me up. . . It kept on and as I started to go down I smelled smoke. . . .'

There was a young chap (4) at the door and I'd hardly got it open when he said, "Your front room's on fire. . ." He was on his way home from a dance and he thought he'd seen flames in there.

I opened the door into the front room and the place was thick with smoke (5). I ran into the kitchen to get a bucket of water but of course it took a long time (6). The young chap asked if there was anybody upstairs. There certainly was – the kiddies asleep (7). I gave him the bucket and ran up. They were awake and their room was full of smoke, too, coming through the floorboards (8). . . .

I told John to get something on (9) and go down, and took the baby (10) out of her cot. Then I realized Jeannie (11) wasn't following. The young chap had started on another bucketful. The kids were crying. I said "Jeannie's still up there" and started to go up but he beat me to it up the stairs and came down carrying Jeannie. . . .

I took over the bucket while he got the kiddies outside but we couldn't manage (12) and the young chap went and called the fire brigade (13). I roused the neighbours (14) and they took the kiddies in (15). Then the firemen came and put it out. Everything seems to be spoilt either by the smoke or the water. My wife'll create (16).'

The most obvious first question is the one prompted by the last casual remark (16): 'Where is your wife, then?'

'She's in hospital having another baby.'

This could give you your intro. Likely points would be: When is the baby due? Which hospital? Who is looking after you and the children? With luck he might say they were expecting triplets! And when is he going to tell her about the fire? 'This afternoon when I visit her.'

This set of questions also disposes of (1), which should have been a query in your mind as to why he said 'I was asleep upstairs' and not the more customary 'We were'.

What did he mean by 'upstairs' (2)? He answers, 'In the back bedroom'. What time last night (3)? 'About 11.30.' This confirms the time given by the official source.

Who was the 'young chap' (4) who helped him? He answers, 'I don't know him from Adam.'

Why doesn't he? 'He never told me his name, never even let me say "Thank you".'

Visions of headlines about 'Mystery Hero' may be occurring to you at this point and you will want all the information you can get about this young man. Ask for a description.

'About 18, funny haircut, tight trousers, but he was very cool and I don't know what we'd have done without him.'

If you can get no more than this, press on to (5): what happened when you opened the front-room door? 'Curtains were beginning to catch fire, hearthrug burning and making a lot of smoke and smell. . .'

Why did it take a long time to get a bucket of water (6)? 'We haven't got a very good flow here, I suppose if it had only taken five seconds it would have seemed a long time.'

What children (7)? 'There's John, he's seven; Jeannie, five; and the baby, Mary. She's nearly three.'

Is the middle child's name Jeannie or Jean? Which schools do they go to? Nothing special here perhaps but it transpires that Jeannie started at the local infants' school only yesterday. Will she be attending tomorrow? 'Yes.'

Where were the children sleeping (8)? 'In the front upstairs bedroom.' Over the burning room? 'Yes.' Did the fire wake them before it woke you? 'Don't know, didn't hear them when I went downstairs but they may have been awake.' The fire itself didn't wake you? 'No, I'm a sound sleeper.' The knocking on the front door woke you? 'Yes.'

Point 9 arises in your mind when he says the name 'John' without further amplification but the query has already been covered in the answers the interviewee gave on (7): names and ages of children. The questions you were going to ask about 'the baby' (10) and 'Jeannie' (11) were also covered.

The phrase 'Couldn't manage' (12) is vague and is worth checking. It turns out the householder was referring to the poor flow of water. But the men might have been affected by smoke or heat.

How did the young chap call the fire brigade (13)? 'By phone.' Where from? 'The callbox on the corner wasn't working, he saw phone wires leading to a house with lights on and called from there.'

Which neighbours (14)? Interviewee roused the people in the adjoining house (this is a semi-detached). Names? Given. Do they still have the children (15)? 'Yes.'

So the statement he gave you is approximately covered. Possibly you can think of more questions you would have asked, or perhaps by the standards of your newspaper this was too trivial an event for an exhaustive interview. Nevertheless, the illustration shows how interviewees should be allowed to have their say first of all; then how the statements should be split up and analysed and followed through even if they produce nothing much.

On such a story as this, however, there are other questions you need to ask, apart from those arising from the interviewee's own story. What was the cause of the fire? Was he covered by insurance? Does he own the house or rent it (never call an occupier 'the owner' unless you know for sure)?

The insurance question is always worth asking because occasionally a family is not covered and a small fire like this can have serious financial complications. Follow up by a question on whether they lost anything valuable; it might turn out they lost a small pet, war medals, grandfather's gold watch. In a modest home like this it is unlikely that anything of great monetary value would be lost but there could be a good angle if they lost something they prized highly.

There are also personal questions to ask about the interviewee; spelling of his name, initials, where he works, local interests, is he a local man, has he been in this house long, etc.

You may want to note down a few points which do not require questions; personal observations such as the house having an exceptionally neat garden now trampled by firemen; or a great deal of chaos in the downstairs rooms which would not please the householder's wife if she saw it.

Coaxing answers

So there it is, a modestly interesting local story created by questioning out of a bald official statement. Stories like this occur thousands of times in a reporter's career and interviewing is the lever that prises them loose.

Try to be interested in the answers you get even if they do not appear very newsworthy. Usually the events interviewees describe are of some interest to themselves. Bear this in mind. Never feel contemptuous of them because they would not be important to you or they do not merit a line in the story you will write.

The garrulous interviewee can be a nuisance but often needs only an occasional guidance back to the main theme of the subject. This type of interviewee will probably give you facts you would not have thought of asking questions about: such people interview themselves.

Checking back

As an interview nears its close, make sure you have obtained replies to all the essential questions you wanted answering. If you have any written questions in your notebook, check back on them before you leave the interviewee. If not, make a quick catalogue in your mind of the salient points in the story and make sure you have all the material you need to write about them.

If the matter has been complicated, it often helps to have a recap at the end of an interview. Most interviewees will not object if you ask, 'I'd like to make sure I've got it right. Would you mind if I go over the main points again with you?' or if you ask for a recap on just a certain aspect.

Telephone interviews

It is not always possible to go to meet the person you want to talk to. They may live some distance away or you may need to talk to several people in a limited time. You must then rely on the telephone.

It is as well not to ring anyone before about 10 a.m. if you can help it, or after 9.30 p.m. If you are ringing someone at their office, try to make it after 10 a.m. and before 4.30 p.m.

You may be able to reach a person later at home but you may waste effort trying, since some spend a long time on the journey and others are hardly home before they are off for an evening out. Often 7 to 7.30 p.m. is a useful time for catching people at home, that is, after they have arrived and had a meal.

When telephoning, try to ask for someone by name, or for their secretary, or for the public relations officer if there is one. If you know no lesser name, then ask for the name of the person at the top. Asking for a name may save you being shunted off to some underling who cannot answer your questions or who has no authority to do so.

When you reach your chosen informant, make it clear straight away who you are, what newspaper you represent (do not rely on your switchboard operator to do this) and why you have rung.

Telephone interviewing requires a simple, clear technique. You need to be clear from the start about what questions must be answered whatever happens. If you are dealing with a complex subject, work out beforehand a form of words which will put your questions simply and clearly.

You also need to be clear, before you start telephoning, about the background; busy people are not going to waste time in unsought telephone conversations with reporters to whom every little detail must be explained and who show no grasp of the subject.

In a telephone interview, never forget that the telephone is an intrusion. If you ring inconveniently a busy person may give you only a bare minimum of their time. When you get through, always show more than normal courtesy; again the interviewee has only the sound of your voice upon which to base a judgement of you. Never forget to thank the person for helping.

Controversial interviews

Broadcasters make reputations by giving a hard interview time to people they disagree with and feel superior to. If someone is condemned by a newspaper interview, it can only be out of their own mouth. Arguing with an informant is a waste of time and gets in the way of the main task, which is obtaining clear, graphic information and opinions. Even on the air, vehemence is frequently a smokescreen behind which an interviewer seeks to hide a poor question that fails to get to the nub of the matter.

Newspaper editors tend to be wary of reporters who let their own view intrude into their reporting (comment-writing is different). If you are to be fair and accurate, you must give a fair hearing to people even though you may disagree with them.

You must also, however, be prepared to ask direct, probing questions. 'How do you justify what has happened?', 'Should there be open-sided wagons in the Channel Tunnel?' The fact that something is explained does not mean it is excusable and acceptable.

You have more time than the broadcasters. If you do not get a direct answer to your question, you can ask it again.

Christopher Dobson writes in *The Freelance Journalist* (Butterworth-Heinemann, 1994) that in an interview a friendly appearance, a soft voice, amiable chatter and an air of sincerity work wonders. Encourage your subject to volunteer information rather than have it extracted like cross-rooted wisdom teeth. When you get to the hard questions, you do not need to ask them aggressively.

Finding the hidden story

Lurking in many interviews is a hidden story which even the sharpest questioning cannot be relied on to bring to light. An offshoot of the Avon tyre company won in 1993 an award for its help to tyre-makers in Asia. Only at the award ceremony did it disclose that much of this help was given by one long-serving employee who worked beyond retirement age. Behind the company story was a human one.

So how might you find the hidden story? Here are a few ideas:

• Listen carefully to what people say. If what they say surprises you, explore it further. Staff journalists can check with the library whether a story is old or new.
• Keep on asking questions – the longer an interview lasts, the more chance there is that something unexpected will be said. It is especially important to keep a telephone interview going. If you dry up the interview will end.

Ask questions such as the following:

'*What difficulties did you overcome?*' – Enterprises usually give the impression that their success was plain sailing. This is rarely true. A butter-fly-rearing project in a remote part of Belize nearly foundered because the building of a serviceable approach road proved unexpectedly difficult. The butterfly experts had to turn road builders.

'What were you doing before?' – A promoter of technology utilization previously devised electronic equipment for modern aircraft.

'What are your plans?' – A new development may be near.

'What are your colleagues working on?' – It could be something of great interest.

At some interviews, the only story is the hidden story. Both the comedian Dave Allen and the athlete Daley Thompson have been known to give interviews at which they declined to answer questions. Daley's stonewalling made an entertaining newspaper article, closing with the publicity officer's inquiry: 'Have you got enough material?'

Dave Allen on television, proved willing to answer questions about his childhood in a family divided in religion and haunted by a hellfire priest. This was an important hidden story because it showed what lay behind his religious satire.

The second interview

A second interview may throw completely new light on your subject. An interview was intended to produce a feature on a new technique for killing germs in operating theatres, but it turned out that the doctors concerned wanted to patent the technique and so opposed publication. A second interview saved the day by disclosing that similar techniques were being developed for killing HIV and other viruses in blood products for transfusion.

There was, in fact, a further hidden story (see Finding the hidden story, above). A *Daily Mail* writer interviewed a researcher who used the same approach to produce a germ-killing toothbrush.

In an interview the Tanzanian government announced it was stopping the cutting of teak. What made an ordinary story lively was an interview with a furniture maker who was faced with having no teak for his furniture.

What an interviewee may be hiding is that his company is about to fail, or that it has been engaged in sharp practice or that it has been less successful than it claims or that he himself or the company is about to lose a contract or job. Your editor will expect you to find these things out. An article published in ignorance could embarrass the paper. How do you find out?

Listen during the interview for any hint that something is amiss. Your informant may brush criticisms of his work aside but the criticisms could be valid or, even if invalid, widely believed. A second interview here with a knowledgeable outsider is a good safeguard.

Where interviews can fail

Most reporters talking to most interviewees on most subjects get more material than they can use. Editors, however, seem to be asking more questions these days, which means reporters must ask more, too.

Bernard Palela, editing the *Business Times* in Tanzania, rarely failed to find at least six more questions he wanted answered on any story submitted to him. He was also usually unhappy with reports based on a single interview.

In Britain the quality papers have got interested in what they call numbers: the facts and figures which uphold, or fail to uphold, the assertions people make.

The phrase 'fresh frozen plasma' in an article for the *Sunday Times* inspired a hilarious afternoon of questioning. How did it differ from any other plasma the sub-editor wanted to know.

It turned out that fresh frozen plasma (from donated blood) is plasma used by local hospitals, as opposed to that sent for processing at the transfusion service's national laboratory, which shows that reporters need to understand precisely what interviewees are talking about.

The Independent article on page 51 stemmed from a paragraph in the newsletter of King's College, London, which referred to a European Union-sponsored effort to stop Europe's Mediterranean countries turning into desert.

What *The Independent* ideally wanted was a sharply defined, overall picture of what is happening, with figures to show its importance, plus cogent examples of how people are affected and suggestions for putting things right. The research so far, however, had collected basic data about climate and about some hillsides and river valleys. The overall picture lacked sharp definition.

Professor John Thornes, co-ordinator of the Medalus project (Mediterranean Desertification and Land Use), was keen in interview to tell the public what was going on. But he did not have to hand the sort of facts, figures, graphic details and human stories a newspaper looks for.

He wanted to assess the impact of erosion on individual farms. Rainfall has halved, he said, and global warming is liable to reduce it further. Plants stop growing when the soil dries out at the end of May. Many are destroyed by fires during the summer. Much of the rain falls in autumn storms which wash away soil from hillsides. Farming has switched from the hills to vegetable-growing in valleys, which uses a lot of scarce water.

The Med slides towards disaster

Soil erosion caused by water-hungry crops and tourism is threatening southern Europe's landscape. By **David Spark**

Tomorrow an international conference begins in Crete to try to prevent a repetition of the horrifying hectares – 28.6 per cent of susceptible drylands – have been at least moderately degraded by human activity. This is the highest percentage of any continent. Moisture may become scarcer as a result of global warming (though computer models offer conflicting answers). If so, the hardest hit use water sparingly, by installing drip irrigation and growing crops under polythene. Nevertheless the agriculture which puts cheap Spanish lettuces and strawber-

Figure 5.1 *Pictures and interviews play their part in the presentation of an important news story – an example for* The Independent

Dr Nichola Geeson, joint manager of Medalus, in interview, recalled the disaster earlier in 1996 when a flood of mud overwhelmed a campsite in the Spanish Pyrenees. Here was erosion in devastating action. It made a good opening for the story.

The Spanish Tourist Office in London said farming takes up 60 per cent of Spain's water supply and domestic use 10 per cent. Warmth and sunlight make it possible to grow two or even three vegetable crops a year, if water is available. Furthermore, the years 1995 and 1996 have both been wet, replenishing the water in underground aquifers.

The tourist office's director pointed out that Spain for centuries has been diverting water from rivers to improve the supply. It is well off for reservoirs.

Dr Jean Palutikof of the Climate Research Unit at East Anglia University said the latest computer model suggests the Mediterranean will get slightly wetter. (This contradicted the earlier belief that it will get drier.)

The article as printed showed what came out of these varied interviews. The interviews, in fact, failed to establish a clear link between the two themes of damaged land and overused water, despite the subsidiary headline (above) which attempts such a link.

Attempts to vet copy

In any sort of interview, telephone or otherwise, resist, if you can, any request that you submit your story to the interviewee before publication. It is unlikely that your newspaper is prepared to surrender its right of unfettered reporting. Occasionally an exception can be made where the story deals with a complex technical subject and your newspaper decides it wants the informant to vet the story for accuracy. In this case the decision to submit the story is the newspaper's.

If your interviewee insists on seeing the story as a condition of giving the information, say that you will put the request to the editor. If the editor agrees, it is usual to submit to the interviewee a print-out or copy of your typescript. Do not give the story to the sub-editors until you have had the vetted copy back again.

Some interviewees are pedantic about phraseology and will attempt to make all sorts of minor alterations to the wording. Always make it clear, as tactfully as possible, that you are seeking confirmation of fact and not changes in style or wording.

6 NEWS WRITING

As you gather your facts after your assignment and make your way with them to the telephone or back to the office, force yourself to decide where your story will begin. In the main, you have two choices. You can choose the most important and striking of the facts you have gathered; or if the basic facts themselves are not of immediate human interest you can choose some more personal and human point which does have this interest.

Here are two good openings: 'The postmen's strike is on – no mail will be delivered today'; 'It was washday yesterday for Mrs E— of Puddletown; but by the time she came to hang her washing out, part of her garden wall had been knocked down to make room for a new bus shelter.'

The first of these sets out some important news in a simple, direct fashion. It tells the reader just how the news affects him or her.

The second is longer. It could have begun: 'Workmen yesterday knocked down part of a garden wall to make way for a bus shelter.' But this would have been less interesting. It is Mrs E— and her washday who win the readers' interest and entice them to read on.

Here is another example: 'Yesterday as she put her joint in the oven for her husband's and children's dinner, Mrs Jones of 5 Dolphin Avenue was one of the first housewives to use W—'s new gas supply.' This is more interesting and imaginative than merely recording the opening ceremony.

Very occasionally, even when the main news is of immediate interest, it is worth delaying it, like this:

The new toy was a bit heavy but nine-year-old Stephen Alton, of Billingham, caught it and threw it back to his brother Philip.
    The window cleaner, Fred Jarvis, glanced over casually during his Saturday round but a second later he was clambering at top speed down the ladder.
    The children were playing with a live mortar bomb.

The graphic quality of this makes it superior to the more straightforward: 'A window cleaner scrambled down his ladder yesterday to stop two children playing with a live mortar bomb.'

Here now are two bad openings: 'For 49 years, with a break for the war, the cathedral has not heard sounds like the note David G— sang yesterday.' And the second: 'Despite the high unemployment among young people in T—, the city cannot be accused of neglecting the education of the young for their future careers.'

The first does not make sense; the writer, in trying to be different, got himself confused. The point of the story was in fact simple. David G— had been in the cathedral choir for almost 50 years. That is what the opening sentence should have said.

The second example might have been acceptable as the opening of a report of a dull speech by a local bigwig. It does not pass muster at all as an opening for what the reporter was writing: an account of his visit to a new teacher-training college a day or two after its first term had begun. This cried out for a more personal treatment:

> John T—, last week a clerk in an engineering office, was yesterday sitting at a different sort of desk, training to be a schoolteacher.

Wherever you decide to begin, never try to say too much at once. If you find your thoughts rushing out, send them all back and insist on one at a time.

Where to begin

If the main news of your story is of immediate interest to your readers, try to grasp the kernel of it from all the interesting side-issues which can come later: A man is in hospital with typhoid. Two people were drowned when their car fell into the river. The Mayor was killed today in a level-crossing crash. These are facts that should go in the first sentence or intro.

Where the news is less unusual or immediately arresting, it may have its particular humanity and human irony. A driving examiner is fined for a parking offence because he did not want to keep an L-test candidate waiting. A man drives a van to do a friend a good turn and is fined because the vehicle is defective.

Two young soldiers were once tried in court for stealing a stone, a rather bizarre offence worth a paragraph; but the story which the case disclosed was a little human drama in itself. Mrs A—, living near a river bridge, heard a scuffle one night. There was a splash and she saw the soldiers running away. Thinking they had pushed someone into the river, she called the police, who searched it for several hours. But all they found was the stone.

Telling the story, as above, was the best way to present a report of this case, since the soldiers pleaded 'Guilty'. It was the human drama, rather than the charge, the fines or the magistrates' comments which made people want to read it.

Some of the most awkward reports to begin are those of news which is obviously important but which is not going to make much impression on the reader unless well presented. Planning officers issued an important statement about the amount of waste land disfiguring their region and about ways of reclaiming it. One suggestion in the course of the statement was for a corps of youth volunteers to help in the work. An imaginative journalist seized on this as the most newsworthy point. It was something practical, something new, something the readers could grasp.

Sometimes you might feel that the succession of incidents you have to report requires a general introduction, like this perhaps: 'Big groups of football supporters went on a drunken tour of the town yesterday, fighting in the streets and smashing glasses in pubs.' This is fair enough, provided you are going to quote specific incidents later which will bear out your opening assertion. You will want to mention at least two big groups, at least one fight in the streets, and the breaking of glass in at least two public houses.

If you cannot do this, a more specific opening is better, as you cannot then be accused of exaggeration: 'Five people were arrested last night when football supporters fought in the main street.'

What is new?

Some reporters make heavy weather of reports following up earlier events. Either they fail to explain the earlier events adequately or, in their eagerness to explain, they kill their report with a recital of previously reported history.

A news story should begin with news. Avoid beginning with an idea which is negative in feeling and whose expression will require words like 'no', or 'not' or 'unlikely'. If there is no news why should the reader read on? If you report some notable occasion you need to open with something new, not with a point which could have been made equally well before the occasion took place.

When reporting speeches be on your guard against being misled by eloquence. What sounds important at the time may look trite in cold print. One newspaper report began:

Europe today offered companies both a dilemma and a challenge, said Sir
A— B—, speaking last night at the annual dinner of the Chamber of
Commerce.

This was scarcely news. In the final paragraph of the report, however, Sir
A— was quoted as saying: 'There are still too many companies in this
country who could be exporters and who are not.' Surely this was a much
more interesting point with which to begin?

A frequent difficulty which reporters present to their readers is the
mixing of facts and comment. If you have to choose between a fact and a
comment about the fact – and both are news since your paper last
appeared – put the fact first. This helps the reader to understand. Look
at this example:

'In view of the Government's Report on future traffic needs, a railway station
would be even more essential,' Councillor Leonard Richardson, chairman of
Guisborough Council, said yesterday. 'Extra buses replacing trains would
have to travel along narrow roads, adding to traffic congestion.'

He made his comments shortly after it had been announced that the
Minister of Transport had agreed to the ending of the train services between
Guisborough and Middlesbrough.

This report should have begun: 'Train services between Guisborough and
Middlesbrough are to end.' This was the news, and it was also essential
to the understanding of Councillor Richardson's comment.

Starting with a quote

For typographical reasons many newspapers used to forbid their reporters
to begin reports with quotations. This rule can be waived and so, if you
feel that a quotation is the most interesting and distinctive feature of your
story, do not be afraid to put it first.

Here is an example from a local paper in which the opening quotation
gives freshness to a rather common-or-garden subject, a schoolteacher's
departure for Australia:

'I just cannot wait to get to the sunshine,' said Marion Hutchinson, of 14
Copper's Terrace, Thornley, yesterday, referring to her new job in Sydney,
Australia.

If your best quotation is a complicated one it is better to hold it back to
support your first sentence, rather than to put it first. The national
newspapers rarely make this mistake. This famous occasion is from the
Daily Mail:

Mr Khrushchev tonight claimed that the Berlin convoy hold-up had been
solved by a Western climb-down. He declared: 'We would not have yielded
and they would have had to move over our dead bodies.'

This opening would have been poorer with the quotation first.

Using a quote at the beginning can cause difficulties if your newspaper's style is to begin stories with a drop letter – i.e. an ornamental big capital letter at the beginning of the first paragraph. A quotation mark in front of a drop letter looks rather odd.

In reporting speeches you should distinguish between expressions of opinion and announcements of fact. If the news point of a speech is an opinion, then you must give it as a quotation or in a piece of indirect speech attributed to the speaker. If it is a fact you can state it as a fact, e.g. 'A new road is to be built from the Dun Cow Inn to the town boundary'; or 'Water is short in some parts of the city'. You can leave naming the speaker until the second or even the third sentence. This gives you a simpler opening.

Opening sentence

Having decided what your first point is to be, your task is to express it in a simple, clear, accurate, direct and precise opening sentence. This sentence should not be longer than it need be. Opening sentences of 40 words or more are to be avoided.

Have another look at that earlier example about the postmen: 'The postmen's strike is on – no mail will be delivered today.' Compare it with these:

1 Professor M—, MA, DSc, has been appointed to the chair of Environmental Studies in the University of L—, with a principal interest in the evolution of the external environment and its effects in N—.
2 While the government accepts the principle of the Report on higher education and will implement its main proposals, this will not be done to the detriment of other branches of education, said the Minister of Education last night.

In both of these, the meaning has been lost in forms of official jargon that are foreign to the ordinary reader: 'evolution of the external environment'; 'implement its main proposals'.

The report of the minister's speech later records his actual words. 'I want to make it clear,' he said, 'that the undertaking in this report will not be at the expense of schools and colleges.'

The whole flavour and directness of this has been lost in the laboured opening sentence. Next time you are tempted to change 'schools and colleges' into 'other branches of education', think again.

Your opening sentence must be direct and precise if it is to catch the reader's imagination and interest. So avoid the formulas of local government minutes that sometimes creep into newspapers: 'Reference was made'; 'The view was expressed that...': 'The value of the Duke of Edinburgh's Award scheme was stressed by...'. Even passable opening sentences can often be made simpler and more precise.

If the facts are technical, do not just hope the readers will understand without help where the meaning had to be explained to you. Show how the technical facts are related to people:

> Research concerning the cells of a water plant found in Scottish lochs and Norfolk broads may in time help farmers to grow better crops, especially in arid countries. By using radioactive particles of sodium, potassium, chlorine and other substances, biochemists are studying how the plant absorbs them....

Often you have to choose what to leave out of your opening sentence to keep it short or within bounds, while still retaining in it the maximum meaning: 'A steelworker was trapped two hours when a girder fell at the Johnson engineering works today.' This does not tell the reader much about the steelworker, his injuries or how he was released. It does say what happened and where it happened, which are essential facts.

Stick to the facts

Whatever you decide to leave out of your opening sentence, always retain its clarity and accuracy. The sentence must be readily comprehensible at first reading. It must also be accurate, not just approximate. Much criticism of newspapers stems from opening sentences which, for the sake of sharpness or impact or simplicity, go further than the established facts. Consider this one:

> Hundreds of dairy farmers in N— are puzzled and angered by a letter they got yesterday from their milk company.

It turned out that only a few farmers were puzzled and angry.

C. P. Scott, an editor of *The Guardian*, was famous for his dictum that the comment is free but facts are sacred. Facts can be curiously hard to stand up. The young reporter who accepts as hard fact an allegation by a union secretary or a management spokesman about an industrial dispute without checking is assuming too much. In reporting an allegation be sure to attribute it to the person making it. In reporting a decision by a council or committee be sure to include any provisos that qualify it. Beware of saying something has happened for the first time unless this is checkable.

Simple and precise

Accuracy apart, you will often have to choose between maximum simplicity and maximum precision. A sentence can be simple and vague; it can also be precise and clumsy. Compare these two openings from *The Times*:

A wife's forgiveness of the husband who put bleach in her gin helped to save him from prison yesterday.

A high-altitude trial launching of Britain's air-launched nuclear weapon Blue Steel was cancelled for technical reasons today only three minutes before the appointed time of firing.

In the first opening, precise detail has been ruthlessly pared away to focus the reader's attention on the two essential facts: that a man put bleach in his wife's gin and that her forgiveness helped to save him from prison. The second opening, on the other hand, is full of detail, gives the reader an exact picture from the start and saves explanation later.

Both methods have their application in provincial newspapers, as in these examples:

A woman was killed at Hartlepool yesterday by the car of a friend she was teaching to drive.

R— J—, the 23-year-old Newcastle man serving a six months' prison sentence at Durham, was still on the run today 48 hours after disappearing from a working party outside the jail.

The second of these is detailed and exact. The first is able to capture the meat of the story in one sentence of eighteen words because the detail of that sentence has been pared away. Compare it with the opening sentence of a report of the same accident in another newspaper: 'A 53-year-old Hartlepool woman was knocked down and killed by a car in Hartlepool yesterday.'

This has only one word fewer; yet it has not the irony which made the accident, in both papers, appear prominently on page one.

The precisely detailed method of intro can also be taken too far. Here is a very wordy example:

Mgr McCann, Roman Catholic Archbishop of Capetown, put forward a proposal at the Vatican Council today that a consultative body of bishops drawn from the entire episcopate, meeting periodically in Rome with the Pope and leading officials of the Curia, might be empowered by the Council to decide certain detailed questions arising from their debates.

This would bore and scare off many readers.

On the other hand, provincial devotees of the spare style often overlook one reason for its attractiveness to the popular national newspapers: that it can hide away the locality of the story and so induce people living miles away from, say, Wrexham to read a Wrexham report. In a local paper this de-localizing is hardly a virtue. It also lengthens the report unnecessarily since the opening sentence has later to be explained in specific terms.

In a County Durham newspaper, for instance, there is no point in an opening sentence like this: 'The smallest partner in a joint committee set up to find jobs for an area has had the biggest success.' This should have read: 'The smallest partner in North-West Durham's job-finding committee, Lanchester District, has had the biggest success.'

The cult of the spare style tends also to bring with it a cult of the indefinite article 'a'. Here is an unnecessarily repeated use of the indefinite article:

> A church congregation will act as the jury in a 're-trial' of Christ, which has been written as a Passion play by a W— Congregationalist minister.

This should have read:

> The congregation will be the jury in a retrial of Christ which the minister of St George's Congregational Church, W—, has written as a Passion play.

The best general rule is to make your opening as exact and precise as you can without making it clumsy. Do not say 'a man', say 'a bricklayer' or 'John Smith, a bricklayer'. Do not say 'a union official', if you can say 'the union secretary'. Do not say 'a firm' if you can say 'Graham and Son, the engineers. . . .' This is especially important in local and regional newspapers. Many readers will know of or work at the firm; the mention of its name will give them a reason for reading the report.

Again, in your local paper, if the place of the incident you are reporting is a town or village in your circulation area, give its name. Do not be satisfied with the name of the county or district. Here is an opening which could have been more precisely expressed:

> A chief source of income for H— village hall may end soon and make it impossible to keep the hall going.

This could have read:

> H— village hall may soon lose its income from school meals. As a result, it may have to close.

It is often possible to split down an opening idea into two sentences for simplicity. This is an example where it has been done:

Midland miners were asked yesterday to vote on Saturday morning working. Each pit will decide for itself whether it will work the Saturday shift to ensure supplies of power station coal this winter: there will be no coalfield decision.

Grabbing the reader

Keep your intro especially short – not more than 20–25 words – when you are reporting an unexpected, dramatic happening. A long sentence will blur the sense of drama and no larding with 'sensational', 'dramatic', 'tragedy' or other pseudo-exciting words will save it. Take this example:

> An airliner belonging to British Airways skidded and slewed off the side of Heathrow Airport's No. 1 runway today after a flight from Malta.

This is all right but, when shorter, it becomes much better:

> An airliner skidded off the runway at Heathrow airport today.

If you ever have to report on a disaster, the best and most tasteful methods are the simplest. Give the readers simple, straightforward answers to their questions. How many people were killed? What happened? What do the eyewitnesses say? Who came to help?

This is not the time to search your vocabulary for adjectives and similes, so avoid this sort of opening:

> It was like hurling a stone into a cup of coffee. But the stone was a mountain. And just before midnight it plunged into the 873 ft concrete V— dam to spill over its side a 150-million-ton liquid cataract of death.

The report from which this opening is quoted told the readers in the second paragraph, almost as an afterthought, that up to 4000 people had been killed.

There is a time and place for adjectives and similes, particularly when the occasion has a feeling of ceremonial. Big national newspapers manage this sort of thing extremely well, as in this opening from *The Guardian* after the successful rescue of three miners in a German pit accident:

> Like celebrities arriving at an international airport, the three trapped miners stepped down the gangway from a decompression chamber today into the mud and safety of a *sugar beet* field.

The *Daily Mail* man caught the scene with even greater precision:

> Three brave men walked out of the steel compression chamber here tonight. Blinking as the light hit them they walked down 25 wooden steps unaided into a churned-up *turnip* field and freedom.

It is a shame that the inquiries of one or other of the reporters had failed to identify what the field had actually grown!

Frequently, as in these two examples, reporters with imagination can give greater meaning to the bald fact which their opening expresses. Here are more examples:

- **Bald fact:** a father and mother have been found dead. ***Intro:*** 'Three young sisters were orphaned this weekend when both their parents met a violent death.' This shows the human result of the tragedy.

- **Bald fact:** a town's War Memorial Committee is to wind up. ***Intro:*** 'After 18 years during which it provided a variety of social activities, never-ending controversy and finally a £30,000 swimming bath, the Northallerton War Memorial Committee is to wind up.' The bald fact has been put into the wider and interesting context of the committee's history and achievement.

- **Bald fact:** a Civic Trust has been formed for the North-East. ***Intro:*** 'There is to be a Civic Trust for the North-East to help in a drive to clear away eyesores and ugliness, and to make the North-East a better place in which to live and work.' To the ordinary reader the phrase 'A Civic Trust' is meaningless. This opening explains it in terms of what it will try to do.

- **Bald fact:** the County Planning Officer has issued a detailed criticism of a proposal for a linear city stretching across County Durham. ***Intro:*** '"Stop the nightmare – I want to get off" is the reaction of Mr J. R. Atkinson, the Durham County Planning Officer, to the suggested scheme for a linear city stretching 40 miles from Darlington to Cramlington.' This opening from a weekly paper cuts through the detail and gives a racy summary of what the planning officer was saying.

Order of facts

Having got down your opening sentence, which is the key to your report for reader and subeditor alike, your next task is to review and check the rest of your facts and organize them into a continuous, fair, readable thread of thought. Besides the facts in the opening sentence, many events throw up other important facts which ought to follow as soon after the opening as they can. You want to emphasize any unusual features. You also want to answer the readers' immediate questions quickly: what happened; who was hurt; am I in any danger? And so on.

At an inquest there was an account of a road crash, a statement that the dead man was not to blame and a request by a solicitor for stricter precautions in future. The explanation was the major fact for the opening, but the other two points needed to come early in the report as well.

Again, consider a major accident in which several people have been hurt. Most reports will begin with the number of injured but other points need to be made soon. Readers want a brief, one-sentence description of what happened. They want the names and addresses of the injured. You will also want to tell readers if someone had a lucky escape and the names of those who distinguished themselves in rescue work. You will want to say how the people in the crash came to be there. You will then want to give any eyewitness accounts.

Here is an example of story construction from another field:

> Drugs with a street value of around £4000 were seized in a series of early morning raids at homes across South Wales yesterday.
> Under the cover of darkness 60 plain clothes and uniformed officers swooped at ten locations in Cardiff, Swansea and Pontypridd in a co-ordinated operation police had been planning for months.
> Twelve people were arrested and a range of drugs, believed to include heroin, LSD, amphetamines and cannabis, were taken away for forensic tests.
> At one house in Rhydfelin, Pontypridd – which has been dubbed the drugs capital of South Wales because of their easy availability – police recovered £300 worth of heroin. . . .

After giving other details of the raids, the story introduces an explanatory quote:

> Detective Chief Inspector Clive Bartholomew, head of the South Wales force's drugs squad, said: ' We were targeting what we would call medium-sized dealers, people who do this professionally and make a living from it. They are in it for the money.' (*Western Mail*)

Constructed in this way, a story has a natural impetus. It answers the reader's questions as the eye descends through the paragraphs. Here is a news story of a very different sort which demonstrates again how intro and supporting material are put together:

> An artificial electronic limb promises to give seventeen-month-old Martin Calder, the youngest child in Britain to be fitted with such a limb, much greater freedom.
> Martin, from Paisley, Renfrewshire, was born with both hands and one leg missing and is adapting well to his new right hand, fitted by doctors at Southern General Hospital, Glasgow.
> Fingers on the tiny hand clench as muscles in the stump of his arm transmit signals from his brain.

As he grows older, doctors hope a left hand and working artificial leg will follow.

'It will revolutionize his life. We are hopeful that he may soon be able to feed himself,' said Mr Mark Broomfield, lecturer in prosthetics at Strathclyde University. (*The Herald, Glasgow*)

If you are reporting a controversy and your report is to be fair, then the major point each side is making should be presented in your first few sentences. It is unfair to set out one side of the controversy at length because it is the newsier and then add the other side only at the end.

You should also set down the main points of major announcements before you become enmeshed in other people's comments on them. Announcement-and-comment is an increasingly common form of news task, as governments and other public agencies grow more and more active and publicity-seeking.

No journalist reporting the budget would hesitate a moment before opening his report with the budget's main provisions: ten pence on cigarettes, six pence on beer and so on. Too many journalists perhaps fail to realize that the same logic of telling the reader the facts applies to other announcements. It is not enough to set down one main fact, follow it with a batch of comment and let the important detail get in as best it can.

Once you have given a fact or a quotation there is no need to repeat it further down when you come to give more quotations or more details. Nor, if two people make the same point, is there any need to quote both of them.

Some journalists open their reports with a summary of perhaps four to six paragraphs and then go back to the beginning to rehearse all the facts in detail, including those already given. This is fair enough on the rare occasions when you need to give a semi-verbatim report of an important meeting, but it can be a waste of space. The Press Association news agency uses the summary method but out of necessity; it has to send out running stories as they develop, and therefore supplies summaries or 'new leads' from time to time to keep the running story up to date. For reporters producing a report all of a piece it is better to resolve the facts into a single logical and unrepetitive thread.

When you are writing a long report on a complex subject you may find at the end of, say, the fourth paragraph that your thread of thought is not moving through the facts in quite the right direction. Some important points are being missed out. If that happens, do not be afraid to go back to the beginning and start again.

If necessary, make a list of the points you want to include in a report and get them into order, or even jot down for yourself an outline plan of the story.

Explanations

You may find that you have established your opening points all right but your next four or five paragraphs are full of explanatory or previously reported material that does not take the narrative any further forward. This is a particular danger with reports that follow on from a report in a previous issue. Far too many journalists expect their readers to read through a long recital of what the paper has already told them before they come to anything fresh. Long explanations early in a news report are death. It is far better to try again. You will almost certainly find that, at a second look, you can pick out the most important explanatory facts and get them into one paragraph.

A long explanation may indeed be needed. Newspapers often fail to explain enough for the reader who has not read previous reports on the same subject. The right place to give any long explanation, however, is at the end of the report or in a separate panel alongside. In the first few paragraphs you need give the readers only enough explanation to let them know where they are.

Here are the third and fourth sentences of an account of the shooting of baby seals on the Farne Islands:

> Two Ministry of Agriculture and Fisheries marksmen, brought down from Scotland and flown to Staple Island in a hired helicopter, did the killing.
> Today and tomorrow they plan to shoot over 200 more female pups or a number of cows and pups in this operation aimed at reducing the breeding potential of the colony by a quarter.

This puts the reader right in the picture without running to length.

The second paragraph of *The Guardian* account, given earlier, of the rescue of three miners in Germany read like this:

> They are in excellent health after spending eight days, caught by floods, in an air pocket 240 ft underground and at a pressure of two and a half times that of normal.

This not only gives the background but in its first phrase takes the report a stage forward.

Notice the precise detail of these examples. Precision helps to establish the difference between one event and another and so avoid the sort of woolly sentence that takes no grip on a reader's interest or mind. Make it clear for the reader what happened and where it happened.

Helping the reader

People learn by relating new information to what they already know. This is why you should resolve your facts into an unbroken thread, taking the reader step by step from your opening points through to the remainder of your information, like this:

> Thieves broke into the H— Workshops for the Blind and stole prizes waiting to be collected after a raffle.
>   They got away with a wristwatch, a travelling clock and £15 in cash. Charles Freeman, secretary and manager of the workshops, said, 'We will have to replace the prizes now.'
>   The prizes were given by traders in the town to raise money for the blind. The raiders broke into the workshops through a first-floor window. Staff discovered the break-in when they arrived for work on Saturday morning.

The reporter has to rearrange the facts to make an unbroken thread of thought from the opening sentences. Far from beginning at the beginning and working through to the end, the reporter might have to begin at the end and work through to the beginning.

The same holds true for reports of meetings. It is no use reporting Councillor Johnson first simply because he spoke first if the one making the most important speech was Councillor Smith. In the report Councillor Smith must take first place.

The thread of thought running through your story should nevertheless be clear, simple, fair, accurate, systematic and unbroken. It also needs to be as direct and specific as possible. Do not write a generalized phrase like 'taking part in a mercy mission to a South Italian village' when you can write the specific facts 'helping to repair a nursery school in a South Italian village'.

Write clearly, so that a non-expert will understand the situation; but do not betray your own previous ignorance to the expert.

Sometimes it is possible to make your facts crystal clear by presenting them in a sort of note form. A light-hearted newspaper account of a Dutch hornplayer's criticism of the Northern Sinfonia Orchestra and of an orchestra spokesman's reply contained this passage:

> **Horn player:** 'The orchestra gives far too many concerts and does far too much travelling about. Instead of playing in towns like Stanley or Whitley Bay, the Sinfonia should be concentrating on engagements in the big centres of population.'
> **Spokesman:** 'I don't think 140 concerts in a year is overworking the orchestra. The orchestra because of the way it is financed has an obligation to small communities as well as large ones. . .'
> **Horn player:** 'The Sinfonia has no porter. Everyone has to do his own donkey work.'
> **Spokesman:** 'Many of the musicians. . .won't allow you to carry their instruments for them.'

This was a lucid presentation of the facts of criticism and reply. It is fair, giving both sides of the argument, which is absolutely essential in any report of controversy. It is also systematic, working through the criticisms subject by subject in a way anyone can understand.

Changing subjects

In reporting, you sometimes have to choose whether to go through your facts subject by subject or speaker by speaker. You must do one or the other. Never shift about at random.

Some reporters make heavy labour of tying their material together in one thread. There is no need for this sort of phrase: 'Another point of view was expressed by Mr Higgs who said. . .' If Mr Higgs was speaking on the same subject as the previous speaker 'Mr Higgs said' will do; or, if you want to stress his disagreement with what has gone before, 'However, Mr Higgs said' or 'By contrast, Mr Higgs said'.

Very often you can so manipulate your material that one sentence leads on to the next without any artificial bridge but occasionally you need to change from one subject to quite a different one. If so, make this clear with some short introductory phrase, like this: 'On the arts festival, Councillor Smith said. . .' This warns the reader of the new subject.

When changing subjects, it is a good idea to leave a bigger space than usual between your paragraphs. This warns the sub-editor that here is a good place for a sidehead or crosshead.

Never leave the reader guessing about the identity of a speaker you are quoting. If you are introducing a new speaker in your report, start the sentence with him. 'Roger Johnson, president of the Brightland Civic Trust, said it was time the town had a theatre. . .' If you leave his name until the end of the sentence the reader will assume that you are still reporting the previous speaker.

Make sure it is clear who the new speaker is. Do not just write 'Roger Johnson' if it is six paragraphs since you mentioned he was president of the Civic Trust.

If possible, save up for the end of your report some interesting fact or wry comment which perhaps will give it a sense of completeness. This is much better than leaving your line of thought hanging in the air.

It is easy to say what should be done in short examples, less easy to do it in a long report when you are faced with a notebook full of notes. Here is a report reprinted by courtesy of *The Star*, Sheffield:

They're at it again . . . for the fourth time this year, in the name of progress, workmen were today digging a trench at the junction of Abbey Lane and Abbeyfield Road, Sheffield.

This tortured strip of tarmac has been gouged, torn and filled in until it has taken on the appearance of a patchwork quilt. The workmen will be finished by Wednesday or Thursday but residents are asking: 'When will they be back again?'

There is a rumour that the road never stays intact longer than a week.

At the beginning of the year, city engineers carved a giant main sewer down Abbeyfield Road, turning sharp right at the junction and proceeding up Abbey Lane.

They dug a hole in the middle, fenced it round with railway sleepers and stayed there so long that when they filled it in a correspondent of *The Star* lamented the disappearance of a 'Sheffield memorial'.

Then the traffic lights had to be rewired, renewed and resited. Up came the road again and down went another trench and another pipe.

Next a junction box blew up nearby. That meant another trench, more traffic queues and more noise.

Now the electricity company are laying a 33,000-volt cable to a new primary sub-station to Totley Rise – in yet another trench.

The reason for all this is – progress. For the electricity company, it is a result of 'the tremendous growth in domestic load in this part of the city', said their Chief Engineer, Mr F— S—. The new main sewer will combat flooding which people in the Beauchief dip experienced after heavy rainfall.

At Beauchief Post Office, the postmistress, Mrs M— E—, has got so used to a hole in the road outside that she no longer notices it. 'It's been going on for years now,' she said today. 'It doesn't bother me any more. One thing I'm sure of; as soon as they fill the trenches up it'll be no time at all before they start digging again.'

G— G—, foreman at the Beauchief Garage just below the junction, says: 'There is always a great big trench somewhere round the crossroads. If it's not one thing, it's another.'

He said that the excavations caused traffic jams all the way down to Millhouses and seriously affected petrol sales at peak hours, when the road was too congested for motorists to drive into the garage forecourt.

What of the future? A City Engineer's spokesman said: 'For the time being that would appear to be it. When the electricity company fill in their trench, there are no others planned.'

This story starts in the right place and also has a proper ending. It is simple, clear and lively. It is, in all probability, fair: the reporter has taken the trouble to speak to electricity company and city spokesmen as well as to the local people. Part of the narrative thread, from 'At the beginning of the year', is chronological; but the chronological passage begins only after the present has been described.

The narrative moves smoothly except between the quotations from Mr S— and Mrs E—, where there is a slight break in the line of thought.

Handling quotations

The reporter in the above example has also successfully solved problems which often give trouble: what to quote and what to paraphrase; and how much of each to include. There are several ways of presenting information gleaned, as in this example, from interviews:

- **Direct quotation:** Roger Johnson said: '. . .'
- **Indirect speech:** Roger Johnson said that. . .
- **Statement of the information** as fact, without reference to Mr Johnson or whoever gave it.

The advantages of direct quotation are accuracy and liveliness.

When an official makes a statement for publication in which every word has clearly been weighed, you should quote it directly. This ensures accuracy and on an important issue it gives readers some original information on which to form their views. If the statement is too long for quotation, then the vital passages should be quoted. Similarly, if you have to include in a news report a letter which your newspaper has received, quote the letter straight.

As for liveliness, every report gains from including at least one direct quotation, giving not just a point but somebody's individual expression of it. Often when you look in your notebook for someone's actual words they make a point far better than you could make it in indirect speech.

Sometimes it is possible by skilful arrangement to tell a whole story in quotations. After a lawbreaker was released from prison, the *Daily Express* once published a moving and graphic account of how, in a chase across rooftops, he had turned back to save the life of a pursuing policeman who had fallen through a skylight and was clinging by his fingertips to its frame. This account was in direct speech and captured the breathless atmosphere of the incident in a way which in indirect speech would have been impossible.

It is permissible to change the order in which sentences were uttered if this makes a more logical sequence and does not damage the sense. It is permissible, too, to correct the construction of a sentence. But the essence of quotation is that these are a person's own words.

If you are giving an approximation of a person's words rather than the words themselves, you must put them in indirect speech: 'He said that. . .'; or if he has answered 'yes' to one of your questions, 'He agreed that. . .'

The main usefulness of indirect speech, as opposed to direct quotation, is that it enables you to condense several sentences of actual speech into a single sentence of your report. People do not usually tell stories, answer questions or even make speeches in a few well-chosen words. Only a few of their words may merit direct quotation.

Avoid the temptation to make people appear more definite than they are. You will not get much more help if you cause people unnecessary embarrassment with the organizations or companies to which they are answerable. Good reporting requires intent listening and a really conscientious effort to understand what people are saying, what they are hinting at and, most important, what they are not saying.

Both direct quotation and indirect speech are useful in making clear the source of your facts. You must always attribute your facts if they are of a kind that may be challenged later and you cannot vouch for them yourself.

But there is no need to say: 'From Mr Jones I learned that he has 26 young men in his care.' All that was necessary was: 'Mr Jones has 26 young men in his care.' Mr Jones is hardly likely to have made a mistake in his estimate and the saving of five words can be important. In most newspapers there is competition for space. A line saved may also save an interesting fact that would otherwise have had to be cut from a report.

The right length

Judging the right length for your reports can be difficult. It will vary according to the type of readership, according to the interest and value of other reports to appear in the same edition, and according to your skill in presenting your material in an interesting way. You may also have been briefed by the news editor or chief reporter on length. Most readers cannot read too much of a report that really interests them or too little of a report that does not interest them at all. Here is some general advice:

Give every fact you can about something the readers are really going to talk or wonder about: a murder; a bad railway accident; a debate of a vigorous local controversy. On any subject, be ruthless with platitudes and with any details which do not help the reader to get a sharper picture of the facts you are presenting.

On subjects you judge to be of lesser interest do not let your report meander vaguely with the thought that the sub-editors can cut it if they want to. It takes a sub-editor twice as long as it should to handle a story if it has to be cut by a third.

Facts and figures

Do not write sentences which tell the reader of a local weekly nothing, like: 'Mr Dickson delighted the audience with his amusing lines and he referred to various places of interest.'

Reports can also be inadequate through the reporter's failure to grasp the subject reported on as a piece of life, not just of record, and hence to give the reader the detail which will bring it to life.

When a leading citizen got a parking ticket soon after parking meters were introduced in Newcastle, the *Daily Express* reporter next day told its readers the colour and number of the parking ticket and the colour of the band on the traffic warden's arm. It is always worth remembering that reporting is about people and about life, not only the recording of events.

To give the reader the sharpest, most lifelike picture, you must get your detail as accurate as you can. Do not write 'Another man said' if you can write 'Mr Charles Smith, of Hillside Road said' or 'Charles Smith, of Hillside Road, a tall, 53-year-old bricklayer, said. . .' If a man's appearance helps to bring him to life in your story, say what he looks like. Whether he is old, young or middle-aged may have a bearing on the way his remarks should be read.

However, if people speak to you as holders of an office rather than personally, it will save both you and them embarrassment if you use names and office without personal details or age. You may not get much future help if you write about 'Blimptown's 47-year-old bespectacled and ginger-haired chief executive'.

In giving a clear picture of a subject or situation you can often find numbers useful. Twelve is more helpful than several; 85 than many. Figures are handy as an indication of size and as an objective test of airy expressions of opinion. Such and such a firm is doing 'well': how well? Such and such is 'always' happening: how often? When did it happen last?

If you have to present a large block of figures or facts about a list of places or people or subjects it is better to give them as a table or in note form than to attempt to string them together in good flowing English.

Entering your text

We have discussed how to structure a news story and how to order your material and present it in the most readable form to the length required. We have looked at the various aspects of news writing and offered guidance to help deal with the problems and options that can arise. We need now to look at the mechanics of delivering your story to your newspaper in time to meet its deadline, to what is referred to these days as 'entering your text'.

In the pre-computer age of only a couple of decades ago the typewriter reigned supreme, whether operated (often with dubious skill) by the journalist in the office or by the copy taker (telephone reporter) who took down the story over the telephone when there was no time for the reporter to get back to the office. The typewritten text, having been vetted by the news editor or chief reporter, would then be passed to the chief sub-editor to begin the editing process that qualified it for its place on the page.

Figure 6.1 *Another edition deadline approaches – a reporter keys in a court story in the news room at the* Manchester Evening News

The computerizing of newspapers and the almost universal adoption of direct input means that all text is now entered directly into the office computer by the writer, whether reporter, feature writer, sports columnist, or whatever, by means of an electronic terminal called a video (or visual) display unit (VDU). This has basically a QWERTY keyboard rather like a typewriter, but with additional command and function keys and, in place of paper, a monitor screen upon which the text appears as it is typed.

Instead of having to start again when needing to change an intro or make heavy corrections the writer can make the changes simply by tapping keys. For this purpose, the text already entered can be scrolled backwards or forwards by a command key so that it can be worked on on-screen. When the text is satisfactory a command key is pressed and the story is sent electronically into the computer, to be retrieved for checking, updating, editing and typesetting as required. The writer's keystroke, subject to whatever amendments or editing is needed, thus becomes the keystroke that sets the paper in type.

It is, in fact, possible to get a computer print-out of the story on paper but in practice this is rarely done unless the writer needs to take the story home or a version of it has to be sent away from the office for checking. Within the office the story exists inside the computer as a series of electronic impulses which can be retrieved by the writer by simply typing in the catchline on the keyboard of the VDU should it need any further checking or amendment. It is otherwise left inside the computer until it appears in its final typeset form on the page to which it has been allocated.

If the reporter feels that he or she has become part of the production process it is not a responsibility that need weigh heavily. In fact, once the story has been typed into the computer the writer plays no further part in the process. The only involvement that could occur would be if the text needed updating or amending in the light of later information – which would have been the case in earlier days with copy typewritten or in longhand. In fact, the use of electronic copy entry gives the writer a powerful advantage over the old system in that corrections can be made easily on-screen (there is even a spellcheck built into most systems), leading to cleaner text free of the changes and crossings out that characterized much typewritten copy. You could say that the ease with which errors can be put right on-screen means that the word-processing function of computerized systems flatters the bad typist (see Chapter 17).

Presentation

The rules of presentation still apply under computerized input, though spacing both vertically and laterally is automatically allowed for in the system. The writer's name, the name of the newspaper and the date and time must be put at the top of the story. Paragraphs should be of the right length to allow for setting in the narrow column widths of a newspaper, and should not be more than 50 words long, with two or three sentences the maximum.

The story must be given preferably a one-word catchline so that it can be identified and retrieved from the computer for the various functions it undergoes. The word you use does not matter much provided no-one else has chosen it for another story. Avoid therefore catchlines like 'fire', 'accident' or 'council'. Choose preferably a word that has a particular significance to the story. While the computer will reject catchlines already in use and will list those that have entered the system by means of page and edition 'directories', it is useful to be able to remember and recognize a story by its catchline.

The story will not need to be entered in folios since the system is not dealing with 'pages' of type, but you will still need to mark END at the bottom of the story, or MFL if more is to follow later. Instructions to sub-editors such as 'Please check spelling of name' should be bracketed into the story as you enter it into the system.

When time is short

It is always worth remembering that writing of any sort – good or bad – takes time. The technique outlined in this chapter makes it possible to produce good, easily read copy in no more time than it would take to produce a disjointed slipshod job. But there will be occasions when you just have not the time to set out your report in full at one go.

If you work for a daily paper you may have to go to the nearest telephone and dictate your story from your notes to catch the edition. When you do this, try to have your first few paragraphs clear in your mind or, if possible, written out before you begin. Then take the speakers you are reporting in their order of importance, not just the order in your notebook. As you dictate, spell out names and unusual words, and ensure that the copy-taker is confident he or she has keyboarded your copy correctly into the system.

Read it through

With many jobs, depending on your edition times, you will have time to return to your office and keyboard your own report. Remember to scroll it back on-screen and read it through. You should be asking yourself these questions as you do so:

1   Does it read all right? Would I as a reader readily understand it? Can I make the English flow more smoothly? Can I mend any break in the line of thought?
2   Does it leave questions unanswered that the reader will want to ask?
3   Does it answer important questions early enough?

It is a commonplace that newspaper reports must answer the obvious questions: Who? What? Where? When? Why? How? Which? Check that your report does so.

Complaints

However conscientious you are, someone sooner or later is going to complain about a story or you may find yourself having to talk to someone making a complaint against the copy of a colleague. If this happens, take down the facts of the complaint and report them to your editor. Never get involved in an argument with the complainer about who was right and who was wrong. Get their name and address. Be patient but firm with anyone who starts by declining to give their name and address or even by declining to say what they maintain is wrong with the report as printed. Point out that you are perfectly willing to have the complaint looked into but only if you know what it is and who the person is. Always be courteous.

If possible, persuade the complainer to put the complaint in writing as a letter to the editor for publication. You can offer to take down such a letter over the telephone, provided you insist that the editor receives a copy in confirmation.

If the complainer threatens an action for libel, decline to discuss the matter any further and say that they must get in touch with your editor.

In any event, give the editor a note of what has happened. If the complaint is of the accuracy of your reporting, you ought to have a note in your notebook which you can transcribe for the editor. If the complaint is against the accuracy of what someone told you, check if possible with your informant to see who was right. Getting both sides in a report of a controversy is one way of safeguarding yourself.

Good taste

A criticism of some newspaper reports is that they lack 'taste'. The trouble is that good taste is indefinable and one reader will strongly defend what another would fiercely attack. A reporter's best guide is his or her honesty. A reporter needs to be frank without seeking to shock; to respect honestly held opinion, however unfashionable.

Complaints about taste usually concern religion, obscenity or the reporting of gruesome details. Obscenity is the easiest to cope with. The Press Council (now the Press Complaints Commission) ruled against four-letter words and most newspapers are brief and circumspect in their reporting of sexual cases in the courts.

As for gruesomeness, try to describe the dead or the dreadfulness of wounds without gratuitous detail. Bear in mind the feelings of relatives of dead or injured people. At the same time, there is nothing to prevent your reporting facts – for instance, that a doctor had to amputate a trapped person's leg.

A note on short reports

Journalists often assume that writing a report of up to 200 words is a simple task requiring no great mental effort. In practice, if you have a stack of facts and only 200 words to express them in, it is depressingly easy to produce a very poor 200 words indeed. Where several reporters in different places may each be called on to provide a short report to build up a general picture it is important to master the craft of the short report as surely as the longer one.

It requires a ruthless paring down of detail to the most essential and the most interesting. Get out of your mind the idea that, since you have only 200 words, the first few facts in your notebook will do the trick and you can forget the rest.

This point is most easily illustrated in the potted biographies which reporters may be asked to provide to go with a picture perhaps of someone in the news. The space may be 30 to 50 words and it is very easy indeed to have a person scarcely leaving school before the 50 words are up.

Alternatively, your subject might be a person of many titles: chairman of this committee, delegate to that, the organization's representative somewhere else. With many jobs and titles you can get well beyond your 50 words and still leave out the most important of the jobs. Remember, too, that a person may be proud of his or her list of titles but it will be almost meaningless to the reader.

There is no answer except to ask yourself, and other people if necessary, some basic questions. What is the person's name? How is it spelled? Where do they live? How old are they? What do they do for a living? What is their main claim to fame? Are they married with children? Have they any public interests? You should finish up with something like this:

Councillor John Smyth, the new Mayor, is 41. He is an architect, married with three children, and lives at 6 Dale Road. He designed the new St Peter's Church, where he is people's warden. As planning committee chairman he was prominent in the High Street shops controversy. He is a Conservative.

7 NEWSPAPER LANGUAGE

Newspaper reports need to be understood by people from a wide variety of educational backgrounds and cultures. This means that long, involved sentences full of clauses are not helpful. Newspaper English needs to be simple and straightforward, the sort of English a busy person would prefer.

Use active verbs, not passives: 'he sang a song' not 'a song was sung by him', 'some people feel' not 'it is felt that...' Wherever possible, use simple tenses rather than 'will have been', 'would have been' and 'might have been'. Never start a sentence with a long clause.

Do not be content with abstract phrases: try to give concrete examples. This is why it is important when dealing with handouts and official reports to seize on any examples and illustrations they give of the points they are trying to put across. If there are no examples and the handout fails to show how its information affects ordinary people, find out.

This chapter deals with some finer points of style; but never forget that the main one is to present your information in a language which the readers will read, which will not bore or confuse them.

Keith Waterhouse put it like this:

- Use specific words (red and blue) rather than general ones (brightly coloured).
- Use concrete words (rain and fog) rather than abstract ones (bad weather).
- Use plain words (began, said, end) not commenced, stated, termination.
- Use positive words (he was poor), not negative ones (he was not rich – the reader at once wants to know how not-rich he was).
- Don't lard the story with emotive or dramatic words (astonishing, staggering, sensational, shock).
- Avoid non-working words that cluster together like derelicts (but for the fact that, the question as to whether, there is no doubt that).

- Don't use words thoughtlessly. (Waiting ambulances don't rush victims to hospital. They wait.)
- Don't use might, would, should and may unless you have to.
- Don't use unknown quantities (very, really, truly, quite).
- Never qualify absolutes. A thing cannot be quite impossible, glaringly obvious or most essential.
- Use short sentences, but not all of the same length.
- If a sentence reads as if it has something wrong with it, it has something wrong with it.
- Words are facts. Check them (spelling and meaning) as you would any other.
- Adjectives should not be allowed unless they have something to say. Red-haired says something. Stunning says nothing.
- Adjectives should answer questions, not raise them. How tall is tall?

It is worth adding to Waterhouse's comment that one of the most overused adjectives in British newspapers is bitter (as in bitter battle, bitter controversy, bitter dispute, and so on). Don't use it. It has lost all meaning.

The problem with codes

If everyone agrees that the aim of newspapers is to communicate with their readers, why do some journalists fail to write plain English? A common reason is that their informants talk and write in codes; and sloppy, diffident or overworked writers allow these codes to seep into the newspapers.

English language papers in East Africa, for instance, commonly employ the language of the international aid agencies. The Commonwealth Journalists Association's newsletter amusingly suggested a set of rules for this particular code:

- The word sector must appear in every sentence.
- Every paragraph must contain at least one of the following: implementation, participation, marginalization, involvement, facilities, multisectoral, resources, respectively, infrastructure or seminar
- Don't struggle to make yourself clear. Add mystique with ritual words of uncertain definition such as positive, negative, governance, stake-holder, capacity building, enabling environment, transparency, sustain-able, agroforestry, biodiversity, beneficiaries.
- Use alphabet soup – WHO, FAO, HIV – wherever possible.

Pompous, vague English is not simply a vice of aid agencies. There is plenty of it in Britain. There seem to be three main reasons. Some officials are uncomfortable with facts plainly stated on paper. They think language should be less revealing, that difficulties should be hidden, that the less dignified things people say should be suppressed. Second, coded English is for many a useful shorthand that is understood by colleagues. Third, coded English (they think) sounds more professional.

But journalism is not about sounding professional. It is about communicating with readers in clear, simple and vivid language.

Sentence length

As you write or keyboard your copy and reread it afterwards, ask yourself whether the words you have used convey your facts and news judgement clearly to the reader at one reading. Are your sentences easy to follow, accurate, direct and unambiguous? Do they read smoothly? Are they dull and pallid: do they capture the life of an occasion and the 'colour' of the people there?

Are your words working for you and the reader, or will your meaning pass the reader by because it is wrapped up in worn phrases, or too many words?

Obviously, your sentences must be simple and this usually means they should be short. It is perfectly possible to write clear long sentences, but it is not easy to write clear long sentences in a hurry, and even less to read them in a hurry. If you find you have written a long rambling sentence, you will usually also find that you can easily break it up into two or three shorter ones. However, do not make your sentences so short that they are staccato and disjointed: they must read easily. The longer a piece of writing the more well-constructed long sentences you will need.

The thought needs to flow smoothly from the start to the finish. Here's one that went wrong:

> Everything from buying shoes, which must have fewer or more than four holes for laces, to entertaining at home, where I never have dinner for fewer than four, is determined by the numbers.

This sort of sentence causes a reader to scan the punctuation marks furiously for enlightenment. The thought in the sentence doesn't flow because the subject :'Everything' is 25 words away from the verb 'is determined'. It is easier to read if it is put like this:

> Everything is determined by the numbers: from entertaining at home, where I never have dinner for fewer than four, to buying shoes, which I prefer with fewer or more than four holes for laces.

Try to make your points directly. Prefer verbs to verbal nouns. 'Before he went' is better than 'before going'; 'after Romulus founded Rome' than 'after the foundation of Rome by Romulus'; 'the Council decided' than 'a resolution was passed'; 'he studied at Cambridge and then joined the BBC' than 'educated at Cambridge, he joined the BBC'.

The right word

Using simple and direct words will help to avoid vague phrases: 'Thinking of buying', not 'Contemplating the purchase of'; 'Some people think that. . .', not 'The renewed emphasis in some quarters is on. . .'; 'This is because. . .', not 'This stems from the fact that. . .'; 'The exhibition also includes a display of small boats', not 'Another feature of the exhibition is a section devoted to the display of small boats'; 'London needed. . .', not 'There was a need in London for. . .'; 'Another sailor, John Smith, said. . .', not 'The viewpoint of another sailor was put by John Smith who said. . .' The *Times Guide to English* style points out that 'The bus sped downhill' is better than 'The bus accelerated swiftly downhill'.

Avoid words such as 'accommodation', 'facilities' and 'available' which act like cottonwool on the readers' minds, preventing them from really grasping what you are saying. 'Shopping facilities' are shops.

Do not be afraid of the word 'said'. It is far better than 'stated', 'declared', 'affirmed', 'grinned', 'continued'; and far, far better than 'claimed', which implies disbelief and should not appear in a news report.

However, on most newspapers, you do not have to sprinkle your copy with 'he said'. One 'he said' in four or five paragraphs is sufficient if the same man is doing the speaking all the way through.

Some newspapers have a rule, largely to ease the cutting and editing of news reports, that every paragraph of reported speech must be attributed to the speaker. If your newspaper has this rule, here are some possible alternatives for 'he said', provided the context is appropriate for them: 'maintained', 'stressed', 'emphasized', 'asked', 'demanded', 'proposed', 'replied', 'undertook to' (for 'he said he would. . .'), 'felt' (for 'he said he felt'), 'thought' (for 'he said he thought'), 'believed' (for 'he said he believed'), 'doubted' (for 'he said he doubted'), 'understood' (for 'he said he understood'), 'denied the council had' (for 'he said the council had not'), 'confirmed' (for example, that something was true), 'disclosed' (something not previously known), 'alleged', 'commented', 'mentioned', 'wondered' (for 'he said he wondered').

There are in fact plenty of possibilities without forcing words into new senses.

Correct English

Do not be afraid of correct English. If you present sloppy or loosely written text, you will mislead the sub-editor and the reader. Words and punctuation marks are not just arbitrary things: they are the code which you and the reader have in common. For your sentences to be easy to follow the punctuation must be correct.

Do not write sentences like these (which actually appeared):

1 'The boundary battle between a builder and an allotments association was mutually frozen.'
2 'Old people in D— may die before the Town Council can rehouse them all who want municipal accommodation.'
3 'Residential schools for persistent truants was one of the resolutions passed at the Synod. . .'
4 'Modern techniques of salesmanship are very scientific, the old foot in the door methods are gone.'

The trouble with (4) is that the writer has sought to make do with a comma when correct English requires a full stop and capital letter; and full stops and capital letters are a great boon to readers. The report should have read: 'Modern techniques of salesmanship are very scientific. The old foot in the door methods are gone.'

The trouble with (2) is the superfluous 'them' which has been left in before 'all'.

As for (1) and (3) how can residential schools be 'one of the resolutions'; or how can a boundary battle be 'mutually frozen'?

If a sentence will not work with the first form of words which comes into your head, try another: 'The Synod wants residential schools to be set up for persistent truants'; 'A builder and an allotments association have agreed on a temporary ceasefire in their battle over the boundary.'

The Germanic practice of running nouns together (boundary battle, damage assessment techniques, cash pile, rescue package) is far too common in British newspapers. It is better to undo this knotted language. 'A prizewinning writer of short stories' is preferable to 'a prizewinning short-story writer'. 'Training in management' is preferable to 'management training'.

Ask yourself whether anyone would speak in the way you have written. Ordinary speech is a good guide for the correctness of newspaper English, though obviously you can rarely tell a newspaper story exactly as you would tell it to a friend: you have to manage with fewer words.

The English used in radio and television news bulletins is a useful guide. The news reader must have a text which reads easily, is in short sentences, and is immediately intelligible. Newspaper style needs these qualities, too.

Words and idioms

Do not be afraid of lively, idiomatic English if it is appropriate to the subject and occasion and best expresses your meaning. If a word or phrase or turn of speech is in common use, then it can have its place in a newspaper even though, as with some slang words, it may be only in a quotation of what someone said.

Use such idioms boldly if they are appropriate. Do not dress them up in inverted commas as though you were afraid of them. To put 'licences to print money' in inverted commas merely draws attention to it as a cliché. Use inverted commas only if you are seeking to emphasize that the word between the quotes was the actual word somebody used.

Choice of word and idiom is governed in part by the subject and the occasion. This does not mean you have to cultivate a pompous, great-occasion style for Royal visits and the like: simple English is seldom wrong. Here are a few paragraphs from Patrick O'Donovan's account in *The Observer* of Sir Winston Churchill's funeral:

> The church, a bare, Gothicized hall, casts its shadow over the plot where Churchill's father and mother lie. His grave was dug in the last empty space at the head of theirs, alongside the path. The headstones here are plain and unassertive. There is no room for magnificence.
> The graveyard stands on a small hill, at the edge of a village street. Churchill chose it for himself and it lies within sight of his birthplace.

Avoid what is called elegant variation as in: Tomkins's next big acquisition could be a year or two away, despite the conglomerate's mounting cash pile.

'The conglomerate's' should simply be 'its'. If the aim is to make the point that Tomkins is a conglomerate, there are better ways of doing it. Perhaps: 'The next big acquisition by the conglomerate Tomkins. . .'

Avoid exaggeration in word and idiom. People do not usually thunder at each other or lash each other.

Slang and contractions

There is a good deal of slang in the private language of people in various trades and communities. Try to avoid it in writing. Write 'radio amateur' not 'radio ham', 'advertisement' not 'advert' or 'ad'.

If usage is the basis of English style every writer is making a contribution to that style. Therefore, if you have any feeling for the language you will want to use words judiciously as a craftsman uses his tools: with respect.

People might say 'lose out' for 'lose', 'meet up with' for 'meet', 'biggest yet' for 'biggest', 'hospitalize' for 'send to hospital', 'finalize' for 'complete'. Such usage in print is sloppy. The *Independent on Sunday* boasted in an advertisement of 'an editorial team of no less than 83 wordsmiths'. To which a reader replied: 'Let's hope none of them has fewer education than your copywriter'.

Ordinary speech, as we have said, is a good guide for solving some stylistic problems that beset journalists as well as a general guide to newspaper English. Is it therefore permissible to use in writing contractions such as 'hadn't', 'didn't', 'I'm' and so on, which are commonplace in speech?

Normally you use the full form, but do not be afraid to use contractions when you are reporting in quotation marks what someone has said. It reads more naturally that way. Quoted speech without contractions has an air of unreality. Also, the language is changing. 'Don't' is now often acceptable in books. Many journalists even on quality papers, no longer refer to a man as Mr.

What about sentences beginning with 'And' and 'But'? Ordinary speech suggests these are permissible but not too often.

Speakers do from time to time emphasize the word 'And'. If their speech were written out, the 'And' would legitimately start a new sentence. In written work a sentence beginning with 'And' is an effective and legitimate way of making the culminating point in an argument; but do not begin with 'And' or 'But' if your sentence reads just as well without it.

Technical language

As a newspaper journalist, try to use words which are in common use and which your readers will readily understand. Never use a technical term you do not understand yourself unless it is essential to the subject. Always consult a dictionary if in doubt about the word's meaning. The effect of much technical language is to remove the subject from ordinary people.

A council's 'capital programme' is meaningless to many readers. 'Capital', the accountant's term for money that is invested rather than spent once and for all, is not sufficiently understood. Another popular technical word is 'infrastructure'. Economists use it frequently to denote railways, ports and other services on which a community and its industries depend. It is unlikely ever to become a word in common spoken use. It does little good, therefore, to put it in an ordinary newspaper report. Try to replace it with a phrase people will understand, perhaps 'roads, railways and other services'.

Here is another example:

> There was a general inverse relationship between the changes in unit value and those in volume, indicating that supply shifts may have been more important influences on primary commodity prices in this period than were changes in world demand. . .

What that means is:

> As the volume of trade increased, prices tended to fall; this indicated that the supply of food and raw materials had influenced their prices more than had any changes in the world demand for them.

English teachers ask, or used to ask, pupils to write sentences showing the meaning of a particular word or phrase. This is useful also for reporters who have to introduce their readers to an unfamiliar word. Often it is a matter of tact; you have to slide in an explanation for your less knowledgeable readers without appearing to talk down to those who require no explanation.

Never throw in the sponge and start a report like this:

> The X— company is to build a cyclohexane and aromatics plant on its N— site. The total production capacity for cyclohexane, benzene, toluene, xylenes and heavier aromatics will be over 400,000 tons a year.

What on earth are aromatics, never mind heavier aromatics and cyclohexane? Later this report explained that cyclohexane was used in nylon manufacture and xylenes for Terylene. These were really the terms in which to present the facts:

> The X— company is to build a new plant for materials used in making nylon, Terylene and dyes. It will be on the N— site. . .

In this way it is possible to get round cyclohexane and even heavier aromatics so as to give the reader some clue to their meaning.

Foreign words

Foreign words present difficulties much as technical words do. You might like to impress your friends with words and phrases such as 'aficionado' and 'Schubert's Lieder', but it is better to say 'fan' and 'Schubert's songs'.

There is no language like English in an English-language newspaper. It is the only language most of your readers know. Only accept foreign words such as 'impresario' and 'compere' (not 'commere') which have been accepted into common use.

If you cannot spell Gelsenkirchen or Mönchen Gladbach, look them up in an atlas or gazetteer. Place names must be checked – even if you think they are right.

Double meanings

Technical and foreign words are not alone in presenting difficulties. Simple English, too, presents pitfalls. Some words have two or more meanings. Always try to restrict a word to a single sense in any one report.

Consider, in a report, on council housing, the word 'home'. A 'home' can be a house where a family lives. It can also be a hostel or institution for children or old people. Never use it in both senses in the same report. Once you have used a word in a particular sense, the reader expects you to go on doing so. The reader also expects you to use the same word whenever you want to convey the same meaning. Introducing a different word will suggest that you intend a different meaning.

Conscious that good English requires variety, journalists are often chary of repeating the same word, and this sort of elegant variation is the result:

> Warwickshire wanted Dudman, Glamorgan asked Laidlaw, Hogan was invited by Hants and Thomson by Kent...
> On Wednesday Richards occupied three and a quarter hours for 50, and yesterday Curtis utilized three hours in getting 46...

The first sentence should have read: 'Dudman was invited by Warwickshire, Laidlaw by Glamorgan, Hogan by Hants, and Thomson by Kent.' The second: 'On Wednesday, Richards spent three and a quarter hours for 50, and yesterday Curtis spent three hours for 46.'

It is possible to give English all the variety it needs without verbal contortions.

The right word order

Try to keep together words that belong together. It is no use writing like this:

> Other modifications (such as enriching the blast with oxygen which gets beyond the 20 per cent thermal replacement limit fixed by blast temperature) to blast furnace practice...

In this example the phrase 'other modifications to blast furnace practice' expresses only one thought. It is quite hopeless to expect the reader to follow the sentence when this thought is split in two by a bracketed parenthesis 21 words long.

To indicate parentheses in newspaper reports it is usually better to use dashes than brackets. Though they may not be good literary punctuation, dashes lead the reader's eye through the parenthesis as speedily as possible, whereas brackets tend to bring the eye to a halt. You might write, for instance:

Other modifications to blast furnace practice – such as enriching the blast with oxygen – offer the prospect of halving the amount of coke needed. . .

Try to make sure, then, that words which go together are read together with as little hindrance as possible. A corollary of this is that your sentences should not appear to link words which you do not intend to be read together. Consider this sentence:

At the hub of the shooting, Islington, a shopkeeper opposite the Camden Head, outside which a Jamaican was shot dead on Sunday, disagreed.

This has the reader worrying. 'Islington? I thought that was a place. Now here's this fellow telling me it's the name of a shopkeeper opposite the Camden Head.'

However, at the third reading it becomes obvious that Islington is the place, and that a slight change of word order can make the sentence clearer:

At Islington, the hub of the shooting, a shopkeeper opposite the Camden Head, outside which a Jamaican was shot dead on Sunday, disagreed.

Commas are useful: the one between 'shooting' and 'a shopkeeper' shows that these words are not to be read together, but it is no good letting commas turn your copy into a bout of hiccoughs. Keith Waterhouse writes that if your commas regularly outnumber your full stops, then your sentences are too long.

The word 'and' can present problems for readers who are puzzled to know which words they should read together:

Christopher has singed his eyebrows and face and once his hands, which were soaked in petrol, caught fire. . .
   Bedrooms are planned away from the living-rooms of adjoining flats and isolated from central corridors and sound insulation is included in the floors. . .
   It costs up to £12,000 a year to maintain its fabric and its music – it has a song school – costs as much as £5000.

Sorting out the meaning of such sentences is too much to ask of the reader.

It is often as well also to split in two those sentences which, though not ambiguous, link ideas that do not go together. The connection of disparate clauses can lead to questionable double meanings: 'He has 12 children and is a night worker.' It can also lead to an unjustifiable assumption of cause and effect: 'His mother-in-law has just come to live with him and he spends most of his time on his allotment.'

The root of this kind of trouble is lazy thinking. In short biographical sketches and similar reports, it often results from a vague dislike for repeating the person's name or for starting several sentences with 'He...'

Variety and rhythm

Almost all the examples so far have sought to show how important it is to write clear, accurate, correctly punctuated English. However, if your report is going to run to length, it needs to be readable as well as clear.

Variety is the most obvious quality which makes English good to read. You need to avoid using the same word, or words which have a similar sound, at the end of sentences which follow each other. You need to vary the construction of sentences, beginning one with subject and verb, another with some phrase. Avoid writing this sort of passage in which sentences of the same construction follow one after another:

> Herself educated at Sherborne, she joined the staff of... A former chairman of... she was for four years a member... Also a former president of... Miss X became...

Rhythm, too, is important. Your final sentence, for example, needs to reach a climax as it ends, not to trail away into nothingness. As you reread what you have written, try the sound of it in your mind.

Keith Waterhouse comments: 'A piece of writing without rhythm is like a load of sand being tipped out of a lorry.'

Numbers

Numbers give a story precision. Too many are confusing and hard to read. Use only the most important ones which clinch the points you want to make. 'The rolling resistance of steel wheels to rails is only a sixth of that of tyres to tarmac' is better than 'the rolling resistance of steel wheels to rails is less than that of tyres to tarmac.'

To make numbers less complex, *The Times* has a useful rule of three: 12,319 becomes in the paper 12,300; 1,234,567 becomes 1.23 million; 0.12298756 becomes 0.123.

Make sure numbers mean what you think they mean. More people are bitten by mongrels than by rottweilers, but this is because mongrels are more numerous, not because they are more dangerous.

Do not accept other people's arithmetic on trust. Do the calculations again yourself.

Political correctness

Political correctness has a good and a bad side. The good side is that it encourages writers to be sensitive to other people's feelings. The bad side is that it produces clumsy phrases, seeks to hide realities behind euphemisms (mental handicap becomes learning difficulty, which we all have) and it sometimes seems more interested in evading criticism than in expressing meaning.

'Environmentally sustainable rainforest ingredients' may make a product politically correct but it tells the reader little about brazil-nut oil or whatever the product contains. The environmental movement has frequently blunted its impact on people by the vagueness and imprecision of its vocabulary.

An organization which seeks to help the old was outraged by the use of 'old people'. But it is hard to see the alternatives – elderly, seniors, senior citizens, pensioners, retirees – as any great improvement. Perhaps the right question to ask is: Does the elderliness of the people actually matter to the story? Anyone over 45 is probably 'elderly' to a 20-year-old journalist.

The best advice on political correctness is:

1   Say what has happened or what people are doing. Don't bother with the 'correct' description: 'ActionAid has supplied seed for grain farmers in Ghana,' not 'ActionAid has helped Ghanaian farmers achieve food security.' The reality of a situation is not changed by a change in the vocabulary used to describe it.
2   Be sensitive to people's feelings, provided you can achieve this without writing clumsy sentences.
    An organization in India is unhappy with the phrase 'disabled people'. It prefers 'people with disabilities'. To meet its point, 'getting disabled

people accepted in society' was changed to 'getting people accepted in society despite their disabilities'.

3   Don't be condescending or patronizing, to readers or to the people you write about. It can cause real offence. Political correctness rightly attacks it.

A marked success of the feminists has been to persuade writers that they can no longer use 'his' or 'him' to include 'her' when making a generalization. It is not now acceptable to write: 'A journalist must keep his articles to the length required.'

R. W. Burchfield in the *New Fowler's Modern English Usage* points out that in such contexts 'their' and 'them' were used in the past, and are widely accepted now, especially in association with nobody, anybody and so on: for example, 'if somebody is not doing their job'.

The use of the singular verb 'is' with the plural adjective 'their' is rather awkward, however, and it is often better to move entirely into the plural: 'If people are not doing their jobs . . .' Certainly, it would not be possible to write: 'A journalist must keep their articles to the length required.' In this sentence, 'A journalist' must become 'journalists'.

Loaded words

Be careful with words which imply a judgement: terrorist, guerrilla, freedom fighter, wildcat strike. The word 'terrorist' implies unjustified violence, while 'guerrilla' implies that violence is justified. If at all possible, just say who the people are and what they have done or said.

The *Times Style Guide* bans all euphemisms for murder. An execution, it points out, is a judicial killing after due process of law under state authority.

Worn phrases

Finally, a note on clichés and worn phrases. One of the temptations when you write reports day after day is that you will begin one in very much the same way as another. Phrases leap to your mind but these only approximate to the meaning you want to convey; and whereas the art of journalism is to show how one thing differs from another, you end by making all things seem the same. One 'oil-rich island' sounds very much like the next. Try to devise and use new similes and images of your own which exactly convey the meaning you want. Note the apt use of a games image in: 'Goldie the eagle went hunting yesterday and scored a duck.'

Be wary of words which fit too easily together in your mind: 'gory details', 'acid test', 'plod manfully', 'hit back'. Acid has gone with test so often that it has ceased to add any meaning to it.

All worn phrases began life as original thoughts and images. Unlike 'hold-up' or 'eyesore', they have not proved apt enough to be accepted into the language. Well-observed descriptive passages are often spoiled by a worn phrase:

> Seven hundred feet below the green whaleback hills, the strong and proud heritage of the miner passed into history. . .

'Green whaleback hills' is fine but generations of politicians and travelogue commentators have deprived 'proud heritage' of all meaning.

In part, it is a matter of context. 'Stick out like a sore thumb' is an acceptable idiom sometimes. If someone used it in a speech or in a comment you had asked for, you would rightly report it in order to lend colour to your report. However, 'Stick out like a sore thumb' can look very pale if it is placed next to a stronger image meaning much the same thing, as here:

> They stand stark above the skyline and stick out rather like a sore thumb.

This sentence should have ended at 'skyline'.

A phrase can yet be given new meaning by its context. One writer gave life to 'old-world courtesy' by linking it with a much fresher phrase, 'new-world brashness'. *Reuter's Handbook for Journalists* commended: 'The writing is on the wall for blackboard manufacturers.'

The last word shall be with Mrs Marjorie Porter, a student at a County Durham weekend school, who showed with this short essay that the most jaded phrase could still be useful:

> It's all very well these writers saying avoid clichés and platitudes; but where would the politician be without a platitude and the clergyman without the cliché? I would never be able to hold up my head if I couldn't hang up my hat on a literary tag.
>
> So I shall take up my pen – which is mightier than the sword – and write a letter in favour of the preservation of platitudes and the continuation of clichés.
>
> I don't want to let the side down, but fair's fair and there should be a certain amount of give and take. I doubt if I have a leg to stand on, but right now I'm going to put both feet firmly down and dig in my heels, and between you and me and the gatepost if I don't get these teachers of the art of writing to join the RSPPACC I'll eat my hat.
>
> This is no laughing matter; I'm deadly serious. You just keep your fingers crossed while I enter into battle armed with only a feather quill and, before very long, you'll see, there'll be two schools of thought and mine will be one of them. I'm determined to get my word in, even if it is only edgeways.
>
> We must weigh the pros and cons of this weighty matter and beg leave to

differ from our mighty leaders of the literary world. I try so hard to take things as they come; but I can't take it all lying down and feel I must call a halt.

One simply must draw the line somewhere! After all, how could I live my life without 'count your blessings', 'keep your pecker up', 'these things are sent to try us': when the pipes are frozen, the electricity is off, there is no oil in the house and it's Sunday? I grant you, I could well consign to the ashes the one which says 'A woman's place is in the home'.

I intend to stick to my guns and even though you think I am crying for the moon, hoping to convert the dyed-in-the-wool anti-platitudinists, I shall soldier on, knocking my head against the very wall my back is up against.

If I took a leaf out of the book of a teacher of writing I would find no familiar conversational tit-bit, no colourful clichés, popular platitudes or silly sayings. It would be like opening a box of poppets to find them all white.

I must take heart: all cannot be lost, and if the literary writers refuse to have coloured poppets in their box of information, I shall open my Pandora's box and sting them where it hurts.

References

Bagnall, Nicholas, *Newspaper Language*, Butterworth-Heinemann 1993.
Hicks, Wynford, *English for Journalists*, Routledge, 1994.
New Fowler's Modern English Usage, The, Oxford University Press, 1996.
Reuter's Handbook for Journalists, Butterworth-Heinemann 1993.
Times Guide to English Style, The, Times Books, 1993.
Waterhouse, Keith, *English, Our English*, Viking, 1991.
Waterhouse, Keith, *Waterhouse on Newspaper Style*, Viking, 1989.

8 REPORTING THE COURTS

1 COURT STRUCTURE

No fundamental difference exists between court reporting and any other reporting. The requirements are the same: to understand what has happened and to report it fairly, accurately, clearly and in a manner to catch the attention of the reader. Fairness and accuracy are vital to give your newspaper the protection of privilege and to avoid injustice to the accused, witnesses and to people mentioned in the proceedings but not involved.

A British MP had to make a statement in Parliament to rebut allegations made against him in a widely reported court hearing. Non-MPs have no similar opportunity. In such cases it could be dangerous to report a denial while the case is in progress as this, in effect, accuses a witness of falsehood. The wording of a denial, even after the case, needs to be cleared with a lawyer.

Magistrates' courts

One or more magistrates' courts sit frequently in almost every English town of any size. There are also county magistrates' courts for out-of-town areas. Magistrates are unpaid. Large towns may have a stipendiary magistrate – a paid lawyer appointed by the Lord Chancellor. A stipendiary usually presides alone, without lay magistrates.

Courts sit more often than they used to do to cope with the increased numbers of brawls and burglaries and to ensure that every contested case is fully and fairly presented. Anyone accused of an offence of any seriousness is likely to have a lawyer, possibly with the help of legal aid. If several people are jointly charged with the same offence, they may well have a lawyer each. Giving evidence, police officers, under the system as it now is, read lengthy transcripts of tape-recorded interviews. Unfortunately, all this makes it more difficult for newspapers to cover their local courts fully.

There is often a conflict of interest between magistrates, who want no unnecessary delay, and lawyers, who are reluctant to proceed until ready. Cases can be repeatedly adjourned to a later date.

Some newspaper editors believe that they should cover the results of magistrates' court cases even if they are unable to report all the hearings. In such cases magistrates' clerks may be willing to tell reporters about the results of cases. Alternatively, reporters can consult the courts' registers of decisions.

An aid to reporting, as well as to busy witnesses, is that contested cases – likely to be the most newsworthy – are commonly assigned starting times, so reporters can know when to turn up for the big case.

Steps have also been taken to speed up hearings. In many cases the Crown Prosecution Service is able to send its evidence to the accused. If no reply is received promptly, the case is taken as proved and the witnesses will not need to give evidence before the magistrates.

People in danger of going to jail have a right to **trial by jury** in a crown court; and on some charges the magistrates must send them there. Committals for trial, once lengthy procedures in which witnesses dictated their evidence to a typist, are now usually a formality, with a file of statements being handed to the magistrates. The defence does not normally contest the case at this stage.

However, the magistrates have to be satisfied that there is a case for the accused to answer, and the defence can ask for the prosecution witnesses to give their evidence. It may believe the case to be so weak that the magistrates (they hope) will throw it out.

If you, as a reporter, report a committal for trial, tell your news editor so that he or she can arrange for the crown court hearing, at which the full case will be heard, to be covered.

The people with the most arduous task in a busy magistrates' court are the lawyers of the **Crown Prosecution Service**. They review evidence gathered by the police and give copies of it, on request, to accused people or their lawyers. They arrive in court with heaped-up files and struggle for mastery of the facts of each case and of the intricate pattern of related cases where, for example, three people are accused of three thefts but only two are allegedly involved in each.

They prosecute the accused or explain why they cannot do so on this occasion, because there are perhaps still 20 witnesses' statements to consider, or banks and forensic scientists have yet to produce reports, or a prisoner has not arrived from prison or the accused faces other charges at the other end of the country.

As a reporter you should get to the courtroom five or ten minutes before the court, or case, is due to start. The magistrates' clerk will be at the table upon which the court's work centres. Opposite the clerk will be lawyers representing accused clients and the Crown Prosecution Service. In some big cities, the police appoint a warrant officer who holds all the papers relating to court cases.

All these people will probably be ready to answer queries. Do not hesitate to put your queries to them. Reporters for evening papers with early deadlines need to find out everything they can before a court or case begins, such as names and addresses of any witnesses. All names and addresses need to be checked against what people say is evidence. Any discrepancies must be sorted out.

The court list, which may have to be paid for, is likely to give names and addresses of people accused, with summaries of the offences they are alleged to have committed. Someone may be accused of more than one offence. The magistrates will normally hear these related cases together but can do so only if the accused agrees.

The offences alleged may be alternatives stemming from the same set of circumstances; for example, a motorist involved in an accident could be accused of reckless and careless driving. If the motorist pleads guilty to careless driving (driving without due care), the prosecution may decide not to pursue the reckless driving charge. Similarly, an accused may plead guilty to theft but have a not guilty plea accepted to the more serious charge of robbery (theft by force).

Charges can also change. At a hearing adjourned to the following week, an accused man faced a charge of attempted murder. Next time he appeared, the charge was reduced to common assault. Such changes must be reported. At the appointed hour the magistrates enter the court; and it is important for reporters to identify who is presiding. It may be the magistrates' elected chairman or deputy chairman or it may, in their absence, be some other magistrate.

Some people will have been summoned to appear in court. Others will have been released on bail to appear. Yet others will have been arrested by the police who must charge them within 24 hours (36 if the offence is very serious) and bring them before a court next day, either to have their case heard or to be remanded to appear at a future hearing.

An arrested prisoner can expect release on bail unless there are strong reasons for refusing it. (Those without a fixed address can be sent to bail hostels.)

A prisoner can also ask for legal aid. What can be reported of remand, bail and legal-aid hearings is normally restricted to the court's decisions, the charges, the names of the people involved, and the accused's name, occupation and address. On no account should you report any reference to previous convictions. Similar restrictions apply to a report of a case adjourned to a later date, or a committal for trial. (For greater detail, see Section 4 of this chapter.)

When the magistrates hear cases, their clerk will ask accused people if they plead guilty or not guilty. These pleas should be reported.

If the offence is one which gives a right of trial by jury in a crown court, the clerk will ask if the accused elects to go for trial. This again should be reported. Electing to go for trial is different from being sent for trial.

People accused of minor offences may plead guilty by letter. This will normally be read to the court.

Almost every case opens with a **prosecuting lawyer** telling the magistrates what the prosecution believes happened. An accused who admits guilt then has a chance to say (or have a lawyer say) why the punishment should be lenient. The accused may also ask for other offences to be taken into consideration (in case the police discover them later). The magistrates will ask if the accused has any previous convictions (or 'findings of guilt' in a youth court).

If the accused pleads not guilty, the prosecutor must call witnesses to establish the facts alleged. It is always better to report the first-hand stories of the witnesses than the second-hand (if polished) account given by the prosecutor. Not everything the prosecutor says may be borne out by witnesses.

The accused or a **defence lawyer** can cross-examine the prosecution witnesses and should question them on any point in their evidence which the defence proposes to dispute. If the prosecutor believes the cross-examination has confused a witness into giving a false answer or wrong impression, he or she can ask one or two more questions to sort out the confusion.

Normally, a prosecutor is not allowed to put leading questions, suggesting to a witness what answer to give. However, the prosecutor can do so, with the magistrates' permission, if a witness is so uncooperative as to be classed as hostile.

After the prosecution witnesses have given evidence, the accused or the defence lawyer may submit that there is no case to answer: that is, the prosecution evidence, even if the defence fails to rebut it, does not add up to proof that the accused has broken the law.

More likely, the accused or defence lawyer will challenge the prosecution's account of events with the accused's own account, supported, if possible, by witnesses. The accused can simply make a statement or can gain greater credence by giving evidence on oath and submitting to cross-examination by the prosecutor.

Magistrates usually hear a case right through but, if it is lengthy, they may adjourn for lunch or even till another day. Reports on the hearing up to the break will probably contain far more of the prosecution than of the defence. It is important to give a good account of the defence in the next edition of your newspaper after the hearing resumes.

When the defence has had its say, the magistrates consider and announce their verdict. If an accused admits guilt or is found guilty, the magistrates have to consider what sentence should be imposed. If they send someone to prison (or 'youth custody' for under-21s), the law requires them to consider first what other sentence would be appropriate. They will therefore ask the probation officer in court for a social report and postpone sentence until a later date. (If the plea was guilty, a report may already have been prepared.)

The probation officer's report can recommend any of a wide range of sentences, orders to do community service being particularly popular with magistrates. For a first offender, the **probation officer** might recommend a conditional discharge (no penalty if the accused does not offend again) or a fine (if the accused has a job).

Offenders before the court for the third time might get a probation order. This compels them to report regularly to a probation office. The probation service will assess the offender and arrange help to encourage them not to offend again. It has, for example, drop-in centres offering adventure activities, literacy classes, help with job-seeking and welfare rights and for mothers with babies.

If offenders continue offending, the probation service could recommend that the magistrates send them to a day training centre. They must turn up there every day for group work of one kind or another. This is the last chance before prison.

An alternative for offenders with jobs is intensive probation. This requires them to attend three sessions a week.

The probation service will never recommend prison or youth custody, but the magistrates may decide in the end to send offenders there. If they jail someone on two or more charges the sentences can be consecutive or concurrent. Someone receiving concurrent sentences of 6 months and 3 months serves 6 months, the two sentences being served together.

Magistrates can order offenders to make **restitution** to their victims. On some charges they must disqualify them from driving or they can impose penalty points which could result in a later disqualification. They can ask them to pay towards the costs of the prosecution: note that being ordered to pay costs is different from being fined. They can give an **absolute discharge** if they feel the offence is no real blot on the offender's character.

They can bind over both the accused and witnesses to keep the peace. Accused people do not need to be found guilty for this to happen.

Someone convicted by magistrates can appeal to a crown court against conviction or sentence or both. The prosecution and the defence can also challenge magistrates' interpretation of the law, requiring them to 'state a case' to the Divisional Court of the Queen's Bench Division of the High Court.

Intriguing **points of law** can crop up in magistrates' courts. For example, if a man is found riding a stolen motorcycle but has asked permission of the person he thought owned it, can he be guilty of riding without the owner's consent?

The Crown may prosecute firms as well as individuals – for example, for operating dangerous vehicles. Magistrates also hear cases brought by local authorities, by voluntary bodies such as the National Society for the Prevention of Cruelty to Children, or even by private individuals.

When you are covering a court, someone might ask you not to report a particular case. Your answer must be that you will refer the request to your editor.

If the magistrates seek to order you not to report something, the situation is more complex. They can order you not to identify a witness under 18. (If you leave the court, make sure no such order has been made in your absence.) It is, in any event, fair practice not to identify an accused under-18 (appearing alongside an adult), since it would be unlawful to identify an under-18 appearing in youth court. (The youth court age was raised to 18 in October 1992.)

Section 4 of the Contempt of Court Act gives courts power to postpone reporting if it would prejudice court proceedings. Section 11 empowers them to ban publication of a name they have directed should not be mentioned in court; but they can use this power only if the administration of justice requires it.

The magistrates can exclude the press and public from their court if they believe that justice cannot be done in a particular case with press and public present. This could happen if private or government secrets are being disclosed in evidence.

Tell your editor about any request or order from magistrates. If they make an order, find out under what section of what Act.

Remember that 'court' is not a sealed compartment divorced from ordinary life. What happens in court has effects and offers reporting possibilities outside it. If there is a case about a dog, warn the news editor or chief photographer so that a picture of the dog can be taken. If someone has behaved heroically, again alert the news editor and photographers.

If you are helping a **photographer** and the picture must be taken near the court, make sure it is taken outside the court premises and does not have them as a background; it is illegal to take pictures within the court precincts. (It must be admitted, however, that television now commonly pictures its reporters against the Old Bailey or some other court building, to give a sense of place to its reports.)

Photographers taking pictures of witnesses or accused near the court do risk a charge of contempt of court if the people pictured complain they were molested. **Artists** can draw pictures of a court scene from memory but must not sketch inside the court.

What makes a case unusual could be a happening after the hearing is over. A man was carried shoulder-high from court after being acquitted in a case of great public interest. Again, after a case concerning two showgirls, the principal point for a morning paper lay in what happened that evening:

> With make-up and cleverly subdued stage lighting masking their injuries, two showgirls went through their striptease routine at X—'s top nightspot early today watched by the biggest crowd the club has had.
>
> Only 24 hours earlier, after leaving the same stage, they were involved in a dressing-room quarrel which ended in them both being taken to hospital.

The second sentence is possible because the fact of there being a quarrel was not disputed in the court hearing.

Newspapers differ in their practice concerning the asking of questions after a court hearing. Some people are anxious to express strong views about verdict or sentence, but it would be wrong to worry someone who is clearly very anxious about the court case and its effects.

Crown courts

As already explained, crown courts hear cases sent on to them by magistrates, either because of their seriousness or because the accused is at risk of jail and has chosen to be tried by jury. A notice is usually posted in the crown court building saying which accused will be tried that day in each court: the notice may not state the charge.

Hearings take longer than in magistrates' courts and since cases may come from a wider area than a local newspaper's circulation it is unlikely a newspaper will cover them all. Make sure your newsdesk knows of any cases of local interest due at crown court, which may be some distance away from the paper's office.

A newspaper which has reported a committal for trial should also report the crown court trial or at least its result.

Lawyers speaking in crown courts are usually **barristers**, also described as 'counsel'. They are instructed by solicitors, who sit behind the barristers and are possible sources of information for reporters.

Finding out when a crown court case is to be heard can be difficult. The courts may send to newspapers in their areas lists of the cases planned for the week ahead. But cases can be switched from the local court to a more distant one. You may then have to ring the distant court daily to discover when a case will be heard, unless you can find a friendly solicitor or police officer to tip you off. The basic problem is that the length of cases is unpredictable and judges must be kept busy, however inconvenient this may prove for lawyers and journalists. The press office at the **Lord Chancellor's Department** (0171–210–8511/8692) may be able to help you with crown court queries. (See also the case discussed in Section 2 of this chapter.)

High Court

The High Court, which sits in London and other large cities, decides the more expensive civil cases, ranging from damages for injuries in road and other accidents to the rightful ownership of artefacts or a headline-hitting allegation of libel. Libel cases are almost the only ones decided by a **jury**. Injury actions can drag on for years until it is clear to what degree the injury is permanent. As in crown courts, barristers normally present cases and are instructed by solicitors.

If a **judge** reserves judgement and you want the result, you may need to make arrangements – possibly by keeping in touch with one of the solicitors involved – to obtain it.

High Court cases may end not in a judgement but in a settlement between the two sides. Thus this *Financial Times* report:

> Talks are under way in an effort to reach an out-of-court settlement in the Outhwaite case, the biggest single legal action in the 300-year history of the London insurance market.
> Mr Justice Saville, who has been presiding over hearings at the High Court since the case opened in October, adjourned proceedings for 'administrative reasons' last Monday.

You need to be on the lookout for settlements. A barrister may come into court and ask the judge to approve one.

It is open to someone defending a High Court action to make a payment 'into court'. The plaintiff bringing the action must then decide whether to take this money and settle. Plaintiffs who refuse and continue the action are liable for the costs of both sides from that time onward if the court ultimately awards damages less than the payment into court.

When an action begins, the two sides exchange pleadings setting out their cases. As a reporter, you may be shown these. But remember that a report of them is not protected by privilege. (See Section 3 of this chapter.)

County courts

Bringing a civil action in the High Court is costly because it is usually necessary to hire a barrister as well as a solicitor unless you decide to present your own case. County courts, where a solicitor can appear, are a cheaper alternative if you are not seeking a great sum in damages or debt. And they sit in most towns of any size.

If you seek only a small sum, you can go to the county court's **small claims court**, which is cheaper still since you do not need to be represented at all. Your small claim will probably be arbitrated on by the **registrar** rather than decided by the judge.

County courts decide on building society applications to repossess houses. They are usually less formal than magistrates' courts; and, since the two sides and the registrar will have reviewed the evidence already, the hearings start in midstream. They might concern racial discrimination or a dispute over a tree or a claim for wages or a claim for damages because a mechanical digger severed a cable and cut off someone's power supply. To win damages, it is usually necessary to prove that the person or firm claimed against showed some lack of care. Journalists can cover these hearings unless they are held 'in chambers': adoption hearings, for example, are held **in chambers**.

If the judge reserves judgement in a case and will give it at a later date, make sure the judgement gets reported.

Some county courts also function as **divorce courts** and/or **bankruptcy courts**. If you cover a divorce case, you would normally (because of restrictions in law) report only the result and what, if anything, the judge says in giving judgement. The court grants 'decrees nisi'. (Nisi is Latin for unless; that is, unless opposing evidence is later brought to the court's notice.) The divorce does not become absolute for six weeks or more. If adultery is alleged, the alleged adulterer has to be made a co-respondent in the action.

Bankruptcy proceedings are complex but the main type you are likely to attend is the public examination of a debtor. In a public examination the debtor is questioned by the **official receiver** (an accountant) to discover what went wrong – whether the law was broken, whether the debtor's assets and liabilities are fully known, and whether assets transferred to someone else should be recovered. Creditors also can ask questions. The registrar presides. He or she does not announce a conclusion but simply closes the examination if the debtor has been frank and all the ground has been covered. The debtor may suggest paying '60p in the pound', which means paying 60p for every pound owed.

The official receiver may admit a reporter to a creditors' meeting. Note that your report of such a meeting is not covered by privilege (see Section 3 of this chapter).

County courts also hear petitions from creditors for the winding up of companies. The result of such a petition can be compulsory liquidation of the company. Note that this is different from voluntary liquidation, which could merely mean that the company wants to close down, not that it is in trouble.

Coroners' courts

Coroners are appointed to hold inquests into deaths which doctors do not certify as being due to natural causes or which they may have been mistaken in so certifying or which take place in custody.

Coroners can be lawyers or doctors. In London, they must be both. They also inquire into **treasure trove**, that is, findings of silver or gold or jewels where the owner or the dependants cannot be traced.

If a death might involve criminal responsibility, the coroner summons a jury to help. An inquest with jury must be held if anyone dies in prison. Coroners can dispense with an inquest if a post-mortem examination shows that death was from natural causes.

Only in the interests of national security can press and public be excluded from a coroner's court. Coroners should tell the press when they are holding inquests.

At an inquest hearing, the coroner will already have draft statements from witnesses and will go through these with them. In some circumstances, the coroner may accept statements unread. There will probably be no reading of suicide notes or psychiatric reports.

The coroner may allow questioning of witnesses by people involved or their lawyers. Eventually the coroner or jury will reach a **verdict**. The coroner 'records' a verdict: the jury 'returns' one.

Juries are not allowed to return verdicts of murder or manslaughter against a named person or to add riders suggesting someone is responsible or liable. An application to quash a verdict can be made to the Queen's Bench Divisional Court.

Often, the verdict is of less interest than the story unfolded by the inquest, as here:

> A convicted murderer was found hanged in prison hours after hearing his fiancée had married the man who put him behind bars, an inquest was told on Friday.

Or here:

> Amateur actor P— Z—'s real life ended in tragedy when he asphyxiated himself just three days after appearing in a successful play. Z—, 57, of X— Close, B—, who made his stage debut in *Happy Families* at the Abbey Theatre, St Albans, had been told by his boss that his contract would not be renewed.

In both these stories from the *St Albans Observer*, the verdict was not given until almost the end.

Where the verdict really is the main interest, you may have to explain why, as here:

> An inquest jury decided yesterday that a 69-year-old man died from brain injuries he received in an accident 11 years ago.

Occasionally, an inquest brings to light some previously little-noticed danger to life that is well worth reporting.

Inquests have their own confusing jargon. Coroners sometimes open inquests simply for 'evidence of identification', which may mean little to readers. Instead of using this phrase, you should say, perhaps: 'The coroner opened the inquest and John Smith identified the dead man as his brother William.'

Find out what the dead man or woman died of and which bones were broken. 'Carcinoma' is cancer. A 'femur' is a thigh bone. 'Hypostatic pneumonia' is, for lay people, 'pneumonia'.

Occasionally, allegations of lack of care are made at inquests. Report them and the replies to them carefully, and any comment from the coroner. If the coroner exonerates someone, say so prominently.

Consistory courts

The dioceses of the Church of England have their own courts called consistory courts. These are presided over by a lawyer called the chancellor, and sometimes make headlines by hearing allegations of misconduct by a church officer.

The chancellor has to grant or recommend a faculty if new objects are to be brought into a church or alterations are to be made there or in the churchyard. For example, a vicar might wish to create a dancing area. The chancellor may hold a consistory court hearing if the proposal is deemed controversial.

The **Court of Arches** is the appeal court from consistory court decisions.

The Church has its own vocabulary. An aumbry, for example, is a cupboard or recess in a church wall often used for reserving the sacrament. If you use such words in your report, do so in such a way that the meaning is clear.

Courts-martial

Courts-martial, in the services, have a function similar to crown courts in civilian life. Soldiers on charges are brought before the commanding officer of their unit; but there are many charges COs cannot try and their task is then to produce an abstract or summary of evidence for a court-martial.

The presiding officer at a court-martial is the president. He will have two or sometimes four officers with him. In more serious cases he will also have the advice of a judge-advocate, a lawyer.

In the United Kingdom, courts-martial often concern service offences, particularly **absence without leave** – a less serious charge than **desertion**. Absence without leave does not mean much to newspaper readers, who can stay away from their work any time without being brought before a court. But absence cases may disclose a human story of a serviceman's troubles and it is in this that the newspaper interest lies.

Note that findings and sentences at Army and Royal Air Force courts-martial are subject to confirmation. Navy findings and sentence are not.

Courts-martial are normally open to the press, provided space is available. There was room for only some of the journalists seeking to attend the court-martial of a gunner who avoided serving in the Gulf War because he did not agree with it.

If there is a military camp or station in your area, make sure you know how to find out about any courts-martial that may be planned. You may need to make a regular telephone call to an officer who arranges them. In the Navy, Army and RAF, notices of impending courts-martial have to be posted prominently at the camp or station concerned.

Tribunals and inquiries

Many legal decisions are made not by courts but by **tribunals** set up to cover particular fields such as employment or the National Health Service. Industrial tribunals are the most commonly reported since they frequently feature newsworthy disputes over dismissal. They usually have one member representing employers and one representing trade unions, with an independent chairman.

Chairmen decide on procedure, which can be informal and can also be laborious, with evidence written down as it is given. A tribunal can sit in private to avoid a breach of national security or of confidence or a disclosure of commercial information.

If you are in doubt about the basic detail of a case, ask a tribunal official or someone involved (but not someone in an emotional state). Industrial tribunals need careful reporting, especially if there is an adjournment with only one side of the case heard. Mistakes in reporting are liable to be pounced on.

If there has been a disaster, such as the deaths of Liverpool fans at a football match at Hillsborough, Sheffield, a judge may be appointed to hold an **inquiry**. Much commoner are the public inquiries into planning appeals and proposals, at which inspectors appointed by the Secretary of State for the Environment preside. The General Medical Council in London hears allegations of misconduct on the part of doctors.

2 HOW TO WRITE UP COURT CASES

Here, with numbered notes and changed names, is a report based on a real case heard in a crown court. It gives an example of court reporting and tells a human story of repeated folly, ending in personal tragedy.

A knife-slash that went right through the victim's cheek (1) led to Jim Handler (2), a 49-year-old East London car dealer, being jailed for four years (3) at Snaresbrook Crown Court yesterday. The jury (4) found him guilty of wounding a former partner, Dick Nelson (2), with intent to do him grievous harm.

After Nelson (5) was slashed, customers at the Huntsman public house, Romford, tried to stop the flow of blood with ice and beermats. He was on a drip in hospital for two days and his face was scarred (6).

Meanwhile, Handler left his home in Milky Way, Dagenham (7), and after a fortnight went to Spain, staying a year. He was arrested after he returned last June (6). In court, each man accused the other of being the aggressor. Handler pleaded not guilty (8).

The jury heard that Handler – who once, as a decorator, painted the court building (9) – lost thousands after investing £20,000 in a car showroom owned by Nelson and another dealer, Tony Hicks (6).

Part of the deal was that he would receive a similar wage to the others, £200 to £250 a week. Nelson, of Sunny Hill, Barking, said this was all the deal amounted to. Handler, however, said that it was his payment for working six days a week and that Nelson also promised him a share of a thrice-yearly 'cut-up' (10) of profit and of commission from a finance company. Further, he maintained, he was to get his £20,000 back, or receive a third of the stock of cars, if he decided to pull cars.

Handler, an ex-Navy man with no previous convictions (11), told the court that the £20,000 was what he had left after selling his house and paying his debts. By investing it in the saleroom, he hoped to make enough money to start in business again on his own (12). 'Dick Nelson told me: "It's a very good showroom, Jim."' (10)

He received £500 from a cut-up of profit but, after five months, decided he wanted to pull out. He felt his partners were hiding facts from him. He alleged that Nelson had hidden a note about finance-company commission under the telephone, and had later shown it to Hicks. 'I thought: "That's underhand." I told Dick I wanted to leave. He said he would speak to Tony Hicks about what money they would give me to go.

'Next day Dick offered me five grand. I said: "I'm willing to take a loss. If we call it ten, I'm willing to settle for that." (10)

'The same day Dick said: "I'll tell you what. I'll give you another two grand out of my own pocket. If it was down to me, you could have all your money."' (13)

He received £5000 and, over several months, part of the £2000 (14). They met at the Huntsman bar for a further payment.

Handler told the court: 'Dick said "I've got a monkey for you, £500."'

'I said "What a funny guy you are, Dick. Most people would pay their debts before anything else. But you have holidays in Greece and builders round at your house and you have all sorts of birds."'

'Dick went absolutely mad. "That's nothing to do with you," he said. "I don't even have to talk to you. I can do my talking with this."'

Handler alleged that Nelson had a knife on the bar. He (Handler) put his hand on it, Nelson hit him with a bar stool and they fought. 'I finished up on a table where four people were sitting. That's when we both realized that Dick had been cut. We stood there looking at each other.'

He threw the knife away outside and later got his first wife to inquire how Nelson was. He left home because he feared what Nelson might do (15).

Nelson, however, told the court that Handler had taken the knife to the Huntsman and had made a sudden attack on him soon after they met. There had been no fight. He put his hand to his cheek and sought to fend Handler off with the bar stool.

George Nixon, a barman, said he saw Nelson fending off Handler: neither of them at that stage appeared injured. John Melly, the landlord at the time (16), said he found blood at the right-hand end of the bar and some had hit the ceiling (17).

Mr A. Myers, prosecuting, said that this was where they had been drinking together. He submitted it was also where Handler had slashed Nelson in anger at the loss of his money. Mr John Lancaster, defending, asked how Handler could have intended to slash Nelson when what he wanted was cash. He also asked how Nelson could wave a heavy bar stool if he was already wounded and holding his cheek. He pointed to the barman's evidence of a fight (18).

The Recorder, Miss C. K. Michael, QC (19), told the jury that, to find Handler guilty, they must be convinced both that he intended to harm Nelson and that he was not acting in self-defence. Handler's refusal to answer police questions about the incident after his arrest was within his rights and should not be held against him (20).

After hearing the jury's verdict, she told Handler he had been found guilty of a most serious offence which had left Nelson scarred for life and that, in spite of his previous good character, he must go to prison for a considerable time (21).

Notes

1   Nelson's appalling wound was central to the case and makes a graphic introduction. Another possibility would have been something said by the judge. She might, for instance, have pointed out the dangers of unwritten business agreements. If Handler had been acquitted, you would need to make this acquittal clear from the start. If someone is

convicted by a majority verdict of the jury, say so, but not if he or she is acquitted by a majority.

2   It is possible in this story to give names and places in the opening sentences without making them too long. It has the advantage of making it clear from the outset who is who.

3   In theory, judges like magistrates should ask for a probation officer's report before sending someone to prison. In practice, there is a reluctance to postpone sentence because the court with its panoply of expensive legal talent would have to reconvene. Some crown courts are experimenting with seven-day adjournments for a probation officer's report. If an accused pleads Guilty, a report will probably be requested and the case adjourned.

4   It is worth making the point that the jury gives the verdict.

5   Courts are very courteous. Accused and witnesses are addressed as Mr, Mrs or Miss. In newspapers, 'Mr' is going out of use and, for men, a plain surname will do (except lawyers). There seems no good reason, however, for referring to women in court reports by their surname alone, if they are given Mrs, Miss or Ms elsewhere in the paper.

6   These paragraphs make use of facts not in dispute between prosecution and defence. Anything in dispute must be attributed to a speaker.

7   Give the street where the accused and witnesses live, since there could be someone else in the town with the same name. Reporting street numbers from court information can, however, be risky.

8   The sentence beginning 'In court' indicates early in the report the line the defence will take. It is important to give the accused's plea of not guilty. If an accused pleads guilty to some charges before a jury comes into court to try him on others, do not report his guilty pleas until the case is over.

9   Handler told the court he once painted the place, and this adds a touch of irony.

10   Using Handler's phraseology adds life to the account.

11   This, taken from what was said in court, tells us more about Handler. Fairness requires a mention of his previous good character.

12   This helps to explain why Handler got involved.

13   Handler alleged Nelson had said on several occasions that it was Hicks's fault he was not getting his money back. This could have been true or could simply have been an excuse. In either event, Hicks was not called to give evidence, so had no chance to reply. Reporting a direct allegation against Hicks would, in these circumstances, have been unfair. One way out of this difficulty could be not to name Hicks in the report. But try to be sure that, in omitting a name, you do not cast suspicion on someone else. Accused people may seek to shift

blame on to someone not involved in the case. Evidence of this sort needs treating with great care but it is tempting to use it if the allegations are against someone well known. Draw it to your editor's attention.

14 This uses what Handler and Nelson were agreed on, and avoids going into a dispute between them over how much of the £2000 was actually paid.

15 This covers Handler's reply to the implication that he had left without showing much concern for Nelson's injury.

16 This makes it clear that Melly is not the present landlord.

17 Given a decision to tell Handler's story in detail, the reporting of barman and landlord is reduced to points clearly relevant to Handler's guilt or innocence.

18 Similarly, the account of what the barristers said is restricted to their most telling arguments. It is better to report prosecution witnesses than the prosecutor's outline of the case. They are likely to speak livelier English, and they may not bear out everything the prosecutor said.

19 The judges in crown courts include High Court judges (described as Mr Justice Smith), circuit judges (Judge Smith), recorders (The Recorder, Mr A. B. Smith) and assistant recorders (Mr A. B. Smith, sitting as assistant recorder). Later in a report, all can be referred to as 'the judge'. But it is never correct to call Mr Justice Smith 'Judge Smith'. Recorders are part-time judges. The title stems from quarter sessions, forerunners of crown courts. QC stands for Queen's Counsel, a status taken up by senior barristers.

20 The judge's explanation of the law is worth covering.

21 So is the judge's reason for the sentence.

To be protected by the law of privilege (see Section 3 of this chapter) against allegations of libel, a court report must be fair, accurate and contemporaneous (that is, published in the first possible issue of the paper). Fairness means reporting what the accused as well as the prosecution has to say. If the accused pleads Not guilty, you must give a generous share of the report to the defence. Whatever you leave out, try to include a report of evidence given by a defence witness.

When a hearing runs on for a day or even longer, as the Handler one did, an evening-paper reporter will need to file a report part-way through, probably before the defence case has even begun. Make it clear that this is an incomplete report of the case, by writing 'Proceeding' or 'The hearing continues' at the bottom. Make it clear, too, that the accused denies the charges and that the prosecution case is made up of allegations, not established facts. The wording 'he maintained' or 'she submitted' can sometimes replace 'alleged'.

It is important to include any indications, from the questioning or from statements, of the defence's point of view. It is even more important to ensure that the paper gets a good account of the defence for its next edition or issue.

The Press Complaints Commission said in November 1991 that it deplored the tendency of some papers to highlight the opening of cases, when dramatic and damaging evidence is given, while publishing only inconspicuously their outcome which may throw doubt on such evidence.

If at any time the jury is asked to leave the court while a lawyer makes a submission (it is possible that some evidence is inadmissible), you must not report the submission until the case is over unless the application is granted and the judge tells the jury the gist of what occurred.

It might be held that the report above is over-generous to Handler. However, it does make clear that, though he told a good and reportable story, the jury did not accept it. The report also includes the main points made by Nelson to rebut Handler's case.

Witnesses deserve fair treatment, too. For example one paper wrote:

> PC X— parked a No Parking sign at each end of a car and then reported the motorist for parking, Z— magistrates were told yesterday.

The following would have been fairer:

> A defending solicitor accused a policeman at Z— yesterday of putting a No Parking sign at each end of a car and then reporting the motorist for parking.

An account which reports events in the order they occurred is easiest to write and follow; and it is justified for the Handler case because the business background makes it more than just a tale of a pub brawl. But usually it is necessary to report the most graphic evidence first and then give the background.

The story in this case falls into two distinct parts – the business quarrel and the Huntsman incident – and these need to be kept separate if the report is to be clear.

No reporter attended the Handler hearing described above: indeed there was only one reporter, from a freelance agency, covering all the Snaresbrook courts – and even he was also attending a case at the Old Bailey.

The lack of reporting of the Handler case is unfortunate. The Huntsman barman did not see Nelson cut, and none of the customers in the bar at the time gave evidence. A newspaper report might have caused one of them to come forward with an independent and different picture of what occurred.

Judges' summings-up ease a reporter's task in reporting more than one crown court at a time. The judge in the Handler case recounted the evidence in detail apart from commenting on the law. It would have been possible to report the case by using what she said and this would have cut the reporting time required from two days to half a day. If you do not hear the case and do not hear the judge, all you can safely report are the charges, verdicts and decisions.

Make sure you check your court copy thoroughly.

Who, where and what?

A court report should try to answer in its first few sentences these five questions: Who was accused? Where does he or she live? What was he or she accused of? How did he or she plead? What was the court's decision and sentence?

If a case is more notable for the humorous story it unfolds than for its seriousness, it might be reasonable to keep the result till the end. There are also complicated cases with several accused or several charges. It may make sense to detail them in a panel printed with your report.

The need to cover basic facts and to use words like 'alleged' can lengthen your sentences and make court reports ponderous. One journalist displayed an acute mind by beginning a bankruptcy court report like this:

> The trouble with X's self-service store was that customers really did help themselves.

Compare the more laboured approach in another newspaper:

> A man who had to use schoolgirls to help him catch thieves blamed shoplifting by customers and pilfering by staff for the failure of his self-service business.

Unchallenged facts from the hearing which will make a good introduction to your report are always worth looking for, especially if they show a human touch, as here:

> A Tynemouth policeman yesterday thanked members of the public who came to his help in a skirmish in Grand Parade.

Or here:

> A man of 68 who has served over 39 years in prison wept yesterday as his counsel asked that he should not be sent to prison again.

This case itself was humdrum but its glimpse of a wasted life made it well worth covering.

If an accused pleads guilty, you have greater freedom in how you tell what happened. But make sure you also report what is said on the accused's behalf. This example is from the *Evening Argus*, Brighton.

> A robber was collared after a taxi driver tailed his getaway car, a court heard.
>
> S— Y—, 31, ripped a plastic carrier bag containing £40,000 in weekend takings from shopworker S— Z— as she walked to a bank in Church Street, Hove.
>
> But a cabbie spotted him running away and raised the alarm, Lewes Crown Court was told. He then followed the getaway jeep, giving police a running commentary on his radio.
>
> Y—, of P— Close, Brighton, was jailed for two years after admitting the robbery but said he was put up to it by another man only 40 minutes before.
>
> Nicholas Hall, prosecuting, said Y— and the driver of the jeep eventually abandoned it, jumped over a wall and ran off. The driver was not caught.
>
> Gerard Quick, defending, said Y— was to be paid £200 for his part in the crime. 'The other man was the organizer. He knew Mr Y— was hard up and in desperate need of money. He is unemployed and his girlfriend had very heavy debts.
>
> 'This was a spontaneous offence committed in desperation.'
>
> Judge Alastair Troup said robbery was a very serious offence but this crime was at the bottom of the scale.
>
> Only £1200 of the haul was in cash and it was all recovered.

The writer has put a lot of fact in his second sentence without making it hard to follow. He has also given plenty of space to the defence. But the first sentence seems unnecessarily vague, given that this is a local case for the paper. It could have read:

> A robber was collared after a taxi driver tailed his getaway car in Hove, a court heard.

Note that robbery is theft by force or the threat of force. It is not another word for theft. Here are a few paragraphs from an *Evening Press*, York, report:

> Eight people needed hospital treatment after a canister of tear gas was discharged outside a crowded York wine bar.
>
> One woman was temporarily blinded and the others suffered symptoms ranging from a burning sensation on exposed skin to severe headaches and nausea.
>
> But the man responsible for setting off the device, which is sold on the Continent as a rape deterrent, escaped with a suspended sentence because of the incident's unusual background.
>
> Doncaster Crown Court heard yesterday that C— X—'s motive for spraying the gas was to break up a brawl which had spilled into a small, enclosed courtyard at the back of Z—'s Wine Lodge in the city centre.

> But the unorthodox method he used to quell the disturbance led to near-panic as customers tried to flee the choking fumes.
>
> X—, aged 24, of P— Lane, York, who at an earlier hearing pleaded guilty to affray, was given a six-month prison term, suspended for a year, and ordered to pay £540 in compensation to the two men and six women victims.

This story required careful handling because it was both humorous and serious. It was important to make it clear before too long that X— did not get off scot-free.

If you have to submit a news report part-way through a case or very rapidly after its conclusion, it helps if you can write out your report of non-controversial evidence as the case proceeds. You thus cut down the number of pages of notes you need to scan afterwards. Magistrates' adjournment to consider their verdict gives you time to catch up, and possibly to have the whole report complete apart from the result.

Always check carefully that you have identified accused people correctly and given correct summaries of the charges and the correct decisions relating to them. It is obviously wrong to say someone was found guilty of a more serious offence than he or she actually was.

In a magistrates' court, it is useful to write the results on the court list against the cases concerned and use this as a check.

Occasionally only three accused may appear where the court list suggests four. Make sure you know which three have appeared and what the magistrates have decided to do about the fourth. If they are to try the fourth accused another day, report only the evidence relevant to the three.

If you have telephoned copy to your office or transmitted it from a portable computer, check a proof or the first possible edition of your newspaper to make sure your copy appears correctly. Check the headline too in case your report has been misinterpreted.

Court feature articles

It has long been common practice to follow up the conviction of the accused in a celebrated court case with a feature article or even a feature page about the convicted criminal, prepared in advance. This material from sources other than the trial cannot be published during the trial because the judge would regard it as contempt of court.

If defamatory, it plainly cannot claim the protection of privilege (see Section 3 of this chapter) which covers a fair and accurate account of court proceedings. But editors presumably calculate that it is difficult to defame someone whose reputation has just been destroyed by a conviction. Caution is needed if a background feature is to be published after the conviction but before the judge passes sentence.

What is now also common, after a trial ends, is for newspapers to present the whole story as a feature or group of features, possibly without an orthodox court report at all. If you are tempted as a writer by this approach, remember that you should still give a good account of what was said by the accused and on the accused's behalf.

Here, from a page of features published by the *Evening Argus* of Brighton after a manslaughter conviction, is a graphically written article with what every feature writer strives for, a strong ending:

Firemen were called to a blaze above a Brighton antiques shop during the early hours of September 24, 19--.

As they carefully picked their way through the wrecked building in B— Place, they stumbled across a double death mystery.

They found unemployed gravedigger G— Z—, 44, in a pool of blood in the kitchen. A cheese knife was embedded in his back and he had been stabbed fourteen times. The index finger of his right hand was almost severed and he had been battered around the head.

His girlfriend, 27-year-old B— X—, was found stabbed, beaten and burned in the lounge. The bottom half of her body was almost burned away and she had to be identified by dental records.

An inquest heard she was alive, lying on the floor and bleeding from a stab wound to the neck, when the fire had started inches from her body.

There was blood in every room of the luxury apartment. Some of it belonged to a third party, thought to be H— L— Y— who lived there. Many of his valuable antiques had been destroyed in the blaze.

Clearly a ferocious fight had taken place. Three knives had been used in the battle. Anything that could be brought to hand was used as a weapon. A saucepan, a mincer, a steam iron and a cider bottle were all covered in blood.

The inquest named Y— as the killer and a murder warrant was issued for his arrest. But he had slipped through the police net and vanished.

Today he was found guilty of the manslaughter of Mr Z— and cleared of murdering Mrs X—.

For sixteen years his case lay on file. Some thought he had been killed by a business enemy. Others believed he had escaped abroad in a consignment of antiques. It was even rumoured he might have killed himself.

Then, last year, a man using the name P— Q— was stopped in a scruffy van near his West London home. A small amount of cannabis was found inside.

Police had doubts about the man's identity. Fingerprints were taken and checked against the records. The man's true identity was revealed. He was L— Y—.

A few notes on style

This piece is not without its problems.

'During the early hours of' – A long way of saying 'early on'.

'Carefully picked their way' – Carefully adds nothing, given the use of the word pick. No one picks their way carelessly. If an adverb goes too easily with a verb, or a noun with an adjective, it can probably be struck out without loss of meaning.

'Stumbled across a double death mystery' – This is journalese. It simply means 'found two people dead', which is more graphic.

'Belonged to a third party' – Odd use of a legal/insurance term. Could simply be 'belonged to a third person'.

A useful tip in a story like this is to try to use the words you would use in telling it to a friend.

3 PRIVILEGE

If you report court proceedings fairly, accurately and contemporaneously, you and your newspaper cannot be sued for libel on account of anything in your report. A headline is also protected if it is fairly and accurately based on statements made in court.

This protection is called *privilege*. It covers what is said or read out during the proceedings by people involved in them. It does not cover explanatory material not given in evidence or to anything said after the proceedings and it may not include outbursts during the proceedings by people in the public seats (though these can safely be reported if not defamatory).

Privilege may also not cover documents (including the court list) used in court but not read out. However, you can normally expect the information in the court list to be either read out or given in evidence.

Fair, accurate and contemporaneous accounts of tribunal and public inquiry hearings are covered by qualified privilege, provided the paper is prepared to accept a statement of explanation or contradiction. Qualified privilege covers a fair and accurate report provided it is published without malice and is on a matter of public concern. It may not extend to a report of irrelevant remarks not of public concern.

Schedules listing occasions of qualified privilege, and some important exceptions, are published as part of the 1952 Defamation Act and its successors.

4 RESTRICTIONS ON REPORTING

Committals for trial, remand hearings and adjournments

As already pointed out, reports of committals for trial before the full trial of a case are restricted. Here, in detail, is what you can legally report, unless the magistrates do not commit the case for trial or an accused asks for the restrictions to be lifted (and, if there are more than one accused, the magistrates agree):

1   Name of the court and of the magistrates.
2   Names, addresses and occupations of parties to the case and of witnesses; ages of accused and witnesses.
3   The charges (these can be in full, not just the summary on the court sheet);
4   Names of lawyers in the case.
5   Decisions of the court, including that on any accused not committed for trial.
6   Charges on which an accused is committed, and the court to which he or she is committed.
7   Date and place to which any committal is adjourned.
8   Any arrangements for bail.
9   Whether legal aid was granted.
10   A decision of the court to lift or not to lift the reporting restrictions.

Similar restrictions apply to remand, adjournment and other hearings before the full trial of a case at a crown court or by magistrates.

You can report committal evidence when the crown court trial is over. (This would require that the defence had asked for witnesses to give evidence at the committal.)

If magistrates commit some accused to a crown court and try other accused in the same case, you can report the evidence relevant to those tried by the magistrates.

Newspapers commonly report the fact that an accused protests innocence or complains of police treatment, though such reporting is not strictly lawful.

Here is a committal report from the *Oxford Mail:*

> Two teenagers were committed for trial at Oxford Crown Court accused of stealing two cars worth £23,000.
> D— K—, 19, of R— Lane, Y—, and a 16-year-old youth from Oxford are charged with stealing a VW Cabriolet Golf Clipper and a Ford Fiesta XR2 from Hertz Car Hire at City Road, North Oxford.
> The 16-year-old is also accused of two offences of driving without insurance and while disqualified by his age.
> Woodstock magistrates granted bail to both.

Note that the paper has not named the 16-year-old, although he appeared in an adult court.

Contempt of court

The law on contempt of court, in its literal meaning, forbids disrupting a court's work or bringing it into contempt. Thus a father was jailed for assaulting in court an accused who caused his daughter's death.

Judges can be criticized, but be wary of reporting anything which impugns their motives or impartiality. Beware, too, of vilifying or molesting witnesses or offering them money for their story. You are also not allowed to tape-record a court hearing unless you have asked permission.

A court can charge people (other than an accused) with contempt if they refuse to give evidence and answer questions (provided this would not incriminate them personally). A court has a right to require journalists to disclose sources of information if it believes the administration of justice requires this. Journalistic ethics forbid such disclosure if the sources have asked to remain secret, so a journalist can be in danger of fine or prison.

Once legal proceedings have begun with an arrest, a warrant, a charge, a writ or the opening of an inquest, the Contempt of Court Act 1981 forbids reporting or comment which creates a substantial risk of the court being influenced. In criminal cases, this means that any pre-trial reports must be written with care.

It also prevents publication of pictures of an accused or wanted person if the identity of the offender will be an issue in the trial. But no one has yet been charged with contempt for publishing a police 'wanted person' appeal.

If you have a picture of an alleged offender, check with the police whether identity is an issue in the case.

The contempt rules no longer apply if an arrested person is released without charge or being bailed, or when the case ends or is discontinued. They also do not apply between a court decision and the lodging of an appeal. But, under common law, a newspaper can be in contempt even before proceedings have begun if it publishes something with intent to influence them.

Magistrates do not have power to punish a reporter or publisher for contempt arising from a report. The High Court would need to take action on their behalf.

Newspapers chafe under contempt restrictions and frequently give themselves the benefit of the doubt concerning what is permissible. For example, the *Daily Mail* (January 1992) reported at some length the death by shooting of a boy seeking to defend his shopkeeper uncle, even though a named man was already charged with related offences. Earlier, several newspapers fully reported with pictures an incident in which a householder shot a planning officer who intended to bulldoze his house. Shooting incidents in fact are usually well covered, even when a named gunman has been arrested.

Newspapers have a problem when a controversial civil case in the High Court takes a long time to reach trial. The *Sunday Times* fought hard for the right to comment on compensation for victims of the drug thalidomide, even though an action for damages against the manufacturer was in progress.

This produced a change in the law which now allows comment on public affairs provided any resulting prejudice to legal proceedings is merely incidental. In practice, commentators have found mere incidentality hard to prove. Nevertheless, newspapers published a great deal of comment on the disputes between Lloyd's underwriters and investors over the heavy insurance losses incurred around 1990, even though the courts were involved.

Contempt of court rules can also apply if a tribunal hearing or judicial inquiry is pending. However, a Scottish sheriff dismissed a complaint against the *Sunday Telegraph* which published an article headed 'Lockerbie "whitewash" warning' at the time of the 1991 inquiry into the Lockerbie air crash. He said there was no chance of the article influencing him.

Department of the Environment public inquiries concern matters of local controversy. Newspapers can hardly be stopped from reporting that controversy.

Reports of tribunals and inquiries must not prejudice any pending court proceedings. (Also, the privilege attaching to such reports includes only matters of public concern and may not cover the reporting of irrelevant remarks.)

Sections 4 and 11 of the Contempt of Court Act empower courts to postpone the reporting of a case in some circumstances and to prevent the naming of someone not named in court (see Section 1 of this chapter). Magistrates and judges sometimes attempt to impose restrictions beyond their powers. If they do this, tell your editor.

Outside Britain, the law of contempt has its own nuances. There seems to be wide latitude for reporting and comment before American trials. In Australia a newspaper cited a constitutional guarantee of freedom of expression when prosecuted for publishing criticism of the National Arbitration Commission.

Crime and accident stories

When you are reporting a crime or accident, considerations of fairness and libel as well as of contempt of court require you to tell the story factually, without implying that a named person may be to blame. The Press Complaints Commission has asked the press to treat early estimates of casualties cautiously.

Do not assume that cars were necessarily travelling in the direction they were facing after an accident. Cars, in carefully written press stories, 'collide' with trees but are 'in collision with' other cars. People are never questioned by police: they help with their inquiries. (If a police officer uses this phrase and you report it, your report is covered by qualified privilege: so the person concerned cannot sue you for libel, alleging the phrase implies wrongdoing.)

Interviewing and reporting people who may be witnesses in a court case needs care, especially if someone has been arrested. Normally, do not report witnesses as making allegations against any named or easily identified person. But your editor may decide to report public criticism after some mishap.

Suppose the police name someone they want to find after a bank raid. You might report:

> Police inquiring into a bank raid issued a description of a man they would like to interview. He is George Smith. . . .

You should not say Smith is a suspect, even if he is.

Here is an example of how a crime story might safely be written:

> Police chased two young men down back streets and over waste ground yesterday after a bank hold-up. Later a man was arrested.

In this report, the young men are not necessarily identified with the hold-up, and the arrested man is not identified with them. Do not write: 'One of the young men was arrested.'

Next day, when the police have charged and named the arrested man, the papers might report:

> Robert Brown, aged 19, of Bow Road, Clifftown, has been charged with robbing the town's Midland Bank yesterday.

A strict interpretation of the law would prevent papers repeating their previous day's story of the chase. However, what the 1981 Act outlaws is *creating a substantial risk of influencing the court.* It is open to newspapers to argue that they are not creating anything at all if they merely repeat what has already been reported.

If assessing a 'substantial risk' of prejudicing a forthcoming hearing presents difficulties for newspapers, it must also present them for the courts. They would certainly react if a newspaper implied that someone facing a charge had a criminal history or had been engaged in earlier criminal activity. But they could hardly proceed against a newspaper for reporting a demonstration in which some of the demonstrators were arrested.

The rule for journalists is to ask themselves whether they think that what they write could influence a magistrate or juror. Always try to check whether an arrest warrant has been issued (and proceedings have therefore begun) if you are in any doubt.

Editors, for their part, have to decide how near the wind they will allow their newspapers to sail.

Young offenders courts

Magistrates hear cases against young offenders under 18 (from October 1992) in youth courts, unless they are jointly charged with adults. In reporting these courts, you must not give name, address or school or in any other way identify the accused or any witnesses under 18. 'Any other way' can include hairstyle, clothing or even a sequence of events given in evidence; or naming a juvenile's home village. The magistrates can release you from these restrictions but only in the interests of the youth offender. The restrictions also apply if a young offender appears in a crown court for sentence.

In your report of a youth court case, avoid words such as 'conviction', 'sentence' and 'charge'. A young offender is accused, not charged; found guilty, not 'convicted'.

Family proceedings

Family proceedings, with magistrates on the bench, have taken over from the domestic proceedings of magistrates' courts (concerned, for example, with separation orders, maintenance orders for wives and children, and applications for consent for under-18s to marry).

They also now hear the care-of-children cases formerly heard in youth courts. In these, the local council or a National Society for the Prevention of Cruelty to Children inspector may be seeking to ensure that a child is properly looked after, possibly by being taken into the council's care. Or it could be a newsworthy tug-of-love, with parents seeking to reclaim a child long settled in a foster home.

Magistrates are entitled to hear these child care cases in private. If they hear them in public, newspapers can report the proceedings, but must not identify the children concerned.

Reports of familiar proceedings are normally restricted to:

1   Names, addresses and occupations of people taking part, and witnesses;
2   The grounds of the application and a concise summary of the charges, defences and counter-charges (or, in consent-to-marry cases, parental objections) in support of which evidence has been given;
3   Submissions on any point of law and the court's decisions on these.
4   The court's decision and any observations it makes in giving it.

If a domestic case concerns the custody of children, the magistrates can order that the children should not be identified.

Do not report any case before it is finished. If your paper decides to interview people involved in consent-to-marry cases after the hearing (to escape the reporting restrictions), make clear that what you are reporting is what was said *later*. In any event, you could arrange for a photographer to take a picture away from the court.

If a husband has broken a maintenance order by failing to make payments for his wife, a report of the hearing is not restricted since he could be sent to prison. If he asks for the order to be revoked or changed, however, a report of the hearing becomes restricted again.

If magistrates hear a case in private, do not try to report it by means of interviews afterwards.

Divorce courts

Newspapers are permitted to report only:

1 Names, addresses and occupations of those involved and of witnesses.
2 A concise statement of the charges, the defence and counter-charges in support of which evidence has been given.
3 Submissions on any point of law, and the court's decision.
4 The judgement of the court, and what the judge said in giving it.

No report can be published until all the evidence has been given.

Rape and indecency

In England and Wales it is now unlawful to identify the victim in any kind of rape case (see also Code of Practice, below). There are a few exceptions: the woman can be named if she is herself charged with a criminal offence arising from the rape allegation; or if the accused persuades the judge that the restriction prejudices his defence; or if the judge decides that the restriction unreasonably restricts reporting; or if the woman agrees in writing to the reporting restriction being lifted.

Newspapers can be prosecuted for publishing detailed accounts of indecencies and perversion or indecent medical details. Newspapers normally do not name child victims of indecent assault.

In incest cases the Press Complaints Commission says the accused should be named but the word incest should not be used and the report should not imply the relationship between the accused and the child.

Code of Practice

The code of practice on which the Press Complaints Commission operates stipulates, among other things:

- The press should generally avoid identifying relatives and friends of people convicted or accused of crime unless the reference is necessary for the full, fair and accurate reporting of the crime or legal proceedings.
- The press should not, even where the law does not prohibit it, identify children under the age of 16 who are involved in cases concerning sexual offences, whether as victims, witnesses or defendants.
- The press should not identify victims of sexual assault or publish material likely to contribute to such identification unless, by law, it is free to do so.
- The press should avoid publishing details of a person's race, colour, religion, sex or sexual orientation, unless these are directly relevant to the story.
- Payments for stories, pictures or information should not be made to witnesses or potential witnesses in current criminal proceedings or to people engaged in crime or to their family, friends, neighbours or colleagues: except where the material ought to be published in the public interest and the payment is necessary for this to be done.

See full Code of Practice, pages 239–44.

5 THE PROBATION SERVICE

Probation officers produce reports for magistrates and other courts on offenders (see earlier in this chapter) and seek to encourage them not to offend again. This can mean seeking out the reasons underlying a series of offences. Probation officers believe that crime is often the result of some emotional disturbance or social problem. They work with people released on licence from youth custody or on parole from prison, who must report regularly to a probation office. Normally, anyone given more than a year's custody or prison is automatically released on licence or parole after serving half the sentence.

Probation officers run drop-in centres, helping offenders develop social skills necessary for a law-abiding life and organize hostels for homeless offenders. They do casework with child abusers and work on crime prevention, encouraging community effort against drug abuse and other evils, and working with police cautioning panels.

The probation service also has welfare units, seeking to help with marriage and family problems and to reconcile couples seeking separation. They make inquiries to help divorce courts decide the custody of children.

Basically, probation officers work for the magistrates of a given area. Their area head is an assistant chief probation officer. The head of a unit or centre is likely to be a senior probation officer. Those working in court will probably have the help of probation service assistants.

6 THE POLICE

For any reporter, the police are in many situations the best source of authoritative information. If there is a road accident, if someone is rescued from the sea or drowns, police generally take names and addresses and build up a picture of what happened.

Police forces have a policy of openness towards the media and will do what they can to supply information provided it does not compromise an investigation or cause problems: they would not, for instance, give names of victims of an accident before informing next-of-kin.

A constabulary headquarters now usually has a press office which may put details of fatal accidents and other incidents on a recorded message. If this is so, ring the message number for the details before telephoning the press office for any clarification.

Restrictions on who may and may not speak to the press have been relaxed, so talk to the officer who knows what you want to know. The press office will help you achieve this. Junior officers may be reluctant to speak for fear of contravening their force's policy.

If there is a major incident such as a motorway pile-up, a press officer will go there and will arrange for journalists to speak to senior officers if possible.

When you have had help from the press office, make sure it gets a copy of your paper.

For minor news, you will still need to call on a local police office of a division or sub-division. You should let police officers know who you are by making calls in person when possible rather than by telephone.

The police ought to tell you of any special court hearing out of the normal run. If you feel you have been denied information you should have had, take the matter up with the press office.

Police outside London are organized in county constabularies, often covering more than one county. Each has its own chief constable and its own controlling authority made up of councillors and magistrates.

A typical county constabulary divides its area into divisions and sub-divisions, or possibly just sub-divisions. A division will be headed by a chief superintendent, a sub-division by a superintendent or chief inspector. Heads of divisions and sub-divisions have varying degrees of autonomy in deciding local policing policies.

A county constabulary might have a separate traffic division. It will certainly have a criminal investigation department, headed by a detective chief superintendent. It might have a fraud squad and drug squad.

In a murder inquiry or other major investigation, nearly every detective in the county force could be brought in to take part.

If you need information from the police, the following are the people to ask:

Local information – The senior officer of the division or sub-division or his or her representative, or the senior detective or crime prevention officer.

Major crime and incidents – The county press office (which may put details on a recorded message).

The Metropolitan Police, headed by its Commissioner, covers the London boroughs (except for the City of London) plus adjacent areas of Essex, Hertfordshire and Surrey. The head of its civilian support services is called the Receiver.

The Met operates the world's largest police command and control network, a computerized system capable of handling 400 emergency calls at once. Communicators taking these calls can consult a computerized gazetteer to locate exactly where a call comes from. It records every telephone box, public building, park and pub.

The Metropolitan police district is divided into eight areas, each headed by a deputy assistant commissioner helped by two commanders. Areas, in turn, are split into divisions and sub-divisions, usually following borough boundaries. Areas are identified by numbers and divisions by letters. Thus J Division covers Redbridge, Waltham Forest and Epping Forest.

The policing of the eight areas is controlled by the territorial operations department, headed by an assistant commissioner who also has a responsibility for public order. The assistant commissioner for specialist operations covers international and organized crime, company fraud, computer crime, the flying squad, the regional crime squad, the criminal intelligence branch, the anti-terrorist branch and the forensic science laboratory. There are also assistant commissioners for personnel and training and for management support (including complaints investigation).

Political responsibility for the Metropolitan Police lies with the Home Secretary. It has forty-one consultative groups for liaison with the boroughs and local communities.

The press bureau at New Scotland Yard puts news bulletins for the press on a recorded message. The Metropolitan Police's eight areas also have press officers.

Useful telephone numbers

Press office, the Lord Chancellor's Department, 0171–210–8510/4
Press bureau, New Scotland Yard, 0171–230–2171
Criminal Injuries Compensation Authority (press queries: 0141–331–2726)
   – awards compensation to people injured by criminals; publishes annual summaries of cases but without naming award recipients or saying where incidents took place
Justice (0171–329–5100) – a lawyers' organization concerned with the administration of justice.
The Law Society (0171–320–5810/11/5884) – the professional association of solicitors
Press office, the Police Complaints Authority (0171–273–6483)
Home Office, criminal justice press desk (0171–273–4600.

The legal references in this chapter have been compiled with the help of McNae's Essential Law for Journalists, *edited by Tom Welsh and Walter Greenwood (Butterworths). This work should be consulted for full detail of the law on court reporting and for case law on the various areas covered.*

9 REPORTING LOCAL GOVERNMENT

Britain is a chequerboard of elected and unelected agencies providing local government services.

Most of England and Wales has district or borough councils with an upper tier of county councils. Conurbations are divided into metropolitan areas whose councils provide the full range of council services. Some free-standing cities such as York also have all-purpose councils. Scotland simply has councils. It has no upper tier.

Schools runs their own budgets and some have opted out of council control. Colleges of further education are also independent of councils.

Journalists have a right of admission to council meetings and to meetings of council committees.

Citizens who believe they have suffered from maladministration by a council can complain to a local government ombudsman. There are three offices in England, Scotland and Wales, and Northern Ireland also has ombudsmen.

The authority for **local health matters** is the National Health Service, headed in England, by the NHS Executive with regional offices in London, Milton Keynes, Bristol, Newcastle, Sheffield, Birmingham and Warrington. At local level there are health authorities (health boards in Scotland) which pay hospital and ambulance trusts for services to local patients. Community health councils seek to represent local people's views to the health authorities and trusts. The Parliamentary ombudsman is also ombudsman for the health service.

Health authorities hold regular meetings to which the press and the public are invited. Trusts must hold one public meeting a year but often hold two. Some tend to drop 'trust' from their title: for example, Dundee Healthcare and Redbridge Healthcare (short for Healthcare Trust).

For the family health service provided by doctors and dentists there is a separate network of committees.

Important local services are provided through the Government's national system of **Business Links** (advice centres) and of Training and Enterprise Councils. It uses the TECs to finance training schemes for young people and the unemployed. TECs are also expected to promote local enterprise. They are private companies so they do not admit journalists to meetings, but they issue information about what they are doing.

For rail, gas, electricity and water, there are **regional committees** to represent the interests of users in the area. The Ministry of Agriculture and the Department of the Environment and of Trade and Industry have regional offices. So do the Highways Agency and the Benefits Agency.

Many and varied local bodies exist besides these national systems. The Government has set up offices for London, Merseyside and other places. It has set up development corporations, to promote development in some urban areas. Area and county councils have set up development partnerships with local companies. Many towns have local enterprise agencies. The North has the Northern Development Company. The West Midlands has the West Midlands Enterprise Board and even West Midlands Special Needs Transport. And so on.

The local councillor

If you work on a local paper, whether a weekly or a daily, you need to live close to your local council because it is a source of news that cannot be ignored – indeed, it must be cultivated.

The average local councillor forfeits a great deal of spare time for no reward apart from some expenses. The return is a debatable amount of local prestige and/or the personal pleasure to be gained from doing a laborious and demanding duty as a hobby just like any other demanding hobby.

Either in committee or in open council, a member who has 'an interest' in a matter being discussed must declare that interest and refrain from voting, and may be asked to leave the chamber. 'Interest' is interpreted in a broad way on the principle that it is better to be too careful than not careful enough. It is most frequently interpreted as 'financial interest,' though not exclusively. It could include holding shares in a national company when that company is being considered as a supplier of some item to the council; or being a paid-up member of a local cricket club if the club's application to hire a cricket pitch is being voted upon.

A borough or district councillor represents a ward – a small portion of the authority's area, a neighbourhood. A county councillor represents a county district, roughly equal to several of the local council's wards. A ward may have more than one councillor. Councillors are good contacts for a reporter because they know what is going on in their ward.

In many places councillors hold 'surgeries' in their wards on, say, Saturday mornings, where people can come and tell them their problems. While many of these cases are confidential, some would benefit from press publicity, or they expose matters of public interest which deserve to be spotlighted by the press.

Party politics in local government results in party groups on particular councils – the Conservative group, the Labour group, etc. – which are formally organized, with a leader, deputy leader, and secretary. They hold group meetings in between council meetings, deciding their collective stance on particular issues, who will be their speaker on particular recommendations, and so on. Often the debate in a group meeting is fiercer than it is in the council meeting.

Group meetings are private, though they have been known to 'leak' to the press. The leader of the majority group on the council is known as the leader of the council, who will speak for all members on non-controversial issues.

Council meetings

The work of the council is mostly dealt with through **committees**, with each committee considering only its own specialized matters. This saves wasting the time of the whole council on something relatively trivial, and enables individual members to specialize in particular subjects rather than attempt to cope with the whole range of issues.

Most of the full council meeting will be taken up with the approval or reference back for reconsideration of the minutes of the committee meetings that have taken place since the last council meeting. Much of this material, if of interest, will already have been covered in your paper. You need to have read these reports and the minutes themselves.

Each set of minutes for a given committee will be in two parts: recommendations to the council, requiring approval, and records of decisions which the committee has been empowered to make by itself. These require only acceptance.

For example, a committee may have the power to accept a contractor's price for certain work if that price is the lowest of all those offered. The decision then needs only the formal ratification of the full council. If, for some reason, the committee feels that another contractor would be preferable, even if the price is higher, such a decision might be outside the committee's terms of reference and the matter would have to be put before the whole council, where it can be debated.

One trap in minutes is that dull, stodgy legal phraseology can obscure a matter of explosive interest. You must resist the temptation to skim through such a passage if the subject matter could be of the slightest news value. Each phrase and sentence must be disentangled until it is clear; then the general drift of the passage must also be reduced in the mind to plain English and weighed against the question: 'Does this have any news value?'

If a minute is debated, it is essential for reporters to listen carefully for the item number or page number so that they know what is being discussed.

Sometimes a committee chairman or other member will move that a certain item should be taken 'in committee'. This does not mean 'in the originating committee' but that the council itself should 'resolve into committee'. If this is agreed, the public and press will be asked to leave temporarily. This should be done only for a very good reason. For example, if the purchase of a certain piece of land is contemplated, the council may wish to debate how much it should pay, over what period, or whether another piece of land would be more suitable, etc. It would not be in the public interest if the seller of the land, or competing buyers, could read this kind of detail in the press before negotiations got under way.

Another example of a justifiable withdrawal is where individuals are concerned – perhaps discussion about an officer's salary scale or state of health.

The council must give a reason for withdrawal into committee. This is normally done in very general terms and, of course, may be reported, for what it's worth. The council should also state, after it resumes open session, what decision was reached 'in committee', if this does not conflict with the public interest.

A difficulty with a large authority is knowing who everybody is. Some councils issue **seating plans**. A snag with this is that a member may move up into a vacant seat in order to sit next to a friend, and if you don't know the members very well the seating plan can then be misleading. You can sometimes get clues to people's names during the actual debate. If several members rise to speak at the same time, the mayor may call on one by name, which solves your problem. Failing such clues, make a note of some visual characteristic of the member concerned and ask a member or officer at the end of the meeting: 'Who is the woman in the black dress sitting next to Councillor X?' If you cover an authority's meetings regularly, the members' faces, names, first names, and appointments rapidly become fixed in your memory.

Usually the actual reporting of council meetings is not especially difficult, but it is essential that you know what they are all about. This is the difficult part. Good **shorthand**, of course, is vital, not only for accuracy but also to capture fast, vivid exchanges between members, without which your report would be less readable. Public figures, too, are more prone than most people to claim they have been misreported when in fact they have rashly said something that turns out to be embarrassing when it is published. A reliable shorthand note is the only defence against such a claim.

Writing it up

Although good shorthand is essential, it is a mistake to take too many notes – a council meeting that goes on for several hours will produce enough words to fill several pages of a newspaper. A reporter rapidly learns to be selective and to take down only the newsworthy bits.

Try to bring back to your office as many of the documents issued during the meeting as you can. You may need these to verify your notes, or sometimes to use their original wording as verbatim quotes in your stories.

If you work on a non-party newspaper, you will also have to learn to sink your own **political opinions** when writing the stories, despite the temptation to choose the best bits of your favoured party's speeches and the worst of the other side's. *An impartial approach is the hallmark of the professional.*

A council meeting, or even a committee meeting, usually produces more than one story – for instance, one main story, three of medium interest, and a handful of bits and pieces. Until you gain experience, it is wise to ask your chief reporter or news editor for advice on how much length you should give each story. You should also draw attention to any items which might be worth following up with interviews and telephone calls.

Try to simplify the stilted local government **officialese** found in speeches or minutes, which can be infectious. Explain or avoid technical terms which the average newspaper reader has never heard of. Such jargon can look formidable but there is no need to be frightened of it. Much is merely circumlocutory – 'Resolved: that this committee do concur in the above-mentioned matter' simply means 'We agree'. This sort of phrasing is fairly easy to sort out with a little common sense.

Many phrases are brief methods of expressing quite complex concepts. They assume that the person reading a report or minute is familiar with the working of local government, and the reporter must come into this category. Familiarity with the concepts behind them is the only sure way to the immediate understanding of this sort of language.

Stories originating from committee meetings or minutes are commonly published before the full council meeting takes place. If you are writing up such an item it is important to make it clear that committee recommendations are at that stage, in effect, only suggestions that will need to be accepted and confirmed by the full council.

The council officer

Most councils now employ a public relations staff, but a great deal of press contact is with the senior officers. It is fair to say that most council officers start out with the intention of being helpful not only with explicit facts but also with background information which helps complete the picture. Whether they maintain this intention depends on how they and their facts are treated by the press.

It is usually a matter of courtesy, unless some other arrangement has been made, to contact the head of a department first. If statements on behalf of that department are to be issued, its chief officer is the one to be given the first opportunity to make them.

On some councils, officers are not allowed to engage in press controversy so that if you wish to criticize some facet of a council's work you must make sure you are not also attacking a council officer who is forbidden to reply.

Where a council is indirectly attacked, for example, in a reader's letter or by an organization, it may also be advisable to ask the council department concerned if it has any comment to make. It may have a valid answer which will save the newspaper from presenting a one-sided, unfair version of the situation.

When a question arises concerning council policy or attitude, rather than a matter of fact, it is usually fairer to approach the leader of the majority party or the chairman of the committee concerned, rather than an officer. Sometimes an officer may refer you to the committee chairman. This is not a case of being obstructive but is because the officer knows, better than you do at this stage, that the matter is controversial or involves policy and is therefore best left to the elected representative.

Radical change

The reporting of local government in the regional press has changed radically since this book was first published in 1966. Stories about local services are common but reports of council and committee debates are quite hard to find, unless there is a major local controversy. Both local government and local newspapers have changed.

In the 1960s, councils and councillors were at the height of their powers. It seemed they could do everything. Experts asked if national social-services charities such as Barnardos were needed any longer. In the 1970s the illusion of omnicompetence died. The government could no longer pay its share of all the many things that councils wanted to do. At the same time there were new things which councils had to do, particularly in social welfare: and there were rising expectations, particularly of schools. So the councils have found themselves in a financial straitjacket which is constantly tightening.

It is not easy for governments to make the straitjacket more comfortable by reallocating cash to help those in greatest need. The only hard evidence of what councils need is what they spent in previous years.

Only councillors and staff involved in planning now behave with the old bossy self-confidence. Other council spokesmen are on the defensive, explaining why they have to cut a few jobs here, why local schools aren't all that bad, why some market traders are leaving or why it was necessary for councillors to travel overseas.

The *Financial Times*, which takes a keener interest in local government than most national newspapers, chronicled a day in the life of the chief executive of a troubled London council. It included a meeting with other chief officers.

'The agenda,' reported the FT, 'covers a litany of problems, involving tight budgets, long waiting lists, asylum seekers and troubles with the private finance initiative and with community care.'

There was a meeting with a housing officer and two tenants. 'The tenants complain about the graffiti, the mould and damp, the dirt, the unpainted stairwells and the undone repairs. The housing officer talks in terms of minutes of meetings and financial years.' The chief executive remarks: 'If I turn up to these meetings, things miraculously start to happen.'

So local government is having to change, though with reluctance, away from the old committees and minutes, and departmental culture that dates from the nineteenth century. Wycombe district council, for instance, reduced its number of committees from twenty-seven to four (on care, the environment, the local economy, and value for money).

Local government is now about management, doing your best for local people with the cash available, getting different services to work together. Local party-political debate has been muted. But the changing scene can be exciting for journalists who take the trouble to inquire into what is happening.

Like the councils, local newspapers have been financially squeezed since 1970. Free newspapers have broken the advertising monopolies which sustained them in the style to which they were once accustomed. On the editorial side, this means they must fight for readers: which means, in turn, that the views of readers are at least as important as those of councillors, council officers and other dignitaries. Readers dictate much of the agenda. Their letters are published prominently. What papers want to know about council stories is how readers are affected.

English local dailies have adopted, to varying degrees, the approach of the highly competitive national press and its philosophy of praise for ordinary people. The *Oxford Mail* publishes the kind of Oxfordshire stories which might have made the *Daily Mail*.

On average, forty or more of these stories a week concern local services. To be published prominently, they must normally have an accompanying picture. This gives a head start to stories about primary schools. The *Oxford Mail* writes about particular schools, rather than schools in general. Common subjects also include plans to build houses (usually opposed by neighbours), other planning matters, and the safety of roads.

Other papers reflect other preoccupations. The *Evening Press*, York, is concerned about tight council budgets and their effect on social services and jobs. It publishes numerous planning stories but a good deal less than Oxford about schools. Both Oxford and York are interested in local issues brought up at parish council meetings.

The *Lancaster Guardian* and the *Worthing Herald* reflect local concerns about planning, conservation and the environment. Lancaster also gives most of a page to a feature about the food safety team.

The *Dundee Courier* and its associate, the *Evening Telegraph*, are concerned about hospitals and health. In contrast with Oxford and York, almost all the housing stories published at Dundee concern people in publicly provided housing.

Against this background, journalists covering local government and services need imagination in understanding their council's work, finding stories day by day and presenting them attractively to the readers, with pictures where possible.

Here are the opening sentences of a story from the *Oxford Mail*:

Prince Charles's vision of Britain is soon to arrive in Oxford.

Residents in the Oxpens area are to have a direct say on how they want their part of the city designed.

City council planning chairman Stef Spencer said: 'It's something the Prince Charles Institute of Architecture has been pushing for.'

What could have been a dull piece full of municipal jargon such as consultation, participation and input has become Prince Charles's vision of Britain. It might even encourage people to take part, rather than feel they have better things to do than go to the 'three-day £20,000 consultation exercise.' An inset picture of Prince Charles enlivens a rather dreary picture from Oxpens.

Councils nowadays provide many reports in advance, which is one reason why the reporting of meetings has declined. Armed with a report, a journalist can seek comment from councillors and others without waiting for the meeting. The resulting story will be briefer than a story from the meeting, and brevity is particularly prized in tabloid papers. It means, however, that committee chairmen and officials get most of the say. It could be worth finding the views of rank-and-file councillors.

The stories to look for

Journalists watch sharply for national stories with local implications: mad-cow disease, policy for pre-school education, food scares, shortages of cash in the health service. A health reporter pointed out that health and hospital stories have to be looked for. They are not volunteered by health authorities and doctors, who tend to be wary of reporters.

So, quite likely, are other local government officers. Local government is astonishingly complex, not only running towns and counties but providing an intricate pattern of services, some of them for individual people. It is hard for anyone except senior professional staff and a few leading councillors to understand the context in which decisions have to be made. Those people who do understand doubt the understanding of outsiders.

This is the challenge facing reporters on local government, health and education. They need to think not just about what the council and the health authority are doing and why, but also about what they might have done and what may be going wrong. The management of housing has been a headache for some councils, particularly in London. Newspapers need to be specially vigilant where there is little opposition to the council's dominant political group.

The local press has strong reasons for wanting to be popular locally. It needs to express local opinion and take up local causes. However, it also needs to see that its own opinions and, if possible, those of the readers are well informed. A proposal to shut anything is sure to stir up a chorus of popular disapproval. A proposal to build anything commonly meets similarly enthusiastic opposition, with petitions and protest meetings. But, if nothing is built, how will the homeless – about whom popular opinion is also anxious – ever be housed?

Journalists should do more than simply join local choruses of disapproval. A thoughtful BBC *Panorama* programme featured a couple who took their son, sick with meningitis, to the casualty and emergency department of their local hospital. There had been a campaign to keep this department open. But the boy died. Only a junior doctor was on duty to treat him and she did not know how to. *Panorama* made the point that shutting underused hospital departments may be unpopular. But keeping them open not only wastes money. It can be dangerous. There may be no senior staff on duty when needed.

There will never be a shortage of people, and of vested interests, eager to defend whatever services a council or hospital trust is now providing. Journalists need to look more carefully, given that budgets are always likely to be tight. Is this service being cut simply because it is the easiest place to make a cut? Is it unduly expensive or has it outlived its usefulness? What money might be released for new services or for improving heavily used ones, by discontinuing what is better provided for elsewhere? If money is being wasted, something important may be sacrificed when the demand for cuts is made.

The **Audit Commission**, which can compare one council's spending with that of others, shows how patterns of spending vary. It raises points of policy. For instance, need councillors spend so much time in committees, their most time-consuming activity? Should services for old people concentrate on those more in need? Or should they be spread across a wider number (which is probably more popular with the voters)? These questions underlie arguments about payments for home care.

Figures for councils' spending are published by the Chartered Institute of Public Finance and Accountancy. Birmingham University has an Institute of Local Government Studies.

One report from the Audit Commission said that benefits fraud is the key probity issue facing local government. The commission is involved in the National Fraud Initiative, encouraging councils to match computer-data and so detect people making multiple claims for benefits and grants. It mentions that the charity Public Concern at Work (tel: 0171–404–6609) receives reports of fraud.

The commission wants councils to introduce registers of interests for both members and officers. It points out, however, that cases of known corruption in local government are few.

10 POLITICS

Opportunities for political stories arise at all levels, from local ward organizations to the House of Commons. It is unlikely that one reporter will have to cover all stages but it is extremely likely he or she will cover individual stories from each level at various times.

A brief summary of political parties' structure and procedure is given on pages 139–43. Local circumstances will inevitably affect the amount of news which can be wrung from them. In some areas a party committee will have nothing to do with the press, regarding its affairs as private. In other areas the equivalent committee sends in reports of its meetings and its officers feed stories to the local reporter.

There is little standardization. A lot depends on personalities and on the past history of press/party relationship. As a general rule, no harm is done by asking that a summary of a committee's business be released to the press, or that a story on such-and-such a topic should be withdrawn from the 'off the record' category. In many cases it may not have struck the party concerned that the press would be interested.

As in other fields of reporting, confidence in the reporter induces confidences from the contacts. Given this good relationship at each level, the field of politics – ward, municipal, constituency, regional and parliamentary – can yield a continuous flow of stories.

At the top level of politics on a provincial newspaper is the **local MP**, who may even be a minister. His or her comings and goings, and speeches in the constituency, are normal material for straight news reporting. An MP's home life is also a matter of interest to many readers whether they voted for or against.

If the MP makes a speech in the House, your local newspaper should have some facilities for reporting it, perhaps a correspondent of your newspaper group in the House, or a regular supply of *Hansard Parliamentary reports* in the office. Some MPs send to their local weekly newspapers the appropriate pages from *Hansard*.

A local MP may also make a speech outside the newspaper's area, perhaps at an area rally or at the meeting of a national body in, say, London. This may be newsworthy and the office will have to arrange coverage. The MP's alignment with a particular movement of opinion should also be carefully noted. In the event of major news affecting that movement, the MP's part in it, or views on it, may make a story.

To sum up: the pronouncements and attitudes of a local MP are of interest to both supporters and opponents and must never be overlooked.

One of the most useful local contacts, common to all parties, is the local **party agent** whose salary is paid by the local party association but who may be either full- or part-time according to the party's support in the area. He or she is always authorized to deal with the press and is in touch with day-to-day matters. If you have any sort of query, the agent is your first contact though they may refer you to an officer of the local party; such officers are always unpaid volunteers.

It is important not to confuse officers of the local party with officers of a local party club. The chairman of the political association may not be the same as the chairman of the political club. Even if one person holds both offices, the functions for each organization are different and largely unconnected.

Another distinction the reporter must be careful to make is that a 'prospective candidate' must always be referred to as such, never as 'candidate' until he or she has been formally adopted after the election writ or proclamation has been issued. 'Candidate' by itself in a heading, referring to a prospective candidate, is allowable providing that 'prospective candidate' is used throughout the story underneath it, since even the ordinary reader can appreciate that 'prospective candidate' is long-winded for headline purposes.

All the parties hold **annual conferences** at which local party associations from constituency upwards are entitled to be represented providing they have sufficient members and have affiliated to the party. Some local groups may decide against sending a delegate or delegates to the conference if scarcity of funds prohibits the expense, but a local group may send a resolution or two to the conference even if it does not send a delegate. Agenda setting out resolutions and indicating their proposers are often issued to the press a week or two before conferences. Some of these resolutions can make news stories in themselves, so their wording and their ultimate fate should be obtained, probably from the party agent.

Your office might consider that a conference is worth covering, either directly or via an agency or correspondent. Direct coverage has the advantage that the reporter can mingle with delegates outside conference hours and may be able to obtain background information which affects the debate.

Independents

Especially in country areas, Independent councillors remain important. Even in urban areas there may be Independents forming a local opposition in districts where the majority party is so strong that candidates from the minority parties would have no chance in an election.

It has also been known for there to be two sets of Labour councillors on a council, following a major split on policy, one group being 'official' Labour with the backing of the National Executive and the others 'independent' Labour, financing their election from their own pockets and not from local party funds. The luxury of two Labour groups can be indulged in if the opposition is not very strong.

Journalists often assume:

1   That Independents act in the same way as any other political group.
2   That Independents are Conservatives in disguise.

Neither of these assumptions is necessarily correct.

If you have Independents in your district it is important to know what they stand for and whether they are members of a group or not. To imply that an Independent is not really independent but attends group meetings could be defamatory if in fact the councillor does not attend group meetings at all.

Where a number of Independents call themselves 'Rent and Ratepayers' candidates, or 'Civics', 'Progressives', or 'Moderates', it is fairly safe to assume that they act as a group. Where members call themselves Independents, there may well be no group, and even when you know there is a group structure it is not safe to assume that every Independent on the council is a member of it.

Remember that, locally, Independents can make nonsense of any attempt to calculate whether one of the major parties has done well or badly in municipal elections. Independents can be elected by a protest vote as an expression of opposition to a particular aspect of the council's policy.

Electioneering

Sooner or later you will have to cover an election. Municipal elections, usually notable in most parts of the country for the apathy of the electorate, do not present a lot of difficulty since, as a rule, the campaign beforehand is not very intense, and the number of candidates (e.g. for a borough election) may be quite large, preventing any really detailed treatment.

Occasionally a local **ward election** – perhaps a crucial by-election having some bearing on the political control of a council – can provoke the heated interest that is usually the prerogative of the Parliamentary election and qualifies thereby for closer coverage.

In any major election your best friends are likely to be the party agents directing the operation of the campaigns. They can tell you where the candidates are going to be and what they will be doing. The candidates themselves, certainly in a hotly contested Parliamentary election, are usually too fully occupied to give you much of a coherent picture. The party agent is the professional, even if only temporarily professional. Contact with the party agents needs to be close and constant, whether by phone or in person.

Party agents are normally only too glad to give you details of the candidate's appearances in the constituency, not only at public meetings where the reporter has a right to attend but also at meetings of clubs and groups which might not normally admit a reporter. With those, a word from the party agent to the organization concerned will usually do the trick to get the press in. News-conscious party agents can also be a help in putting you on to stories that arise from vote canvassing and other party activity.

An enormous number of words are poured out in even a moderately well-contested election. For a local weekly paper, this raises problems – a single candidate may make at least ten **speeches** in the constituency in the course of a week, and the paper, unless it is extremely partisan, cannot report all of them anything like fully. There may be three candidates, making a total of at least 30 speeches for that week's issue. The daily paper also has to compress, since a single speech may run to 3000 words or so and the paper allocates space for only 300. Clearly, selection – rather than the difficulty of reporting everything that is said – is the main problem. This is made more onerous for a non-party newspaper by the need to select with true impartiality, not only the amount of space given to each candidate but also the prominence.

Fortunately, candidates making ten speeches in a week are going to repeat themselves a great deal and the repetitions can either be omitted or greatly condensed. There will probably be a party line on general topics such as foreign affairs, home economic policy, defence, etc. The party's views on these will be well known.

But if the candidate deviates from the party line on a given topic – say, defence – this can become news. It will usually be signposted by the candidate who may explain why he or she has deviated on this issue. This deviation may offer a chance for some interesting copy.

Independent candidates have no party line to deviate from, but their views can usually be treated on their merits as either provocative or conventional lines of thought. Reporting Independents has the advantage that an Independent's platform may contain ideas that are fresh to your local election arena, making for good copy.

During an important election, with daily press conferences, various issues will crop up from day to day, and the candidates' reaction to these will also provide more exciting copy than normal party-line attitudes.

Candidates hit out at one another, commenting on remarks their opponents have made and thus inviting rejoinders. Obviously this sort of thing is good copy; there is nothing readers enjoy better than an atmosphere of personal contest about an election.

These three factors – deviation, immediate comment, and personal attack – enlivened by verbatim quotes are the jam which many newspapers prefer to the perhaps rather monotonous bread and butter of the underlying, repetitive speech about party attitudes. Any one of them could divert the whole local campaign on to an unexpected course.

Accuracy is of paramount importance in reporting politics in general and elections in particular. A candidate who bases an attack on what turns out to be **misreporting** of an opponent's remarks, and then has to withdraw, is not likely to be very pleased about it. The candidate may even attribute inaccurate reporting of his or her own remarks to political prejudice by your newspaper – a charge which is difficult to answer if the inaccuracy can be proved.

Since most candidates weigh their words fairly carefully, many either read their speeches or learn them by heart from a written copy. Ask for a copy of the speech with which to check your notes, or against which to check the candidate's actual words if the copy is given out in advance. Some party agents may be obliging enough to have a copy specially made if they know in advance that you are likely to ask for one.

This helps a lot in the case of a local candidate's remarks but does not always cover you for speeches by visiting dignitaries. They may not have a copy of their speech. Even where a copy is provided, if they are experienced politicians they will be capable of adding some unscripted passages which may be the best parts of their speech. If they are big names, this sort of extemporary addition might have national importance. Shorthand is the only real answer for this eventuality.

Another part of an election meeting not covered by a script is the questioning. Well-aimed **questions** can sometimes tempt unexpected hot news answers from the person on the platform. The speaker may be sorry later about what was said, and here again shorthand is the only reliable standby. Political speakers who make indiscreet remarks are only too ready to attribute them later to misreporting and you may have to justify what you wrote.

Newspapers need to establish the candidates as personalities, which means stories, notes and pictures about spouses and children. If you are working for an impartial newspaper you must be careful in the area of feature writing and comment: do not write an enthusiastic piece about candidate A and follow it with a less enthusiastic piece about candidate B. You may unintentionally be affected by the personalities of the two people.

If the campaign shows signs of dullness, and the candidates a reluctance to commit themselves on something of strong local interest, they must be approached with specific questions. Ask them what they think of these issues – pin them down, get them to reply if they will.

Some newspapers run their own quizzes for candidates, asking each one for answers to a standard set of questions. Usually these quizzes are organized at high level on the newspaper, but the young reporter might be asked to take part if the answers are being given verbally.

Newspapers and newspaper groups also organize polls, either about contentious issues or on the result of the election nationally, locally, or both. Some of the forecasts of results can be surprisingly accurate.

Election procedure

Electoral procedure in Britain is, of course, common to all parties and elections are a fertile field for political stories, since politics that stems from high principles comes down in practice to obtaining votes. If you know what the procedure is going to be, you are in a good position to extract the maximum amount of copy from it.

The **writ** authorizing the election is sent to the returning officer or acting returning officer. The former in a borough would be the mayor, and the latter usually the chief executive, who, in practice, carries out most of the duties involved and receives a special fee for it.

After receiving the writ the returning officer must publish a notice of election not later than 4 p.m. on the second day after the writ is received. The political parties' candidates and independents may then be nominated up to a limit of, in general elections, 3 p.m. on the eighth day after the Royal Proclamation, or (by-elections) the ninth day after receipt of the writ in county constituencies, or the seventh day in borough constituencies. Sundays and holidays are not included.

This is the law but, in practice, the returning officer will usually state the deadline much more simply, e.g. '3 p.m. on Wednesday'.

A candidate has to be proposed and seconded and supported by eight other people. He or she must also nominate an agent, and must hand over a deposit (in parliamentary elections) which will be forfeited if the candidate fails to secure a minimum of one-eighth of the total votes cast.

If your newspaper requires the popular election photography of all candidates and their party agents making their nominations and handing over their money, most returning officers will arrange a time and place convenient to all. This does, after all, save them having to be photographed three or four times with individual candidates.

If you wish to attend the **election count**, you should be prepared to sign a declaration of secrecy, promising not to divulge anything connected with the ballot papers, and you may also need to arrange for a photographer to sign too. Having made this declaration, you may then be free to wander about among the poll clerks when they count the votes. It is permissible to take note of how ballot papers stack up if they are arranged according to candidates. But the relative proportions of the stacks fluctuate as time passes and to say that 'X was winning early in the count' would be dangerous, since ballot papers from polling stations in only a certain area may have been counted first, perhaps from the city area of a Parliamentary constituency containing both city and countryside.

Usually the polling stations close at 10 p.m. and the principal part of the count starts as soon as the ballot boxes reach the returning officer. Some areas postpone the start until the next day. A count, whether for Parliamentary or municipal purposes, is worth attending partly for the immediacy of the news it produces and partly for the opportunity of meeting political contacts at a crucial moment. 'Everybody who is anybody' in the political life of the area is there.

When the count is over, the parliamentary candidates' expenses are listed and checked. Maximum limits are imposed by law to ensure that no party has an advantage over its opponents because it can afford to spend more. These expenses are calculated from the time the prospective candidate is adopted as the candidate. Money spent on propaganda between elections is not counted as a contribution to a candidate's expenses, though it may eventually be of benefit.

Party organization

Here is a summary of the major parties' structure and procedure.

Control

Conservatives: The Conservative and Unionist Central Office, with professional staff. Responsible to the party leader for administration and organization.

Labour: The National Executive Committee elected at the annual party conference and composed of trade union, Co-op and local Labour Party representatives. Secretary is a permanent official.

Liberal Democrats: The Federal Party, comprising three state parties – one each for England, Scotland and Wales. Every member on joining is automatically a member of the Federal Party, the relevant state party and the relevant local party. Three Federal committees cover, respectively, executive, policy and conference matters.

Regional

Conservatives: They have no regional organizations apart from unions of constituency associations, sometimes *ad hoc* (see Constituency).

Labour: The party formerly had federations of constituency Labour parties roughly covering county council areas, but functions now mainly taken over by twelve regional councils composed of delegates from constituency and borough Labour parties, trade unions and Co-ops. Each council has regional executive committee and regional organizer. Aims include: 'to co-operate in joint political action' and 'to ensure better co-ordination of local government policy'.

Liberal Democrats: Twelve regional parties each appoint representatives to the Council of the Regions of England. The English Conference, drawn from English members of the Federal (national) Conference, is the sovereign body of the party in England and elects the co-ordinating committee for England. The main organs of the party in Scotland are the conference, executive and policy committee; in Wales the council, national executive and policy sub-committee.

Constituency

Conservatives: Each constituency has a Conservative association which appoints a committee. There may also be specialized advisory committees reporting to the constituency committee. The association is usually known by the name of the constituency although it may cover more than one constituency.

Labour: Each constituency is covered by a Labour party known by the name of the constituency, which elects a general management committee of delegates from ward parties, trade unions, Co-ops, women's section, youth section, etc. In a convenient geographical area with perhaps more than one parliamentary constituency a linking organization is formed of representatives of each constituency party. Where there is a county constituency it has delegates from the Labour parties in the various towns and rural areas.

Liberal Democrats: The basic unit of local organization is a single constituency, known as the local party. It is open to any local party that wishes to combine with adjacent local parties, subject to a ballot of members.

Ward

Conservatives: Each ward within a constituency has its own association known by the name of the ward plus the words 'Conservative Association'. The ward association is represented on the constituency association.

Labour: Each ward has its own Labour party which has representatives on the constituency party. Groups of villages in a polling district might also form a Labour party.

Liberal Democrats: The wards are looked after by the local party.

Other groupings

Women's Conservative Associations and Young Conservatives operate at ward, constituency and national levels and hold annual conferences. Labour Party Women's Sections operate at constituency, regional and national level, but not often at ward level. The controlling body is the National Council of Labour Women, holding an annual conference. The Young Socialists operate at ward, constituency or borough level and combine into the Federation of Young Socialists, with a controlling national committee, and hold an annual conference.

Municipal elections

Conservatives: Each ward executive committee selects a council candidate if it is able to. The nominee has then to be approved by the constituency association, which can also provide a candidate from a panel if a ward is without one.

Labour: The constituency or borough party invites nominations from ward or other subsidiary parties and a suitable list is endorsed by the general management committee, which also decides the number of seats to be contested.

Liberal Democrats: The local party is responsible for selecting local government candidates.

County elections

Conservatives: An agent is named to cover the county division which may or may not coincide with parliamentary constituency boundaries. Each ward in the division may nominate a candidate. If there is more than one nomination for a vacancy the executive of the constituency association makes a selection.

Labour: The constituency or borough party collects a panel of names of suitable candidates, some of whom may have been nominated by wards, and the ward(s) within the county division make(s) a selection from this. On being confirmed, the candidate is then nominated by the ward(s).

Liberal Democrats: The local party (or parties if more than one) within the county division is responsible for selecting candidates.

Parliamentary elections

Conservatives: Conservative Central Office maintains a list of approved candidates and any constituency association may apply for a selection of, say, thirty or forty names. The constituency's executive committee appoints a selection committee which decides on a shortlist of perhaps six candidates. These are invited for interview before the selection committee. The name or names recommended are then presented to the executive committee; if more than one, the executive committee makes the final choice. The person selected is put before a general meeting of the constituency association for adoption as prospective candidate. Before the election a further general meeting is held to adopt this person as the Parliamentary candidate. If the local committee accepts a candidate not on the Central Office list (for example, a local resident) the choice has to be approved by Central Office.

Labour: A Parliamentary candidate must be a trade union member if eligible to join a union. Organizations sending delegates to the constituency party are entitled to submit nominations. The National Executive Committee also has approved lists which it may offer to the constituency. The constituency examines all nominations and sends them to the NEC for approval. The shortlist of approved names is then put before a constituency selection conference consisting of all delegates to the general management committee. Candidates may speak and be questioned. A ballot is then taken and the winning candidate's name is submitted to the NEC for endorsement. After this, a further general management committee meeting formally approves the winner as prospective candidate, and he or she is later adopted as Parliamentary candidate.

Liberal Democrats: Parliamentary candidates must be from an approved list drawn up by the three state parties.

European Parliament

Euro-constituencies are usually made up of two or more British constituencies. European Parliament members (MEPs) rarely deal with matters confined to their area, though occasionally there might be a debate in the Parliament on a subject affecting the MEP's area – perhaps to do with an industry that employs local people. Contact with MEPs cannot be maintained as regularly as with a local MP. MEPs might contribute occasional reports to local newspapers about what has been occupying them, or about their stance on a particular issue.

Political parties in a Euro-constituency spring to life normally only when a Euro-election is imminent; most of them are too large and diffuse to go in for the activities routinely carried out in British constituencies. Local associations and parties form loose alliances to select a Euro-candidate and work for the election. Selection is on the same lines by parties as selection of a parliamentary candidate. Press contact with the election organization can easily be made via the parties involved. After the election the constituencies' collaboration tends to lapse.

11 BUSINESS AND INDUSTRY

Business and industrial news can range from a little story about a company employing 30 people making an obscure product not on sale to the general public to a front-page lead about a major closure in a coal-mining area which can throw thousands out of work. Readers' interest in an industrial story, however limited in extent, is good for circulation but it leaves the reporter no room for error. Many of the interested readers will have personal, first-hand knowledge of what the story is about. Get a minor fact wrong and the reader's faith in the story is shaken.

Industrial news is concerned with either the product itself, its distribution, development and sales, or with the various influences, negotiations, disputes and decisions that are involved in production. Understanding of the product itself is not so hard to attain as you might imagine. If an electronics factory in your area makes a breakthrough with some new development, you may have to cover it.

You can start off from the basis shared with most readers – a lack of knowledge of electronics – but can ask question after question until it is clear what the new development is about, and why it is new. This must then be interpreted in simple language for the readers.

Technical people are usually helpful in explaining things. One suspects they take a kindly pleasure in displaying their knowledge. But make sure that in explaining a product or process to you they use simple language that you can follow. Do not let them get away with technical terms that you cannot understand. Then there is no chance of your interpreting wrongly.

In many stories you will not need to know anything technical at all. The local refrigerator factory which manages to sell some of its output to Eskimos provides a news story with this success. How the refrigerator works is immaterial.

Reporting on business presents good news opportunities. Even local weeklies give business its own page but much of the space devoted to business in local papers is wasted on free advertising copy and dull pieces about new services for businessmen. Yet your area probably has numerous people with fresh ideas for making a living.

Dotted round the British provinces you can find silversmiths (e.g. Lancaster and Kendal), an ostrich farmer (near Penrith), a designer of stoves for Ethiopia (Corsham), a maker of sisal-processing machines (Chard), an expert in photographic chemicals (Woking), a designer of trams and tilemaking machines (Dudley), organizers of Himalayan cycling expeditions (Keswick), a restorer of oak beams (Skipton), a leading publisher on Africa (Oxford).

There are trades you never thought about, such as selling cocoa shell for garden mulch and collecting second-hand clothes for resale overseas. A woman washing clothes in rural Namibia could be wearing a Benetton jumper collected in your town.

Charity shops are almost taken for granted. But there must be a story in how they're doing.

Businesses related to science and computing cluster around universities; craft businesses around holiday areas. Improved communications mean people can work in out-of-the-way places.

Keep an eye on advertisements in newspapers and magazines. People with a good idea need to advertise for customers.

You can also learn about businesses and business people from the many organizations set up to encourage them: the Government's network of Business Links, local Training and Enterprise Councils, local enterprise agencies, development corporations, chambers of commerce, local councils' development offices, council-business partnerships.

If you write about a business, always insist on having figures of turnover and profit. Business people may not be keen to give these, but you can reasonably ask because you are giving them, in effect, free publicity. Figures showing the business is doing reasonably well safeguard you against the possibility that it is in trouble.

Writing about business requires a certain wariness. An apparent success story is not always quite what it may seem. Listen for any snags which, though brushed aside now, could bring damaging publicity later.

Knowing the firms

If you are given the chance to report industrial matters within your newspaper's area, you must first set about making sure you know all the industries in it. You may know some already. Many are probably advertising for staff in your newspaper, so check the advertising columns and list any firms whose names are not familiar.

If the newspaper's area contains a district well known for a particular type of product, such as leather, go to the public library and read the leather trade journals and magazines. Again, with these, read the advertisements too, because some local firm hitherto unknown to you might be advertising. Even in an area where the newspaper already has good industrial contacts, these things should be done periodically because industry is not static; old firms close, new ones open; new products are marketed, and new processes become available from the research laboratories.

All these firms' names should be written in an indexed book or file, together with addresses and phone numbers. Such details tend to snowball. After some time you should have not only the firms' names, addresses and phone numbers but also details about people concerned with the firms: active directors, managers, shop stewards, union officers. This index will eventually become a very important item and it needs to be kept up to date.

Ask to be sent to your area's trades council meetings if they are already covered. If they are not, an approach should be made to the trades council for permission to cover. Almost any major trade union officer in the area should have a record of the trades council secretary's address.

Trades councils

Trades councils claim to be the founders of the Trades Union Congress though, oddly enough, in England they are not affiliated to it (because the TUC ruled out dual representation); in Scotland they are. They have always played a part in local labour matters but their scope is not clearly defined. A trades council, in fact, is a loose linking of all the trade union branches in a single area, which may be a particular town. In a less densely populated area, one trades council may cover several small towns. Trades councils join together in county associations. These, along with trade unions, are represented on TUC regional councils.

The membership of trades councils ranges from white-collar supervisory workers to general labourers. All have the common factor of being delegates to the trades council from their union branches.

If you are allowed to cover it, a trades council will provide stories of its own arising from the discussion. Some of them will have to be handled with discretion. But probably the greatest virtue of the trades council to a reporter is that covering its meetings will give you names of firms and union branches which you possibly never knew existed in the area. These can all go into your little black book or its equivalent for future reference. In addition, you will get to know individual delegates and several of these will undoubtedly hold office either in their union branches or in shop stewards' organizations at their work.

Eventually your indexed book or file should contain the name of every union branch in your area together with names and addresses of as many of the chief union officers as possible. In an industrial area there will be a large number of branches covering a variety of trades. In some large factories there will even be several branches of the same union. Several thousand members of the XYZ Union working in the Blanktown Umbrella Factory could not all attend one branch meeting at the same time and the administration of such a branch would have been too formidable. Therefore the membership of the union at that factory was split up into the No. 1 Branch, the No. 2 Branch and the No. 3 Branch.

Union branches may produce some stories of their own: for example, a presentation to a member of fifty years' standing who may have a good story to tell about 'the old days' of unionism and industry in the town. In any case, the names of branch officers come in handy later.

Disputes

Regrettably, names come in most useful when there is trouble: a dispute. The reporter who has no existing contact with unions at the time of a strike or a dispute is at a serious disadvantage.

Strikes are much rarer than they used to be. The law now requires ballots beforehand and prevents action against firms not directly involved in the dispute. This prohibition makes strikes less effective, but they could still occur in your area.

A strike is normally called by a union or confederation of unions, usually after unsuccessful negotiations with employers. In an official strike the union pays strike pay to its members. These payments are usually far below members' normal earnings. If the strike goes on a long time the union's funds may dwindle to the point where it has to seek financial aid from other unions.

An **official strike** may be national or local or even confined to one factory. It must, as we have said, be preceded by a ballot of members and the ballot paper must say who is authorized to call the strike.

An unofficial strike is where a workforce withdraws its labour without prior union consent. Unofficial or wildcat strikes can be called by shop stewards after an on-the-spot disagreement with the management. They may take the form of a **sit-down strike** where the workforce do not leave the factory. If they are short (less than a working day) and the workforce leave the factory premises and subsequently return they are called **walkouts**.

Unofficial strikes are much rarer than in the past because of the jobs situation, the fragmentation of the workforce into smaller groups, and because of legislation. Unions are liable in law for a strike called by one of their officials, and shop stewards do count as officials. A union can escape liability by dissociating itself from the strike, but the employer then gains the right to dismiss some of the strikers. Normally the employer must dismiss all or none. Shop stewards are not authorized to call official strikes.

A **lockout** is rarer and is a sort of employers' strike, where employers consider workpeople have, in some way, broken an agreement and retaliate by closing the factory to them. In some cases production may continue with non-union labour and the original employees remain locked out.

Efforts might be made to blockade the factory. Union members might attempt to stop materials and supplies being taken in, though they would not be permitted to use force to do so; it usually boils down to their having a serious talk with lorry drivers. They might also attempt to dissuade 'blackleg' workers, this being the term used for anyone who goes on working during a strike or lockout.

All these terms have specific meanings and the reporter must be careful to use the right one. On occasions there might even be disagreement about whether a dispute is a strike or a lockout, especially in disputes over a long period where both strike and lockout have been applied at different stages. In these cases the arguments of both sides must be given and the whole thing referred to as a dispute. To select the terms 'strike' or 'lockout' would be to favour one particular side's argument. Care must particularly be observed in headings on such stories.

Where a factory is 'blockaded' in either a strike or a lockout the people outside the works who attempt the blockade are known as **pickets**. The law is usually there, too, to see that no force is used. Generally a reporter will approach pickets for information because they are readily available, but remember that, in the main, they are usually only union members doing a specific task without having any authority to speak for the union or union branch. Anything they tell you must be regarded in this light.

In industrial disputes it is important that both sides should be fairly and fully reported, even though a strongly political newspaper may knowingly play down the case for one side or another. Either side may consider it advisable at a given stage to say nothing to the press at all. In this eventuality, the fact should be reported: 'Mr So-and-so, managing director of the umbrella factory, said the firm had no comment to make at this stage.'

Thus readers will be able to realize that the information in the story comes from one side only through no fault of the newspaper. A labour dispute often means touchy tempers, and failure to contact all the people concerned can bring your newspaper heated accusations of being partisan.

It is always worth going to the place where the dispute (or any other industrial news event, for that matter) is taking place. You will get a better idea what the fuss is about than you get from official spokespeople anxious to show their own side in the best light. Be careful with figures and their meaning. Employers tend to quote gross pay, including overtime. Strikers talk of 'take-home' pay after tax and other deductions.

In any dispute there is usually some attempt at **conciliation**. There is ACAS, the national conciliation service. In some industries there are standing bodies set up for this purpose. Get to know the names of union regional officers in advance and put them in the little black book. If a dispute does break out, you may be able to reach this person before other reporters and get an important statement.

Disputes have become more diverse. They may concern discrimination or the fate of pension and other rights after a takeover or privatization. They may well result in some form of legal rather than industrial action.

Shop stewards

'Shop stewards' is the general term for people who may be known locally by other titles such as 'workers representatives', 'floor delegates', etc. They recruit new members for their union within a particular factory, make sure dues are paid, and report to the union on matters in the factory which may require union action. But probably their most important function is to act as a direct link between the workforce and management.

In a small firm this will be done only as and when necessary but in a large undertaking there will probably be a committee, meeting regularly, composed of management representatives and shop stewards. These committees have various titles. 'Works committee' or **'works council'** are popular ones. They deal with a broad range of matters affecting conditions of work in the factory.

The shop stewards themselves may also have their own committee from which, of course, management representatives are excluded. The chairman of such a committee is referred to as the 'convenor'.

In large plants the stewards, whatever their job might be, are paid by the management to be shop stewards only and do not participate in everyday production work. Some have offices of their own. Shop stewards cannot be removed by the management since they are elected by the workforce, but a shop steward is subject to being discharged like any other employee.

The employers

In industrial reporting you must remember that there are two sides to everything since industry is a collaboration between capital and labour, whether the capital is supplied by the state or by private individuals. Your contacts cannot be among the labour side alone. People on the labour side are more difficult to get at: you cannot go into a factory department and talk to someone operating a machine. The **management** side is usually more accessible and you can, in effect, go into a manager's office with only slight formality, though an appointment is more courteous. In some cases a local management may refuse information and in this circumstance you should find out the address of its head office and pursue inquiries there.

In addition to being more accessible to your inquiries, managements will tend to seek you out if you are the newspaper's industrial reporter. Principally, they will come to you with news of their products, new contracts, expansions, export triumphs, new developments, etc. Since they do this, it lessens the need for group contacts among managements, and indeed managements tend to form groups much less than the labour side does.

Your paper may frown on free puffs in general but, when a firm approaches the industrial reporter with an item about a new product or a new process, the item may have a strong news value because it affects people's jobs and livelihoods. An example would be where a local sweet factory announces it will in future also manufacture jams and marmalade. In the news columns, as a general item, this would be a free puff for the new jam but as an industrial item it has a different value: it foreshadows more machinery, another sales organization, new staff, promotions, transfers, more wages in the town. The securing of a new contract means further security for workers who might otherwise be laid off, as in the shipbuilding industry, where continuity of employment is directly related to orders for ships.

If your paper publishes, or could publish, features on local industries, even on individual factories, a good way of getting in at a particular plant becomes available. You will be given a conducted tour; you will meet the management and even the owners themselves if it is a small undertaking; you will understand what the firm is doing and how it is doing it. This means more names for your little black book.

Keep an eye open for local firms which do **unusual work** but do not tell you about it, perhaps because they do not see it as local news. Many small firms do work for major overseas projects, others for Oxfam or UNICEF. Even villages and small towns can prove to have business links with distant countries.

In a given area where one trade tends to be predominant, employers form themselves into a federation on a local basis: 'The Blanktown Umbrella Trade Association.' It may or may not open its meetings to the press but it could probably be induced to supply reports and, apart from their intrinsic worth, these might also provide ideas for detailed follow-ups. The local association or federation strengthens your contacts on the management side.

In some trades, such as steel and engineering, the employers' association may cover a very wide area. In a large town or city employers of many different trades may band themselves together in a **Chamber of Commerce**, a sort of businessmen's trades council. Do not confuse it with the shopkeepers' Chamber of Trade, though the latter may occasionally call itself a Chamber of Trade and Commerce. The Confederation of British Industry has regional offices.

Company publications

Many undertakings have publications of their own, or **house magazines**. An industrial reporter should be receiving these, including those which cover undertakings in the area but which may be published miles away.

Usually they will give you some grains of information. Unfortunately, many are published monthly or quarterly so that the news tends to be stale. However, there may be some dateless item which you can use; and, in any case, familiarity with a firm's house magazine will help you understand the ramifications and operations of the company.

Some firms which are limited companies will supply you with copies of the **annual reports** to shareholders, from which news may be derived. Large companies may publish the annual report as an advertisement in a national newspaper. Keep an eye also on the financial pages of national newspapers for news of companies which own local undertakings or for news of dealings in their shares.

Annual reports and other statements of profit and loss are important to newspapers because they indicate how healthy companies are. Will they expand or survive? Have they written off bad debts or losses on contracts? Have they the money to pay dividends to shareholders? Are they trying to raise more money by a 'rights' issue (a request to shareholders to invest more cash)?

Reports do need careful study. The profit could have gone up simply because buildings are re-valued. It could be illuminating to read last year's report also. There may be inconsistencies.

Employment and industry services

Britain has a network of local Training and Enterprise Councils (TECs), whose responsibilities include youth training and other government training schemes. TECs are employer-led, with members from trade unions and education. There is also a network called Business Link.

Jobcentres and unemployment benefit offices come under the
Employment Service, an agency of the Department of Education and
Employment. Jobcentre managers are worth getting to know. Not only
can they give you spot news items (The Blanktown Umbrella Factory is
seeking more workpeople) but they can tell you about employment trends
(fewer married women perhaps being employed locally).

The Department of Trade and Industry advises and encourages enterprises, and seeks to ensure fair competition with the help of the
Monopolies and Mergers Commission and the **Office of Fair Trading**.

Wales and Scotland have their own government industrial agencies: the
Welsh Development Agency (01222–828–6931), the Development Board
for Rural Wales (01686–626965), Scottish Enterprise (0141–248–2700) and
the Highlands and Islands Enterprise Board (01463–234171).

English regions will now also have development agencies. Some set up
their own earlier. Many councils and local groups offer enterprise and
employment promotion services. So do British Steel and coal companies
in areas which have lost steel and coal jobs.

Some privatized industries have acquired government-appointed regula-
tors: Offer (Office of Electricity Regulation, press, 0121–456–6234/6208);
Ofgas (Office of Gas Supply, 0171–932–1606/7); Oftel (Office of
Telecommunications, 0171–634–8751/2); Ofwat (Office of Water Services,
0121–625–1416/1342).

The Health and Safety Executive (press office: 0171–717–6700) oversees
the safety of industrial premises. It has local offices. Air and water pollu-
tion by industry are curbed by the Environment Agency, which has
regional offices.

The **European Commission** is likely to acquire growing importance as
a promoter and regulator of industry as well as a source of help for areas
with too few jobs. It operates regional and social funds as well as funds
initially set up by the European Coal and Steel Community for job-losing
areas.

The London press office of the European Commission is on
0171–973–1971. It also has offices in Belfast (01232–240708), Cardiff
(01222–371631) and Edinburgh (0131–225–2058). The Commission's
switchboard in Brussels is on 010–322–299–1111.

Winning their confidence

It is important that your information contacts should have confidence in
you. Employers or employees resent incompetent or indiscreet reporting
which they think may damage or threaten their livelihood. With this sort
of work you will usually be working among known contacts rather than

among people casually encountered as with general news reporting, and these contacts will dry up immediately if you are hamfisted.

If you can gain your contacts' steady confidence the job is half done. Managements may then tell you off the record when a large contract is in the offing, to be confirmed by a telephone call when it is signed; union branches may invite you to hear an important and newsworthy speaker and trust you sufficiently to let you sit through the private business beforehand, confident that you will not make use of it.

Knowing that people trust you with details of the way they make their living can be a source of great satisfaction as well as giving you useful information.

12 REPORTING RELIGIONS

Religion continues to play a part in the life and self-image of British communities and has increasing importance as a source or component of controversy, in government (Northern Ireland), writings and speeches (Salman Rushdie) and such areas as Sunday trading and schools.

Islam, with well over a million adherents in Britain, sees all aspects of life and government as subject to religious precepts and this has implications for politics, local government, education, dress, feminism and the secular consensus on which public affairs are based. At the local level especially, it makes news. It has no organized hierarchy of spokespeople; but groups of Muslims may form to express a particular view.

Reporters frequently have to cover other less headline-catching religious news especially locally: services, new buildings, youth clubs. Indeed, if they fail to keep in touch with local priests and ministers, they may miss many stories.

The essence of religion is often not news in the usual sense; it lies in what religious people would regard as eternal truths. All the same, there usually is something to be reported at a religious gathering. People may have travelled a long distance to be there. An important speaker may have something striking to say about the modern world or recent events or may present an intriguing account of some far-off place featured in TV news stories, giving you an opportunity to bring into your paper a breath of a wider world.

Most readers may not belong to a religious organization, but they may be interested in religious beliefs as they affect other people. And, as in the Sunday trading controversy, they may themselves be affected by other people's beliefs.

At special services, local people may read lessons, sing solos, lead prayers. Be aware of what you see: a full church, the robes of priests, the flowers, sunlight coming through stained glass. This all helps to bring a religious occasion to life for the reader.

Always treat such an occasion with respect and make sure you understand what is going on. If you do this, you do not need to write stilted English. You can describe an outdoor procession as you see it. If some children look tired or wave to Mummy, say so.

Weddings

One of the small jobs on a local weekly paper is to write up a wedding from the details on a printed form. Accuracy is essential. Remember that the cutting will quite likely be sent far and wide.

Reporters may be self-conscious about the sameness of wedding reports, but there is no point in variation for its own sake. A straightforward presentation is usually the best. If there is something unusual about the wedding, by all means start with it: for example, 'Brightland hockey team formed a guard of honour for John Smith and his bride. . . .'

Your report should say what the bride and bridegroom do for a living and where they work, with any claims they may have to local fame.

A woman 'is married to' a man; she does not marry him. And it sounds better to say that a priest conducted the wedding, rather than 'officiated'.

Priests and ministers

Religious people boast a complexity of titles. Reporters must master them even if national papers and television sometimes fail to do so. Reporters meet most often the priests and ministers of the churches and parishes in their area. If a priest or minister is called David Smith, he is properly described as the Reverend David Smith (or, if he is Roman or Anglo-Catholic or Greek Orthodox, he could be Father David Smith). Never call him Rev Smith or the Rev Smith, since Reverend attaches to his Christian name, not his surname. As the epigram puts it:

> *Call me Parson, Brother, Friend,*
> *But do not call me Reverend.*

Later in a report, the Reverend David Smith becomes Mr Smith (or, if he is a Catholic, Father Smith). If he has a doctor's degree, he will first be Dr David Smith and later Dr Smith.

Fully ordained ministers in the Roman Catholic, Anglican and Greek Orthodox Churches are normally described as priests, those in other

Christian denominations as ministers. Many ministers are now women (e.g. the Rev Margaret Smith; later Miss [or Mrs] Smith). The Church of England also has women clergy. They, too, take the style 'the Rev'.

Priests and Church of Scotland ministers normally take their titles from their parishes, other ministers from their churches. Thus the Reverend David Smith might be minister of Blanktown Park Methodist Church; or he might be Vicar (or Rector or, if Roman Catholic, Parish Priest) of St Paul's (not of St Paul's Church).

The vicar of St Paul's in the village of Muddlecombe will describe himself as Vicar of Muddlecombe. Similarly, the vicar in the main church of the town of Blanktown will describe himself as Vicar of Blanktown. Assistant priests in a Church of England parish are called curates; if they minister in a parish's second church, they are curates-in-charge. You can check the names, titles and parishes of Anglican clergy in *Crockford's Clerical Directory* or a diocesan yearbook.

Some senior clergy have courtesy titles. An Anglican vicar might be Canon David Smith; a Roman Catholic parish priest Monsignor David Smith. You need not give people more than one title. Thus the Rev Dr David Smith in a newspaper is Dr David Smith. The Right Rev Monsignor Canon David Smith is Monsignor David Smith. Similarly, the Lord Bishop of Blanktown is the Bishop of Blanktown.

Bishops are responsible for a diocese, usually the size of a county. Roman Catholic and Anglican bishops covering similar areas normally take their titles from different towns and cities. Thus the Church of England has a Bishop of Chelmsford, while the Roman Catholic Church has a Bishop of Brentwood. Bishops also have assistant bishops. The Church of England calls them suffragans and gives them a title from some other town in the diocese. The Roman Catholic Church often gives them a title from a far-distant place.

Bishops have the style 'the Right Reverend', but frequently hold doctorates. If David Smith is a bishop but not a doctor, you would describe him first as the Right Rev David Smith. Later in the report, in these less formal days, he could become Bishop Smith. Archbishops have the style 'the Most Rev'.

The Church of England has three other common appointments: archdeacon, dean and rural dean. An archdeacon has oversight over a large part of a diocese, particularly for the upkeep of buildings and other administrative affairs. He has the prefix 'the Ven' (for Venerable) and, if this is again David Smith, he can later be called Archdeacon Smith. Similarly, if Smith is a dean, responsible for the cathedral in Barchester, he is the Dean of Barchester, the Very Rev David Smith, and later Dean Smith (if you talk to him, you can call him Dean or Mr Dean).

Rural deans have oversight over several parishes besides their own and will be responsible for their work if they have no priest. Their job carries no special prefix but they are often canons.

The Church of England

The Church of England has two archdioceses, or provinces, York and Canterbury. The Archbishop of Canterbury, Primate of All England, is senior bishop but government is shared with the synod, which has houses of bishops, priests and laypeople. He is also senior bishop of the Anglican Communion, the churches throughout the world which resemble the Church of England in style. They include the Church of Ireland, the Church in Wales and the Episcopal Church of Scotland. In Scotland and the United States, members are called Episcopalians.

The Church of England is comprehensive, that is, it encompasses clergy of widely differing theological views from freethinkers to fundamentalists (who insist on the literal truth of the Bible) and from Anglo-Catholics, who stress dignity and ceremony, to Evangelicals, who stress enthusiasm. The Charismatic movement, emphasizing that Christians can be inspired by God, has strengthened the Evangelical wing and has affected all the British churches, even the Roman Catholics to some degree.

In a parish, the vicar has the help of a parochial church council and of lay officers called wardens. There may also be a lay reader, licensed to conduct services other than communion.

Note that Church of England clergy are ordained deacon before being ordained priest.

The Roman Catholic Church

The Roman Catholic Church is made up of dioceses which enjoy a wide measure of independence. Their bishops meet in the Bishops' Conference of England and Wales, at which the Archbishop of Westminster presides. There is a separate conference for Scotland. Both the dioceses and the conferences have lay consultative bodies.

A parish priest may also be responsible for a school provided by the parish but largely financed by the local authority. Apart from the parish structure, there are many orders of priests, monks and nuns which operate worldwide. Nuns (styled Sister) now often wear civilian clothes and may be members of parish staffs.

The Church of Scotland

The Church of Scotland (The Kirk) is the national church north of the border. It has a parish structure; so you would describe, say, the Rev

David Smith as minister of St Andrew's Parish Church, rather than of St Andrew's Church. The Kirk is organized through a series of 'courts' of which the supreme is the General Assembly, which meets yearly. Parishes are grouped into presbyteries. At the local level, kirk sessions are groups of elders, ordained for life, who help the ministers in the pastoral and business life of congregations. There are also deacons: men and women commissioned to work in the church. The Moderator of the General Assembly is elected annually and bears the title the Right Rev while in office; afterwards the Very Rev.

The Methodist Church

The Methodist Church groups its churches into circuits and these, in turn, are grouped into districts. A district has a chairman, whose work is akin to that of a bishop. A circuit has a superintendent minister who is responsible, with the circuit meeting, for its work. Many services are conducted by local preachers, who are laypeople. Church lay officers are society stewards. There are also circuit stewards.

The governing body for the Methodist Church in England, Scotland and Wales is the Methodist Conference, which has an annually elected President. There is a separate conference for Ireland.

The United Reformed Church

The United Reformed Church was formed by Presbyterian and Congregational churches mainly in England and Wales, although some remain independent. It is organized into twelve provinces, has an annually elected Moderator and its chief administrator is the general secretary. Local churches have elders, who help to serve communion.

The Baptist Church

The Baptist Churches are independent congregations but many come together in the Baptist Union. They practise adult rather than infant baptism. Deacons in a Baptist church are people who help to run it.

The Afro-Caribbean Church

The Afro-Caribbean Churches are also independent congregations and use a variety of names. They come together in three main groupings; the Council of African and Afro-Caribbean Churches, the Joint Council of Anglo-Caribbean Churches and the International Ministerial Council of Great Britain.

Council for Churches

The Council of Churches for Britain and Ireland brings together all the major churches, including those with black leadership. Scotland has Acts (Action of Churches Together in Scotland), Wales has CYTUN (a Welsh acronym meaning Churches Together in Wales), Ireland has the Irish Council of Churches and England has Churches Together in England. Many local councils of churches have switched to the Churches Together title.

Christian Aid is the overseas development agency associated with the Council of Churches for Britain and Ireland. The annual Christian Aid Week raises money also for Cafod (the Catholic Fund for Overseas Development). Many Evangelical churches – Baptist and Anglican – contribute to Tear Fund, another overseas development agency.

Islam

Islam is the religion of a book, the *Koran*, containing detailed advice on how to live and pray. Young Muslims learn about it at schools set up by their mosques. There are also distinctive systems of Muslim names and it can cause offence to get these wrong. There is, for example, no such name as Abdul. The 'ul' or 'ud' common in Pakistani and Bangladeshi names (e.g. Alimuddin) is a linking word.

British mosques are administratively independent of one another. They may be community and counselling centres as well as places of worship. The priest who leads their religious life is an imam. This is also his title (e.g. Imam Alimuddin). There may be a local council of mosques, or two local groups of mosques with different emphases. Long-established mosques such as that of Regent's Park, London, may act as guides for others. Groups of Muslims come together to campaign on particular issues (as in the Salman Rushdie affair).

Hinduism and Sikhism

Hinduism – apart from the Hare Krishna movement – is a family-based religion rather than one with universal beliefs and practices. Families are grouped together and intermarry in castes – which are themselves large, extended families – and the caste system has travelled with them to Britain.

For newcomers, caste offers a ready-made and welcoming community in a strange land. Caste groups have set up social clubs, cricket clubs, temples. Only where Hindus are few are different castes likely to share a temple. However, castes do come together in associations to campaign on behalf of people of Indian origin.

Sikhism is reformed Hinduism, developed in the Punjab, original home of the bulk of the Indians who migrated to Britain. Although Sikhs take pride in having abandoned the caste system, Sikh groupings have if anything been strengthened by the journey to Britain and this has led lower-caste Punjabis (for example, the Ravidasi) to set up their own temples or to convert to Buddhism, which is caste-free.

Judaism

Just as the Christian faith in Britain is principally represented by the Established, Nonconformist, and Roman Catholic Churches, so the Jewish faith also has three main forms. They are Orthodox, Reform and Liberal.

The Orthodox form has the most adherents. In the Greater London area, where the majority of Orthodox synagogues are amalgamated into a union known as the United Synagogue, the word 'united' in a synagogue's title denotes that it is Orthodox. Elsewhere in the country, if the form is not indicated in the title (e.g. Blanktown Reform Synagogue or Blanktown Liberal Synagogue) then it is almost certainly Orthodox.

The Orthodox services are conducted entirely in Hebrew, except for the Prayer for the Royal family and the sermon, whereas the average Reform synagogue uses a percentage of English and the average Liberal synagogue English and Hebrew about equally.

Other differences are that in an Orthodox synagogue the women sit in a special gallery or at the back, separate from the men of the congregation. The men wear hats or small skullcaps called cappels. In a Reform synagogue a head-covering for men is also usual and in a Liberal synagogue optional. The women wear hats whatever the synagogue.

If you are sent to a Jewish service and are not certain which practice is followed, take a hat anyway: you can always leave it off. To attempt to enter an Orthodox synagogue without a hat would be as offensive as a male reporter trying to enter a Christian church with his hat on.

In the first instance in a report, the Jewish minister should be referred to in the same way as a Christian minister, i.e. as 'the Rev. . . .' followed by initials and surname (not surname alone). Subsequently he may be called either 'Mr. . .' or 'Rabbi. . .' followed by surname.

There is a slight trap here insofar as not all ministers of synagogues are Rabbis, which is a title achieved by scholastic attainment. If in doubt, you must ask which is the correct usage. To call a Rabbi 'Mr' in a report would be on a par with referring to a Catholic priest as 'Mr'. In any case, the term 'minister' is correct: 'In his sermon, the minister said that. . .' The

Reader in a synagogue (the Cantor) is always given the courtesy title of 'the Rev. . . .' followed by initials and surname.

The Jewish faith has no hierarchy and in the organizational sense there is no one standing between your local Rabbi and the Chief Rabbi of the United Hebrew Congregations of the Commonwealth who is referred to as 'the Very Rev. . . .'

In the London area, however, there is a court of five judges who adjudicate on legal matters and who, by the extent of their learning and authority, are superior to a Rabbi; their field does not extend to administration and organization. Similar judges also sit in provincial centres in courts of three, not five.

An individual member of such a court, who would, of course, be highly respected in any Jewish community, is a Dayan – Dayanim is the Hebrew plural. Some Dayanim have doctorates and in this case it is usual to refer to one as 'Dayan Dr. . .' followed by initials and surname. If he has no doctorate he is simply 'Dayan' (initials and surname). For subsequent references he may properly be called 'Dayan' (surname). The authority of the Chief Rabbi and Dayanim extends only to the Orthodox form and not to the Liberal or Reform synagogues, which are independent communities.

The major festivals of the Jewish year are: Chanukah (Festival of Light) which lasts eight days and occurs at about Christmas; Passover, near Easter; Purim, about March; Pentecost, near Whitsun; New Year and Day of Atonement, about September (the New Year is a solemn and not a frivolous occasion); and the Feast of Tabernacles, about October. The dates fluctuate in the same way as those of Easter and Whitsun, though the Jewish festivals are based on the Jewish calendar and not on the Christian one. Another major service in the Jewish year is held to mark the anniversary of Israel's Independence Day. This takes place around May and is usually accompanied by a social celebration too.

If your newspaper wishes to cover Jewish worship, it should ask the Jewish minister(s) about attendance at these services and other details connected with them, in the same way as it probably checks up on Easter and Christmas services with local Christian clergy. There could also be an interesting feature article (interesting because of the Christian's familiarity with the Old Testament), perhaps with pictures, on such a festival as the Feast of Tabernacles. Such events as the consecration of a new synagogue or synagogue hall are also reportable; if you are in touch with a local synagogue you will hear about these events in advance and can ask for your newspaper to be invited.

A word of caution is necessary about photographs. No picture may ever be taken in a synagogue during a Sabbath service or festival service and special permission is required to take photographs in a synagogue or its precincts even if a service is not in progress.

The number of organizations attached to a synagogue varies according to the area served but it can easily run to twenty or thirty. These may include groups for women, young couples, and young people, a Zionist society, young Zionists, women Zionists, study groups for young people and for adults, a range of Scout and Guide groups, charity committees, and representation on a Council of Christians and Jews if one exists locally. The activities of many of these groups are reportable to some extent.

A synagogue has a Board of Management which deals with matters of administration and organization, but not of faith. In the United Synagogue there is a London head office to which major items, such as a proposed large financial expenditure, must be referred for approval. The local Board deals only with local affairs. The secretary of the synagogue is automatically the secretary of the Board.

Most synagogues publish a sort of 'parish magazine' just as a church does and you can ask for copies to be sent to your office. The magazine will contain information about coming events at the synagogue (for the diary) and other items of information customary in such magazines.

The Jewish Sabbath is on a Saturday, from sunset Friday to sunset Saturday, and during this period certain activities are forbidden to the pious. Special British legislation has been passed to encompass this, relating, for instance, to the closing of places of employment.

Other British laws apply to the Jewish slaughter of food animals in accordance with religious laws; Jewish marriages; registrations of births, etc. If a Jew objects to marking a parliamentary ballot paper on a Saturday, he is entitled to have his vote recorded by the returning officer. In court a Jew is entitled to take the oath on the Pentateuch, which is the first five books of the Old Testament, and he has the privilege of covering his head in court while he does so.

References

Church of England: *Crockford's Clerical Directory, Diocesan Yearbook* (of the diocese), Parish magazines.

Roman Catholic: *Catholic Directory*, Diocesan Calendar.

Methodist: *Minutes of the Methodist Conference* (lists Methodist ministers), Circuit 'plans' (these are quarterly tables setting out who is to preach where within a circuit; they give the names and addresses of ministers, preachers and officers).

The Baptist Handbook, The Congregational Year Book, The Salvation Army Year Book, The Jewish Year Book.

Useful telephone numbers

Church of England Press Department	0171–222–9011
Catholic Media Office (England and Wales)	0171–938–2583
Church of Scotland Office	0131–225–5722
Catholic Press Office (Scotland)	0141–221–1168
Council of Churches for Britain and Ireland	0171–620–4444
Baha'i Information Office	0171–584–2577
The Buddhist Society	0171–834–5858
Islamic Cultural Centre (Dr Al-Ghamdi)	0171–724–3363
Board of Deputies of British Jews	0171–387–3952

13 SOME THOUGHTS ON SPORTSWRITING

It is easy enough to report sport adequately; it requires inspiration and great care to report it really well. The reason is not hard to find. The sport section is the most predictable in your newspaper. Every week for eight months the doings of Blackpatch United will be recorded and by April one match can easily sound very much like another. In the many months since those midweek previews, so chirpy last August, your team has subsided again into the middle-of-the-league-table rut. Yet these repetitive sporting rituals, with their interplay of chance and skill and the inevitable 'if onlys', are for large numbers of your readers their main contact with the drama of sport. Outstanding moments are remembered for a lifetime.

Sports reporting therefore needs to be more than simple, fair and accurate. It needs the imagination to grasp the way people feel about their team, the pride they take in a victory by their team and their town. Good sports reporters are often notable stylists.

It also requires the most careful attention to the match. When a goal is scored, you need to know who scored it, how the move began, and who passed the ball to whom. At cricket you need to know whether it was a catching chance that the wicket-keeper dropped. You need to know how that batsman who was scoring so well came to be bowled: did the ball spin into his wicket? Did he misjudge where it would bounce? You can, of course, ask these things afterwards but you may not have time and chance. Always, therefore, pay attention.

Watch carefully for any incidents: the batsman who thought he was not out; at rugby and Association football, the reason for penalty kicks since you will need to give an explanation in your report. The crowd is suddenly aware that two players are squaring up to each other. They will be reading your report to discover what the fuss was about.

Going to a match

If you are on the diary to cover a sporting engagement, make sure you get to know something about the game if it is one you have not watched before. Few people leave school without some knowledge of Association football and cricket but only a minority perhaps have ever attended a championship golf match or game of lacrosse. If it is a game you know little about, find someone in the office who knows it better. The Sports and Pastimes section of *Pears Cyclopaedia* gives a succinct description of most games and their rules. When you go to the match, sit or stand next to one of the officials.

You will want to know the names of the players in each team so you can identify them as they play. In the big leagues in soccer – Association football – this is no problem today, for the players have their names printed across the back of their shirts. Many smaller league clubs still have only numbers, however, and there is no guarantee that number nine on the field is the same as the one given on the programme. You probably know your team. Collaborate with a visiting reporter who knows the visiting team.

If you have an imminent deadline you will need to telephone copy probably at fixed intervals to catch editions. The use of mobile telephones has made this a lot easier for the sports reporter. It is still useful to have a runner to telephone copy for you while you concentrate on watching and writing up the match. Some evening papers have their own telephones at football grounds and sometimes at cricket grounds. If you have no mobile or office phone you might be allowed to use the club telephone. This can cause delay, however, and reliance on a public call box can cause even worse delay.

Faced with such problems the best thing, especially for important matches, is to make an arrangement with a private house near the ground to use the phone, sending your runner to put over copy at the required times.

At the match try to get a seat under cover especially if the day is far from sunny and you have to telephone your newspaper. Writing on or reading over the phone from rain-sodden paper is no fun.

Try to get clear in your mind the main questions that you will inevitably have to answer. Who played? Who scored? How did the score come about? Who played especially well? Was there a big crowd? What was the weather? Did the weather affect the game? Was the ground wet or slippery or hard or snow-covered or firm? Was the ball slippery (rugby) or heavy (soccer)? Watch whether players use unusual boots because of the conditions.

If you are reporting for an evening paper, you should know how many words you are required to telephone and at what times or stages of the game. It is important to stick to the times and the number of words. Sports editions of evening papers have to be produced quickly on Saturday afternoons and so reports must fit the spaces allocated without need for cutting. Also, newspapers can accept only a limited number of telephone calls at the same time. If your call is wrongly timed, it can throw the telephone plan out of gear.

Before the match starts you can telephone the names of the players. Check with an official what changes there may be from previously published team lists. You can also say what the weather is like and how big a crowd there is. Should the club have an accurate attendance figure you will want to collect it: find out when you can do so.

Eventually the match begins and you may be faced with the task of telephoning perhaps 150 words to an evening paper after the first 15 minutes. Your best plan, rather than to take notes, is to write out a report as the game goes along. Perhaps something like this:

> On a grey damp day at the Willows, a large crowd saw Blackpatch United attack from the kick-off in their home league match against Brightling Town this afternoon. Jones took the ball down the right wing; and Johnson, the Brightling goalkeeper, saved from Jim Keith, Blackpatch's high-scoring striker.
>
> Although Blackpatch did most of the pressing, Brightling scored first after five minutes. The Brightling strikers burst through the middle for Raymond to shoot into the net from 15 yards. . . .

Obviously you will hope to reach your 150 words about the time the match has been in progress 15 minutes. However, a spate of scoring or other excitement may defeat you. You may then have to cross out some of your earlier copy to make room for the later incidents. At 15 minutes you should be ready with your 150 words at the telephone, or you should have them ready for your runner.

You then continue with your report, writing the number of words required for your next telephone call, perhaps at half-time. The main thing is to keep cool, keep your report simple and get the score right and the scorers' names right. The readers will excuse you most things but not the wrong score or the wrong names of scorers.

For football and similar games, it is useful to have a stopwatch with you. Set it to the kick-off time at exactly the moment the game starts. Each score can then be recorded accurately minute by minute, and you will know how much injury time is played after the first half would normally have ended. At the moment the game restarts for the second half, set your watch to the time it should have restarted. This again will give you the time of scores and the amount of injury time.

Writing your report

Good sports writing, unlike news writing, is a mixture of fact and **interpretation** spiced with **comment**. It thus shares some of the elements of

Figure 13.1 *How a good picture can enhance a sporting occasion – another award-winning effort from young* Hull Daily Mail *photographer Richard Walker showing how the Great Britain Rugby League team celebrated a try against Australia at Manchester*

both news and feature writing. The reader wants more than just a deadpan recital of who did what, and looks to the comments, the opinions and the assessment of the writer on what has taken place out on the park.

If you are not up against the clock – for example, if you are writing for a morning paper, a weekly or a Sunday paper or you are covering an evening match for next day's evening paper – you will have more time to produce the sort of polished result sports readers want. A mere description of the game is not enough. If Briggs played well, draw attention to those parts of the game which demonstrated his skill. Analyse to the best of your ability the debut of a new player in the team, or the first outing of a player previously injured or out of favour. Did you notice if the goalkeeping was suspect as in the previous two games? Or is the conceding of too many goals due to a growing weakness in the defence?

For a weekly paper published towards the weekend your main task may be to look forward to the next match rather than back at the last one. An analysis of the one just covered might be the basis for **speculation** about what could happen at the next fixture, which might be against a very different team. Perhaps an important player has been injured or suspended.

In writing up the match you have just covered you should have two main aims:

1   To capture any vivid and memorable moments in the play.
2   To establish, in a blend of comment and fact, whether and why you thought the match was good to watch, or an important result, and why the winners won.

Never forget that sport is a drama. It has moments of inspired life: at cricket, for instance, the sudden capture of wickets, a batsman's brilliant century, a thrilling partnership; at soccer, a rush of goals; at rugby an exciting ending as the side well behind strives to get equal. Do not be afraid of giving attention to moments like these. These are the things that become the headline and intro to your story; the rest of the game can come later in your report.

Here is how one newspaper led its report of a dramatic soccer game at Newcastle upon Tyne:

> There is still magic born and bred on the Tyne. As Newcastle United regained the leadership of the FA Carling Premiership before 36,577 impassioned spectators yesterday evening, the story revolved not around the League of Nations players remarkably drawn into an area once destitute, but around Peter Beardsley, playing his 700th competitive club match in England.
>
> Beardsley captained Newcastle, the club he had supported as a boy. He scored, almost inevitably, the first two goals. . . .

Note how **statistics** – an element beloved of sports fans – play their part in the intro.

Among the sports reporters' greatest difficulties is achieving variety and maintaining interest when reporting the same team week in a week out. Comments on the play and assessments of the players are in danger of becoming repetitive if that is all the match report consists of, although in every match you must watch for the players who change and control the course of the game. A reference to the **weather** can help in pushing a match report along:

> A swirling wind rolled in from the North Sea to handicap anybody tempted to measure a pass yesterday afternoon. Hit and hope was the order of proceedings and United ultimately triumphed because their defence made fewer errors under pressure. . . .

At cricket and rugby union you will have to watch more keenly than at other sports to spot the players who are really making a difference. At cricket, most medium and fast-medium bowlers look much the same in their action at a cursory glance. You need to distinguish between the short-of-a-length, keep-the-runs-down bowler and the man who is trying to do something interesting with every ball.

At rugby union, the activities of the backs and the wing forwards are usually obvious enough, but it could be a forward who is really winning the game and since the forwards work as a pack he may not be easy to spot. Watch for the success of second-row forwards in getting the ball in the line-out, and watch for the speed with which they and the front-row men get about the field.

Imagery will help the writer but try not to use the more obvious images too often: 'hammer', 'punch', 'battle of giants'. Few matches are clashes of supermen. If you shout at the top of your voice every week, your state of frenzy will grow less and less credible.

While watching a match always keep an eye open for the **tactics** employed. These are most obvious in cricket where fielding captains can choose which bowlers to use and what field to set, while batsmen can choose whether to take or avoid risks. Tactics are fairly obvious in rugby where a side winning the ball can choose whether to pass it along the three-quarter line or have it kicked ahead or keep it among the forwards. Even soccer, where tactics are less obvious, is not just a game between two teams who play well or badly. A team can have a tactical plan of how it hopes to score and how it hopes to prevent its opponents from scoring. It can have prearranged series of moves which it hopes to make should opportunity offer. If you are aware, for example, of the way in which one visiting side's style and tactics differ from another's, your report will be helped.

At soccer the sources of tactics are the managers; and interviewing the managers, or indeed the players, has become a popular way of adding variety to match reports. Do not give undue prominence to a manager's comment if the facts of the match are much more interesting than what the manager says about them. If the manager can manage only 'I think it was a fine game, with plenty of good football', you can leave him until the end.

A manager's comments, however, made the intro in this match report:

'There is only one cure for the position we are in and that is hard work,' Brian Laws wrote in the manager's column at the front of the match programme. The directors of Grimsby Town disagreed. Their answer to the problem was to dismiss Laws last Friday.

Words and openings

In any event, be wary of the worn phrases of sport – 'fine, open game', 'ding-dong battle', 'stung by this reverse' and so on. Do not be tempted either by the trick of saying the same thing in two different ways, as a method of achieving variety: 'They were without Muller their centre forward who has a leg injury, and Wilden, their centre half, who was kept out of the side with influenza.' This is merely a long way of saying: 'They were without Muller their centre forward who has a leg injury, and Wilden, their centre half, who has influenza.'

Good sports reports obey the same rules as good news reports in their **structure**. They need to start well, with the most interesting fact. They need to answer the obvious questions: What and where was the match? What was the score? Who played? Who scored what? Since rugby scores are of varying character and points value you need to make it clear early in a rugby report what the actual scores were:

> Warwickshire are once again the champion county of England, for here on Hartlepool Rovers ground they defeated Durham by a try, three dropped goals and a penalty goal to two tries and a dropped goal.

Sports reports like news reports need an unbroken line of thought from start to finish, and they need to end well. Here was a good ending:

> No one in Wales is complaining now. Even the man who paid £200 for three stand tickets thought it was worth it.

As in news, you do not need to start chronologically at the beginning and move through to the end. You can start at the end of the match if this was the most exciting.

Do not forget that sport is news. Here, on the face of it, is a perfectly satisfactory opening: 'With two days left in their six-day Test match, the West Indies were in a commanding position at close of play yesterday.' However, the headline gave the game away: 'Test match umpire pelted,' it read. The second paragraph had caught the headline writer's eye: 'Police escorted the umpire off the field at the close. About a dozen empty beer cans and bottles were thrown in his direction.' This was the place to start.

As in news, avoid wordy openings like this:

> In a game which was full of energetic but erratic play and which saved nearly all its scoring until the last 10 minutes, S— completed a double victory over H— by three tries to one. . . .

Avoid openings which are negative in feeling: 'The English senior cross-country championship developed too predictably to arouse excitement.' Yawn! Yawn! Why bother to read on?

A simple intro yet with a feeling for occasion is more likely to score, as in the following examples:

A larger than usual crowd tempted out by the wan sun saw Luton beat Stockport by the odd goal in five – scored just two minutes from the close.

Wales kept alive the hope of playing in the World Cup finals next year with an inspired 4–1 win over Greece at Cardiff last night.

In the body of the report the writing and choice of words should reflect the pace and fortunes of the game. The following bit of an account in *The Times* sports pages of an Aston Villa v Nottingham Forest match is a useful model:

Lee's first miss, finding Oakes's outstretched hands after Woan's immaculate cross, was negligent. His second was simply laughable. Lee had already beaten the goalkeeper, but his shot was so tame that Tiler was able to make up ground to clear.

Colour and variety

As well as having accuracy, a sports report can be given colour and variety by a discerning writer. An eye or ear for the unusual will bring the writing alive, as in this hockey match:

Olton pride themselves on the family spirit within the Women's National League Club so it was almost too good to be true to hear their teenage striker Kerry Moore yelling 'Mum' when she wanted a defender to release a long ball down the line. Lyn Moore duly obliged and the talented former England Under-18 player set off on another of her weaving runs.

The Birmingham team are justifiably proud of fielding the mother-and-daughter combination. . . .

And in this report of a women's golf tournament:

It was her fourth home victory this season and her 48th career win. Even having to stay in a nunnery, where the water was icy cold when she took a morning shower, did not stop Davies. Nor did high winds on the fourth day. . . .

The colour can come from a player's unusual physical characteristics, as in this basketball match:

It was for flattening Daniel Hildreth, very much an agent-provocateur for Ware Rebels, that Michael New was expelled from Newcastle Eagles' first-round tie nine seconds from half-time. 'He was lucky I only pushed him,' the 6 ft 9 in centre said after his team's 102–70 victory.

Or from the jollies that attend university rugby:

Amid the flurry of league and cup matches, Cambridge on an autumn afternoon offers a timeless appeal. The students contesting a vigorous match in their usual lively manner, the familiar after-match gathering beside the coke fire in the main pavilion before retiring for tea and sticky buns at Selwyn College . . . .

Vocabulary

One thing that the young sportswriter has to master is the terminology of the game that is being covered. Here it has to be assumed that the readers, whether the report is to do with soccer, horse racing, ice hockey or lacrosse will be familiar with the vocabulary and the basic rules of what they are reading. They do not require you to explain what 'offside' or 'heavy going' mean and they will look askance if you call a hockey stick a bat or confuse a free-kick with a penalty.

It is a good idea for the trainee sportswriter to study how the professionals handle special vocabulary in passages like the following:

Despite this advantage behind the scrum, only a point separated the two sides after an hour when Logan had capitalized on smart work by Scott Hastings for a converted try which left the scoreline 20–19 in Australia's favour. That followed a try by Campese, who rounded off a sweeping crossfield move, the platform for which had been a 50-yard driving maul . . . (**rugby union**).

Faldo dropped a second shot on the 450-yard ninth to turn in 34 but his two-three start to the inward half against the par of three-four meant he had thrown down the gauntlet to the rest of the field.
At three under par he shared first place with Spain's Ignacio Garrido . . . Garrido turned in 34, eagled the long 12th and made amends for a bogey on the 15th by collecting a four on the 561-yard 17th . . . (**golf**).

But Thorburn then attempted an imprudent double to a middle pocket when, taking into consideration his vast experience and defensive mindset, all and sundry expected a safety shot. The red failed to find its target, Higgins eventually doubled it himself and went on to complete a clearance of 42 to draw level at 3–3. Scotland eventually won 6–3 (**snooker**).

Enqvist turned up the heat on that fierce backhand to break back to 2–3 and then levelled the scores with three aces to win his serve to love. From then on a succession of aces – 20 in all – kept Kafelnikov at bay. It was a bit too much for Kafelnikov, who eventually gave up the ghost and his own service to go 5–6 down and then stood back to watch Enqvist serve out the match with four more aces (**tennis**).

Midweek sportswriting

If sports reporting were solely of matches it would be simple, but readers do not want their sport only on Monday and Saturday. They like it

Tuesday to Friday as well, and for newspapers it is a good policy to cater for the enthusiasm of such an important body of readers. You are unlikely to escape on any evening or weekly with writing only match reports. On provincial weeklies published towards the weekend, for example, your main emphasis will often be on the coming match and associated items rather than on last Saturday's result.

Midweek sports pages are an opportunity, not just a chore, but you need a touch of imagination to make them so. Avoid the frenzied approach which blows up casual gossip into a crisis; but also make sure you are not found without a thing to say when your sports editor asks for your weekly contribution to the **chat column**.

Sports reporters who follow a particular team invariably keep a record book. They write down the weekly results and scorers and who played. From time to time their book gives them interesting bits of information: that John Smith has played in 50 successive games; that Phil Jones has scored 18 tries this season. Sportswatchers are interested in statistics and will even bet on them.

Keep in touch with club officials for news of next week's teams, for newcomers, soccer transfers, details of midweek matches. If you follow a cricket side make sure you get the dates of midweek Cup games which are often fixed at short notice. If you want to make your sports pages interesting, remember two things: sports reporting is about people, and there are other sports beside soccer, rugby and cricket.

Most reporters recognize that if a footballer gets married it is news, but do they recognize readers' wider interest in people they see on the games field? What do sports people who are not professionals do for a living? Are they married? How many children have they? What do their wives think about their involvement in sport? If a player attains a notable record do an interview with the person behind the sports figure.

In writing a **sports feature** it is important to conduct interviews away from the dressing room. This way a rapport with the player is more likely – and stale clichés less likely.

The local hockey, tennis or basketball team might be less fashionable than the football or cricket club but readers who never cared anything for hockey will fill with pride if the team in their town suddenly starts beating all-comers. Keep an eye open too for the success of individuals – not just the local star swimmer or athlete but some unknown or second-rank competitor who has suddenly done well.

Officers of the **Sports Councils** in the UK are working all the time to encourage people to take part in sports and games. Their philosophy is that everyone can enjoy some sport or other if only they can find the right one. They encourage less well-known sports by running courses or giving help with organization. There is an upsurge, perhaps encouraged by the

Olympics and the Commonwealth Games, of people wanting to try individual games or sports rather than team ones. The Sports Council office in your region can tell you what courses are running in the area, and perhaps the names of any local man or woman who is making a name in a sport you never even thought about.

With lesser-known sports in your area such as fencing, archery or Kabaddi, if you cannot attend all their fixtures try to encourage secretaries to send in results. If your newspaper will accept the expense, devise a stamped addressed postcard on which the secretary can fill in results and score figures.

Do not forget **schools**. They will be delighted if their local paper takes an interest in them. Adult readers and former students will be interested, too, and it all helps to give the sports pages variety and extra news. It is possible to compile tables of schools in things like soccer, rugby and cricket, showing how many matches they have played, won, drawn and lost, and what goals and points they have scored.

Sporting reference books

The following are useful to have in a sports department for background information and records – and to settle disputes; some are vital to sports journalists:

Soccer: *Rothman's Football Yearbook* (comprehensive for players' details, clubs, leagues and European information); *News of the World Football Annual; Playfair Football Annual* (both pocket-sized, comparatively cheap and packed with essential information plus records and milestones in the game); *Barclays League Football Club Directory; Rothman's Football League Players' Records* and *European Football Records* (European national and international competitions); *County FA Handbooks;* the *Official FA Yearbook* (useful for addresses and telephone numbers).

Cricket: *Wisden's Cricketers' Almanac* (details of previous season's match and individual records, both county and test, including test matches played anywhere in the world); *Playfair Cricket Annual* (pocket-sized record of past results and upcoming fixtures); the *Official TCCB Book of Statistics; The Cricketer* (informative monthly magazine with current season's results, records from cricket all over the world and other useful material); *Benson and Hedges Cricket Yearbook; Cricketers' Who's Who* (likes, dislikes, nicknames, etc.).

Rugby union and rugby league: *Rothman's Rugby Yearbook* and *Rothman's Rugby League Yearbook* (comprehensive for both codes).

Boxing: *Boxing News* (weekly) and *Boxing Monthly* (reports and statistics); *British Boxing Yearbook* (annual review of the fight scene).

Athletics: *Athletics Weekly* and *Athletics Today* (for reports and statistics).

Golf: *The Royal and Ancient Golfers' Handbook* (comprehensive records and full publication of the game's complex rules); *Benson and Hedges Golf Year* (well documented).

Tennis: *ITA Official Handbook; World of Tennis* (both packed with facts and figures).

Horse-racing: *Racehorses of the Year; Horses in Training; Directory of the Turf* (all mines of information).

General: *The Guinness Book of Records.* Darts, snooker, American football and motorsport are all well supported by regular magazines containing results, profiles and ongoing statistics.

14 SUMMARIZING

Summarizing is bound to occupy a good deal of a reporter's office time. Such tasks include taking the gist of what a speaker says and condensing it to a few words; taking a short handout, report, or contributed item and making an even shorter news item out of it; reading through a long report, possibly from an official source, and extracting a story from it which is perhaps only 2 or 3 per cent of the length of the original. It means rejecting a lot of the material altogether as well as condensing the remainder.

The short report

A report of a few hundred words can be scanned fairly speedily in a few minutes. Learn to do this without attempting to take in details.

If it is an official report couched in formal language this is not so easy. Getting an idea of the main theme is the object of reading it through the first time. Then ask yourself 'What is this all about?' Try to give yourself an answer in one sentence. See if there is a passage in the original which roughly coincides with this sentence as a check on your conclusion.

Now reread the material in detail. Mark the salient facts together with any sentence or passage that has a human interest which, though not essential, nevertheless throws light on the subject. If space permits, these items may make interesting quotes.

The long report

You will find in the course of time that it is not unusual for someone to drop a 50,000 word report on your desk and expect a 1000-word version of it back by lunchtime; not just a straight summary but one that highlights the important and the unusual. This is journalism as opposed to mere précis-writing. The procedure is more complex than for short material but there are points of resemblance.

Look at the start of the report: there may be an executive summary. Then at the end: there may be lists of conclusions and recommendations. These could form much of the substance of the news story you are pulling from the report. But in using official or technical material avoid the jargon that often goes with it. This will help to make your own report lively and readable.

Then start the long job of skimming the remainder, not such a quick scan as you would give short material at a first reading but nevertheless not a line-by-line reading. Mark everything that catches your attention. Employ a system of marking that indicates relative interest:

- A single vertical line for an interesting passage.
- A double line for something more important.
- A treble line for something sensational.

Make a note of page numbers of important points or put markers in the book. You do not want to have to leaf through perhaps 50 or 100 pages every time you need to refer to one of them.

When you have finished, ask yourself two questions: 'What is this all about?' (again) and 'What are the most interesting points?' The second question is necessary with longer material because the answer to the first may be too general. Take, for example, a director of public health's report on the health of the town. The answer to the first question is: 'It is about the health of the town in the year 19--.' The answer to the second is: 'A big rise in deaths from lung cancer which the director says on page 12 is directly due to smoking' and 'A sudden rise in overcrowding at local hospitals which results in...' etc. Both these items in the report should have your three-line mark against them, or your equivalent symbol.

One or two of these points will make your intro, plus a firm relating of the point to the source from which it comes which should also be stated in or near the intro. Never attempt a sort of omnibus intro containing a list of points almost ad infinitum:

> The director of public health's report for 19--, issued today, says there has been a big rise in deaths from lung cancer which the director says is directly due to smoking; a rise in overcrowding in local hospitals; a drop in infant mortality but a rise in the death rate compared with the rest of the country ... and so on.

After writing your trial intro, incorporate summaries of as many of the marked passages as your length limit allows and in the order of priority of importance. This will include the three-lined passages, many or all of the two-lined, and perhaps some of the single-line ones. Each has to be condensed on its merits: a three-line passage of 150 words may have to appear in your report as a single sentence. A direct quote here and there from the original material, if it is simple and vivid and if there is the space for it, will brighten your report by varying its rhythm.

Occasionally you may find you incorporate all your marked passages one way or another and still have allocated space left open to you. Make a quick check through to see if there are any more interesting bits. If not, do not pad out with odds and ends, which will only spoil your report, not improve it. Point out to your news editor or chief sub-editor that you do not think the original material will make the length that has been set; after all, you have read it in detail, they have not.

A 'trial intro' means the intro that first occurs to you after the first read-through (short material) and the marking of important passages (long material). This is a useful way of getting down on paper the instant impression the material makes on you and it should be simple and vivid.

However, detailed reading of the material may bring out a point or two that really ought to go into the intro, and your 'trial intro' then has to be amended. If you are dealing with complex material demanding a carefully balanced summary in the opening, keep your 'trial intro' in mind as you read through the material and see how you can bring into the opening sentences all the important sections and aspects of the material that you have marked.

In dealing with either a short or a long piece of material the principal mistake is to go at it bald-headed, sitting down to a loaded keyboard with the material before you open at page one and hoping to construct a story as you go along. This method will produce a disjointed and distorted version and can waste more time than it saves. The main thing in writing any kind of summary is to have clear in your mind before you start what it is all about. If you know this, you can tell your readers more easily.

Here is a word of warning. Reports usually carry an embargo which prohibits their use in newspapers before a stated time. This may be the time of a meeting to which the report is to be presented and the embargo is an effort to ensure that all newspapers start square and that, chief reporters and news editors permitting, all reporters writing about the report have time to read it first. Always observe embargoes; they are usually justified. You will embarrass both your editor and the people who issued the report if you do not.

Balance sheets

When you first encounter a balance sheet which you have to summarize you tend to try to draw some conclusion from the two totals at the bottom. Since they are both the same, and apparently have no relation to anything, at first sight this can appear unrewarding.

The main items to look for are the balance and the principal items of income and expenditure. Strictly speaking, a balance sheet for a year's activities can be presented only by an organization that has no appreciable goods or property – e.g. a drama society, residents' association, local welfare organization, etc. Where the organization has property or other assets with a market value it must give an account of their current value – this is a true balance sheet, and an account of the year's financial transactions would then be called an income and expenditure account. The two sets of accounts are normally presented together, sometimes with an explanation by the treasurer and sometimes without. When the accounts are presented at an annual meeting of an organization, members have the right to ask the treasurer questions about the accounts.

With conventional presentations a credit balance (a surplus or 'profit' on the year's working) is the last item in the left-hand column above the total. If it is a debit balance (a loss) it occupies the equivalent position on the right. This is the nub of the account and may be all you need.

Some of the individual items on either side may be worth notice. Here is an income and expenditure account produced by a hospital's League of Friends:

	£		£	£
Gifts and contributions for the benefit of the hospital patients and staff, and sundry donations*	1036	Subscriptions, donations, and collecting boxes, including Christmas appeal		445
		Bank deposit interest		4
Gifts approved to be purchased*	180	Interest and dividends on investments (gross)		66
	1216			
Administration expenses, including printing, stationery, postage, telephone, secretarial services and miscellaneous expenses	418	Flag Day		151
	1634	Surplus on shop activities after salaries and expenses	1437	
		Less depreciation	113	
Surplus of income over expenditure for the year	532	Provisions for repairs	30	
	£2166		143	1294
		Surplus arising from branch functions		206
				£2166

*Both itemized in detail in original.

Two items stand out: the £1036 spent on gifts and contributions (with a further £180 approved for spending); and net takings in a shop of £1294. In spite of the heavy expenditure there is still a surplus of £532 (bottom left).

This indicates that something is going on in a modest way and, if you are not already acquainted with this particular League of Friends, it would be worth looking into. In fact at this hospital the League has built and equipped a general-store type of shop in the hospital grounds, selling to staff and patients, and is using the income from this to provide items of equipment and welfare facilities for staff and patients – quite an interesting story, followed up.

A further set of figures (as under) was issued to show the total value of the League's assets:

	£	£		£	£
Accumulated fund			*Fixed assets*		
Balance as at end of			Shop premises		
last financial year	3023		and fixtures		
			At cost	1744	
			Less grant	1000	
Add Excess of				744	
income over					
expenditure for					
current year*	532		*Less* depreciation	142	
	3555				602
Add Surplus on			Shop fittings		
realization			At cost	250	
of investments	59		*Less* depreciation	65	
		3614			
Provision for shop					
repairs		60			
					185
					787
Provision for					
purchase of					
gifts to hospital*		180			
			Quoted securities		
Sundry creditors		1200	At cost		1807
			Current assets		
			Stock for shop –		
			at cost	936	
			Income tax		
			recoverable	14	
			Debtors payments		
			in advance	30	
			Balances with		
			bankers		
			Current account	1117	
			Deposit account	206	
			Cash in hand	157	
					2460
		£5054			£5054

*Both items brought over from the income and expenditure account on foregoing page.

Note how subsidiary sums are done slightly to the left of the main columns and their totals taken into the main columns.

The item at the top left (£3023) was what the League was 'worth' when this year started. To this was added the balance from the current year and £59 surplus on selling investments to produce a figure of £3614 to show what the League is 'worth' this year, provision already having been made for shop repairs, gifts to the hospital, and creditors.

Having seen from these figures that there was an amount of money lying around doing nothing, the League committee approved the spending of £1000 in whatever way the staff and patients' representatives suggested. As a rule, this type of balance sheet, indicating the overall financial position of an organization, is of less topical interest than the income and expenditure account which gives up-to-date information on how things have turned out for the organization during the current year.

Both sets of figures have been certified correct by an auditor, usually some qualified person outside the organization who approves the accounts prepared by the treasurer. There may be more than one auditor.

The word 'profit' has been used in this section and is fair enough when lightly applied to the year's surplus for, say, a residents' association. However, it has a strict and specific meaning for commercial organizations, both in accountancy and income tax usage, and should never be automatically applied to, say, the difference between purchase price and selling price. You could inadvertently be implying that a seller is making an excessive profit. If a man's business depends on his reputation he might take action about it.

15 FEATURE WRITING

Young journalists will find that the term 'features' in a newspaper office is used to describe all those editorial items which are not news. A feature article frequently shares a timeliness with the news in that it can arise out of a news story, but in practice the features department will also find itself handling such diverse items as the weekly crossword puzzle, the chess and bridge columns and even the cartoons.

A feature article nevertheless is generally a piece of writing in which, unlike news writing, facts are accompanied by a point of view. It can have a variety of aims and the writer has more scope in style and vocabulary, in comment, description and personal reaction than would be possible with news writing, although the idea is to communicate with the same readers who read the news pages.

While most newspapers employ specialist feature writers it will often fall to reporters to provide general background features to the news or to complement material on the news pages, or even to contribute to special pages built around some seasonal topic such as holidays, a Christmas issue or consumer guides. Such a task can be a valuable experience for the young reporter intending later to specialize. The purpose of this chapter is to guide reporters when faced with such tasks.

Every well-edited, well-balanced paper has a proportion of feature articles which force their way into print because the paper would be demonstrably poorer without them, and its readers less intrigued and less well informed. News, as we said, can be the peg for them: a feature may comment on events, tell the story behind them, or cast light on some less well-known aspect of life and society within (or without) the orbit of the readers. It can also merit being used simply by being entertaining, introducing a breath of humour to a page, though timeliness remains important.

When Samoa beat Wales at rugby the *Daily Mail* took a novel angle by publishing a feature about the rejoicing back home in Samoa. When

Gorbachev's colleagues tried to overthrow him the media looked for every bit of background they could find to explain what was going on, even at the risk of what Rupert Murdoch once called reporting in width – that is, writing round the news without adding much to understanding.

Even timeliness can pall, however, and as major events recede into history only those features with something fresh and illuminating to say will command the readers' attention. When the British government announced a new route for the railway to the Channel Tunnel the *Daily Express* published an article by a woman living in an area blighted by the announcement of the previous route. This had a necessary element of surprise. Instead of giving yet another airing to an old controversy the feature drew attention to the human cost of bungled planning.

A leading African journalist, Willie Musururwa, used to attack what he called speech journalism, reporting speeches rather than the news. The British media is far from free of this; yet anyone who has watched a TV debate knows that debaters may obscure an issue rather than illuminate it. A good feature gets behind the debate to what is really going on.

Strikes are an example. News reports normally cover what the companies or the unions say. The feature writer's job is to find the nub of the dispute, the things that have really upset people and set the whole thing in motion.

The best features are usually about people. Nigel Spivey established himself as a contributor to the *Weekend Financial Times* with an account of a Vietnamese family settling uneasily into a British city. He knew the family well and so was able to share, and touchingly describe, its experience.

Finding ideas

How do you find good feature ideas? One way is to take note of the questions that occur to you and your friends about the news, about what is on television, the area in which you live, the people in the news. Readers will have thought, if only half consciously, of similar questions and will be interested in your answers. One writer, operating on these lines, made a feature out of the rubber bands from bundles of letters which postmen had begun to drop in the streets. Another explained why the Inland Revenue was asking people not to pay their tax by cheque – because thieves were stealing the cheques, altering them and banking them in accounts with names like A. Revenuoli.

Health subjects win great attention, though it is important to avoid raising false hopes by publicizing unorthodox cures you cannot evaluate.

Newspapers tend to prefer health features which concentrate on the people affected rather than the science. Good feature ideas can lurk in advertisements, often the more specialized ones in smaller-circulation magazines, because it is through advertising that people with new ideas may seek to bring them to attention. Read as widely as you can in specialist magazines and other papers that might yield up the sort of ideas you can use.

Anniversaries and birthdays are worth watching for. They supply a timeliness and a 'Why now?' for some intriguing or historical subjects which would not otherwise get an airing.

Illustrations

Once you have decided on a subject, what about illustrations? Most features need illustrations but make sure when you have found the right pictures that they tell the same story as the text. Discrepancies occur even in the national dailies, with a woman perhaps being described as beautiful alongside a picture which tells a different story.

Maps need special care. They are often printed quite small and you will need to ensure that place names are legible. If the printed map is half size the lettering on the original will need to be in at least 14-point or 18-point so that it comes down to average reading size. Make sure (another trap) that the place names on the map are spelt the same way as in the text.

Interviews

Assembling material for a feature, even one produced at short notice ('A quick backgrounder on that traffic black spot – you've got just an hour and a half') usually requires at least one interview. Most people explain themselves more simply, freshly and graphically in speech than on paper. Professionals wary of possible repercussions tend to hide their thoughts behind the written jargon of their trade.

Face-to-face interviews are best. They give the person interviewed more confidence and can allow unexpected facts and ideas to surface. They also give the interviewer more time to think beyond some initially prepared questions.

Arranging, travelling to and carrying out face-to-face interviews take time. You may be forced to use the telephone, especially to talk to several informants over a wide area. This method serves well in any case if you are simply asking for a few facts or gathering opinions (see Chapter 5).

Behind the facts

The two key questions in a radio interview are: What is the situation? What are you (or they) doing about it? In a newspaper feature another question is of great importance: How did things come to be the way they are? For a newspaper has more space for words than radio and can concern itself with background.

Company reports, for example, describe the company's situation and plans. This may be hard to appreciate without a knowledge of how the company came to engage in its particular activities and what problems it has had. Good features are not simply descriptive; they tell a story, adduce evidence, draw conclusions. They can also benefit by having a touch of drama.

As for people, there is often some event – a road accident, even a war of independence or a political purge – which has set their lives on the present tack. For a profile feature of the person you need to identify and recall that event.

Features about things need to be brought to life. Fuel-saving stoves in Ethiopia sounds an unpromising subject, but they are used by women who work up to 17 hours a day baking bread a piece at a time.

Comment

We have said that writing a feature allows you more latitude than a news story. You can, for instance, include comment though it should arise naturally from the facts you are handling; facts should not be selected merely to support an argument. It can confuse or annoy a reader to come across a completely different account of the same situation from another writer with a different axe to grind.

But having rehearsed the facts and the arguments, you do need to reach a conclusion. Good features do not sit on the fence.

Be aware of what your paper has already published on your subject. You do not have to agree with it but you should take account of it; otherwise it looks as if you do not read your own newspaper.

Good beginnings

It is not a good idea to reserve what you have to say to the last paragraph. There may be a case for a surprise ending – though these are the exception – but usually you should make plain in the opening paragraphs what you are about. You need to grasp the reader's attention and to avoid confusing the sub-editor, who has not been where you have been or spoken to the people you have spoken to and is probably wondering what on earth you are on about.

One way to grasp attention and avoid confusion is to start with a crisply told story which embodies what the feature has to say:

> Armed with two passbooks stolen from our house, a woman impersonating my wife drew £10,250 in two days from building society branches in North London.

This is a story in a sentence. It has an element of surprise; few account holders would know that it was this easy to take money from their accounts. And it draws attention to the building societies' security problem, the subject of the article.

Here is the start of another newspaper feature:

> 'I like my life. I like your life. I drive carefully,' said Mr Singh, a one-time economics student as he ducked and weaved his black and yellow scooter-driven cab round the India Gate.

This has colour (literally). It says something about Mr Singh and gives an impression of his strange cab for those who have never seen one like it or experienced the hazards of Delhi traffic. If your feature is dealing with a new place and new people and does not give an impression of them you might as well have stayed in the office and used the telephone.

Here are the opening paragraphs of a feature by Chris Holt in *The Northern Echo's* magazine *Echoes*:

> It's a hard way to earn a living, smashing it out of the rock under the hills where you live.
>
> The seam at Clarghyll colliery is 17 inches wide – only just worth working – and yet that's what miners work under Alston Moor, plodging a mile along a waterlogged tunnel each day to reach the face.
>
> With picks and shovels they hack and sweat coal out of the hill the way all miners did 60 or more years ago.
>
> When the coal industry was nationalized after the war, some of the less lucrative collieries were left in private hands, allowed to work under licence from the National Coal Board.
>
> 'With us it's all manual work,' says John Williams, an Alston miner for 31 years and owner of Clarghyll. 'It's broken off the face with a pick and thrown out of the seam to be put into tubs with hand shovels.'
>
> 'It's not really a job for a man that's not in peak physical condition.'
>
> He is a big man but, like the landscape, unthreatening.
>
> Above ground at Clarghyll, England's three most northerly counties meet in sleeping hog's back hills, green, mauve, yellow and bracken-red.

This feature article starts with a short graphic scene-setting sentence amplified by a second longer one which gives the story both a geographic and a subterranean location, and invents an expressive word, 'plodging'. Note that the seam is 17 inches wide, not 'just 17 inches wide' as they would say on TV.

The fifth paragraph makes the story personal with John Williams and what he has to say. The writer then gives an impression of him which leads into a description of the scenery that also puts Clarghyll on the map of England.

'Sleeping hog's back hills' overeggs the pudding a little. Why not simply 'hog's back hills'? But bracken-red adds something to red and explains it. To have said at the same time meadow-green, heather-mauve and autumn-yellow would have been overlush.

Here is the start of a profile:

> Veteran journalist Henry Ofori recalls the day when he was taken to Accra docks. Among the goods being brought ashore from surf boats was a crate of whisky.
>
> A docker held it above his head and dropped it. Then he and his colleague held it over a bucket and filtered the liquid through muslin. Everyone got a cup. 'This,' said Henry, 'was my first introduction to feature writing.'

Ofori's story of the dockers is entertaining. It also establishes him as a writer with a sense of humour who appreciates other people.

Building the text

Always look out for the fact and phrase that adds sharpness to your article. Be humble enough to realize that some people express their ideas better than you can. Your task is to tighten the words a little – most people use more words than they need – without losing the graphic touches of the original.

Never overwhelm the reader with facts and figures. Seek out those that add most to what you want to say. If you need to give many figures put them into an accompanying table or chart. Check them to be sure they mean what your informants say they mean. Errors in arithmetic can easily occur.

Check, too, the spelling of names, including place names and especially foreign names. It saps the credibility of your feature if you appear not to know where you have been or to whom you have spoken.

If you feel your feature might be defamatory sort out the provable facts from the airy allegations and stick with the facts. Your piece will be none the less effective.

Like a news story, a feature needs to have its material arranged in a clear unbroken thread of argument.

Here is an enterprising follow-up of a national story by Stephen Lewis of the *Evening Press*, York. It is easy to follow, presents clear facts crisply and has a good ending. The quotes are brief and to the point and come from named informants. In this case the text took up only a fifth of the feature, the rest being pictures and headline.

Greedy Brits whose eyes are bigger than their bellies are throwing away almost £1 billion worth of fresh food every year. Housewives and househusbands in York are no better than anyone else when it comes to eating food before its sell-by date.

Top of the list of rotten food that ends up in the bin is exotic fruit like mangoes and avocados, according to an *Evening Press* survey. Salad greens and vegetables such as courgettes also end up in the dustbin.

Nationally, a survey by the Frozen Food Information Service today disclosed that every week families are throwing out £18 million worth of fresh food.

York families contacted by the *Evening Press* say that about 5 per cent of the food they buy goes to waste. That's about £2.50 a week for a family with a £50 food bill.

Patsy Thackway, 50, of Hull Road, York, admitted: 'When I go shopping, I see a lot of things that look nice. We just never get round to eating them. Christmas is terrible. We bought half a dozen mangoes and we ate only two of them. The rest all went out.'

Leslie Oxtoby of Gillygate said his family throws out about £2 worth of food a week. He added: 'It's fruit that goes bad, things like the odd banana. Also, lettuces seem to go brown very quickly these days.'

York University student Fiona Botham, 21, admitted: 'I just buy things that look good at the time and never get round to eating them.' It's usually fruit and some vegetables. And courgettes.'

Only Ian Denton of Pocklington claimed not to be a waster. Ian, 48, a chef at Full Sutton Prison, said: 'I'm good at whipping up dishes from leftovers – although the dog does tend to get lots of scrap food after Sunday dinner.

'My advice to people would be: Don't go shopping when you're hungry, and try not to cook more than you can eat. Lots of people just cook too much.'

As for your red-faced reporter, a cursory investigation of my fridge uncovered stale bread, sour milk, off-colour leeks and a rotten Chinese cabbage.

Some writing tips

Reread your text carefully. Never leave a rushed sub-editor any chance of misunderstanding you, or to make an inaccurate guess at what you mean or who you are referring to. Be especially careful if the subject is in any way technical, both in words and context. Don't leave the sub-editor with an impossible job of checking, or with any possibility of reaching a wrong conclusion.

If you are quoting several informants it can be dangerous to introduce a new one halfway through a paragraph; if the second half of the paragraph is cut to shorten the piece any later quotes might finish up with the wrong speaker. You will have left a trap.

When writing in a hurry it is more important to get the piece finished than to worry about every awkwardness of expression. Nevertheless, feature writing does offer a chance for literary ability. This means using your skill to catch clearly and succinctly what you have to say, not constructing over-elaborate sentences of over-long words. Short sentences are best even in a feature provided you include a few long ones to prevent too breathless a result.

An occasional well-constructed long sentence can be very effective. Here is Mark Steyn in the *London Evening Standard* writing with indignant scorn about TV franchise allocations:

> A year or two after the franchises are awarded the companies go kaput, the new management takes over, the commitment to broadcast twenty hours per week of religious programming and commission two contemporary operas each month is abandoned and the IBA or ITC or CBT, or whatever it'll be called next, quietly turns away, like a genteel spinster faced with a derelict urinating on the tube platform.

This was a feature which took a complex situation and found a simple devastating line of comment.

It is a pity to cut a well honed piece of features prose. Remember that if your piece is too long for the space it may be cut by the features editor before it even reaches the sub-editor who will then not have the benefit of your original text. Most features space is planned. When possible, find out the space and see to it yourself that it fits.

Finally, a feature needs a firm ending: a comment to wrap up the argument, a touch of humour crisply expressed. Here is the end of the Ofori profile quoted above:

> Henry Ofori is glad he's a journalist: 'I wanted to be involved in professional work I could do till I dropped dead.'

A note on leaders

The leader, or editorial opinion of a newspaper, is not an item that a young journalist is likely to be called upon to produce, although it has been known to happen. Alex Glasgow, a satirist of the 1960s, used to sing about the reporter who was asked to write the leading article for his paper and immediately reached for 'exacerbate', 'castigate' and similar long words.

Dayo Duyile, director of the Nigerian Institute of Journalism, has good advice for leader writers in his *Manual For African Journalists* (Gong Publications, Lagos):

> Be exhaustive in finding and checking facts, but be brief in setting down background information – don't tell the whole story over again. Go straight to the point, and don't leave people in doubt where your paper stands.
>
> Be upright in your views and forceful in their expression. Be consistent with what your paper has said before. Watch out for flaws in your logic. Write with dignity.
>
> Don't be wordy: say what you want to say and then withdraw.

16 ARTS REVIEWING

Some editors have no particular policy about arts reviewing and permit each review to go through on its merits. Where the review is signed or initialled the public can accustom itself to that particular reviewer's standards, but when there is no overall standard between one review and another and there are constant changes of staff it can confuse someone trying for instance to follow local drama seriously. If your paper has no policy on this subject, this chapter may help you make up your mind about what sort of approach you are going to take.

Writing for a local paper, the type of arts review you compose is governed by the readership and the sort of arts activity in the area. Writing for a highbrow monthly (on the theatre, for example), you would be considering quite different aspects, your comments consisting perhaps of an examination of trends influencing the producer and how the production matches up with an earlier production. Writing for a popular Sunday national, you might be required to produce only one pithy paragraph on whether the production is good entertainment or not.

Arts reviews share the timeliness of reporting in that they are concerned with the first night of a dramatic production, musical concert or film; the publication of a new book or the opening of an exhibition. In other respects they should be approached as a feature: they contain comment, opinion, assessment, reference to background material and an element of persuasion. The reader expects this. The writer is inviting the reader to share his or her point of view.

This may be a tall order for the young reporter who from day one in training has been imbued with the requirements of news gathering and newswriting. Yet there is a similarity of structures if not of content with a news story. A review requires an intro that gets to the heart of what the reviewer is writing about. There should then follow any necessary description, assessment of the production/performance in its various aspects plus some sound reasons to support the writer's viewpoint. There should also be some technical knowledge, or at least technical awareness, of what is being written about.

There are general principles common to all forms of reviewing. The reviewer needs to consider (in varying degrees) the following:

1   The aims of the playwright/composer/choreographer/author.
2   To what extent these are being fulfilled by the production/performance, etc.
3   The skill and quality of the performers/singers/musicians/dancers, etc.
4   The quality and significance of the work of the producer/conductor in creating the production.
5   The effect on the audience.

Such assignments will come the way of young reporters, providing often a first taste of feature writing.

For those who take to these creative opportunities like a rush of blood to the head there will be seasoned hands about to spell out the pitfalls that await. Some well-known reviewers write more for the benefit of other reviewers and hope to be regarded as clever. Do not, the wise mentor will say, let the glitter of a smart phrase seduce you from being unbiased and fair, especially with amateur productions.

There are other general points to observe. If you are sent to cover a play of a sort you do not personally like, do not let your prejudice show through. If it is a play that has been put on many times, as it can be with amateur companies, do not spend a lot of space recounting the story. An exception would be a new play, perhaps one by a local author. Here you would have to consider the plot and quality of writing as well as the performance.

Shaping your review

A reviewer's response to a play or concert or even a book may seem a long way from a report on an accident or a by-election, yet there are elements in common in the construction of both pieces of writing, A review, within loose parameters, may consist of:

1   **Intro:** the salient thing that strikes the reviewer – an actor's or singer's performance, or an aspect of the production, or the fundamental point made by the author.
2   **The plot or story line** (in books, plays, television programmes, etc.): this, unless it is very well known, is best told in terms of who the main characters are and what they are doing and how the leading actors/singers, etc. are interpreting them.

3 **Development:** other aspects – the remaining performances, style of words or dialogue, lighting, hidden message, authenticity, any other aims of the author or producer/director, etc.
4 **Conclusion:** summing up of the various parts and success of the production/concert/book, etc.

Amateur theatre

On a local paper your most common reviewing assignment will be amateur drama. This is a phenomenon in which the housewife becomes Portia by night, the shop assistant Peer Gynt, the bank manager The Mikado.

You need not be afraid of giving an adverse review, however, if you feel your criticisms are justified – though you may have to prove it point by point if the editor gets a nasty letter. At the same time, do not lose sight of the fact that amateurs have to act under the disadvantage of doing a daily job at something else.

A review of amateur drama should always be courteous, which is a different thing from being servile. It should also never fail to be constructive. A brief paragraph about one actor, 'So-and-so failed to convince as the butler,' is really a poor return for several months of work. Why did he fail to convince? Was he miscast? Was his make-up poor? Could he not be heard? Was he not very well on the night?

This principle of being constructive is important. It can be applied in many ways: the female lead would have been more audible if she had kept her voice up at the ends of sentences; the lighting over a crucial part of the set needed to be brighter; the pace in the middle of the third act should have been faster to build up to the climax. The adverse criticism is still there but it is cushioned by constructive comment. Amateur actors or producers will feel less aggrieved by a constructive review even if its total effect is damning. If you know your stuff, and if they do too, they will reluctantly have to agree with you.

This brings us to an important aspect: the reviewer's attitude. Should he or she attempt detailed technical criticism, or should the reviewer be merely a typical uninstructed member of the audience?

When you are inexperienced in matters of the theatre something can be said for the second attitude, despite the fact that a reporter, in having to write a review after the performance, has a sharpened perception and is unlikely to be typical of an audience. At the beginning of one's career, probably with little experience of watching plays and with even less knowledge or experience of the theatre, there is hardly any alternative for the young junior but to adopt the role of ignorant bystander, judging the play solely by its impact as he or she finds it.

In this role you have an easy task if the show is an obvious success or an obvious disaster. Your internal sounding-board will be working well because the faults or virtues will hit so hard. It is the in-betweens, which are the most common, that make the job more difficult: the play that does not quite come off, or which is oddly satisfying though it has a lot of faults. As an ignorant bystander you are going to find it difficult to tell your readers just what went wrong, or what went right, and the readers will want to know.

This is not to say you will not 'get by' when you are reviewing minor productions. Whoever marks the diary is not, in any case, going to put you down for major plays by accomplished or professional companies until you have learned the ropes a little, enough to write significantly about the play and the acting.

Turning as a reviewer to the type of group presenting a play – an important consideration – you will find in the main there will be two sorts.

Group A resolves to put on a play as one of a series of social events throughout the year: a children's party, car rally, gala dance, bingo session, outing, annual dinner, annual play. Its object is to have a bit of fun, to get the members of the club together, to allow histrionic members to let off steam (however badly), to do something in an organized way which will pass a cheerful evening, raise some club funds, add to the esprit de corps of the organization. The audience, too, will differ from a normal theatre audience. It will be composed of other members of the group, wives or husbands of the players, neighbours and friends.

In this closed circle one can only truthfully review the play as a social event. The main question to be answered is: did it achieve its objective? If it did it is a success, pretending to no artistic merit and hardly to be blamed if it failed to display any. If it did have artistic merit, so much the better.

Group B is the competent drama society formed by people interested in drama, who mostly have experience in presenting it, who know what they are doing, who aim at presenting a work of art to be judged by artistic and not social standards.

This group has to be reviewed by higher standards than you adopt for Group A. Again, you must bear in mind the group's objective but you must also assess to what extent it achieves its objectives and how this production compares with the past standard of the group. Above all, the reviewer for such a production must be reasonably expert. You cannot afford to drop any clangers because these people know their stuff. To quote an exaggerated example, if you write about the sudden failure of the lights in Act 2 when in fact it was supposed to be a dramatic blackout your editor may be asked why he sent such an idiot to see the play.

Your perception has to be on top form. The faults will be less obvious than Group A's and the successes too will be achieved by a complex combination of factors. Group A will be hurt by a sharp criticism: after all, it did not set out to be the Old Vic company. Group B will probably welcome a tough review provided it is fair, constructive, and informed.

An awkward chasm opens here into which the well-intentioned junior might fall: how do you tell Group A from B? Your newspaper should know. Someone in the office ought to be able to tell you what standard the group can reach. Who is most likely to have this knowledge will vary from office to office. But someone will know the difference between the Women's Friendly Play Group and the Blanktown Thespians (founded 1902). After a season of play reviewing, if you survive, you will know the difference yourself.

Continuity as a theatre reviewer, whether you are referring to Group A or Group B, is most important. You need to be able to tell either group how this week's play compared with last autumn's or last year's, to trace the development of an actor (especially in Group B) from walk-on parts to bigger roles, from a sudden flash of comedy to a comedy lead. It helps the player if you can compare his or her current performance with the one in the previous play.

News angles

Do not forget that on a local newspaper you are a reporter as well as a reviewer. Any group effort might have a story in it, if you can find it, and the production of an amateur play spread over weeks or months of rehearsal need be no exception. Try to have a word with the producer after the performance. A player you thought had made a hash of a part had in fact been given it only the night before and had made a remarkably good job of it considering the short notice. It would have been unfair if you had criticized the performance on the assumption that they had been rehearsing for months.

The producer might also give you a news story in its own right which could be split off from the reviews on to a news page: the lighting equipment blew up a few hours before the play started causing a fire put out primarily by the leading lady; the cast spent a few frantic hours scouring the county in various forms of transport for alternative equipment and were finally lent some by a local factory . . .

Professional theatre

Whereas amateurs usually follow well-trodden paths in the selection of scripts, professional theatres present a higher proportion of new plays. The professional theatre, if you have one in your newspaper's area, is not very likely to be assigned to you regularly in the earliest stages of your career but it does occasionally happen – if you are a drama graduate, for example, or if you have theatre experience.

Here the company is not merely presenting a play as a work of art, as Group B amateurs do, but as a work of art for profit. It invites the patronage of the general public, not merely a following of personal friends, and the public expect to get value for their money. Members of the cast are not hampered by daytime jobs, and can rehearse thoroughly and they have probably received professional training of one sort or another, which should eliminate the possibility that the play will be a complete washout.

From the artistic standpoint you will have to assess by how much it falls short of a standard, a task which calls for experience, balanced judgement and technical theatrical knowledge. The last-named is essential if you are dealing with a production which attempts some experiments in either production or acting.

You have to be able to judge how well these experiments succeed in comparison with the conventional method, or the method you judge would be the orthodox one. If you do not know what the orthodox method would have been, you can hardly judge the success of the departure from it.

The principle of continuity of reviewing, which applies to amateur shows, applies even more to a repertory company where a member of the company one week may be playing a country vicar, the next an international thief and the next a down-and-out. A man normally cut out for the heavy type of role may have a shot at a part in light comedy and make a surprising success of it.

Casting itself becomes more important with a repertory company where the producer has a fairly limited selection of players. Ingenuity in making use of them can sometimes be detected. A girl who usually plays lesser parts may be promoted one week to the female lead in a Shakespeare play. The very fact of her promotion as well as details of her success or failure in the role will be of interest to people who have seen her one time or another in the smaller parts. Many repertory players get a personal following of people who are interested in their progress. Who knows where this progress might end? Small-part repertory players have gone onwards and upwards to become great names in the theatre, leaving behind them thousands of playgoers who can say 'I knew her when. . .'

Another point to watch with professional acting is a commercial one: does the audience get good value for its money? This is not as difficult as it may sound at first. For the bulk of the public, rightly or wrongly, an evening at the theatre is not spent solely for the appreciation of the arts. It can even at its worst be a sort of family outing. If you are reviewing a play which is being presented several times after your review is published, it may influence people who wonder whether the play will suit them or their family. Will it be worth going to see?

Is it reasonable, therefore, for you to make it clear how the production stands as entertainment. A gloomy experimental play may be worth doing and may be brilliantly done and you should say so. But it may not appeal to people who want only an evening out; again you should say so. You will not help the serious theatre by ensnaring people into it. Conversely, a light musical may have a wide public appeal and yet be artistically of little merit. Again, state both views.

Theatre: basic background

By now it should be clear that if you want to give an honest review of a play of some quality, amateur or professional, you must have at least some basic knowledge of theory and practice. No one will suggest you should know so much that you could produce a play yourself at the drop of a hat, or take a leading acting role in a good production. Perhaps the British people are inhibited by the cult of the amateur. In some countries the would-be newspaper play reviewer might take a drama course at a university, so that when it comes to reviewing he or she knows as much about the technicalities as the company does. A brief examination of some of the elements of stage production will save the average young journalist having to acquire such knowledge by trial and error.

Producer is a word that has been used here a few times but you may not have considered what a producer does, particularly as some amateur groups are now following the film world's lead of having a producer and a director, or are calling the producer the director.

Though the precise functions vary from group to group, broadly speaking, the producer is the person responsible for the whole presentation of the play: stage production, acting, lighting, make-up, perhaps even things like publicity and box office. Some authority is delegated, e.g. lighting to a lighting engineer, box-office matters to a business manager.

Where the programme states there is also a director, as in the film world, this person will be responsible to the producer solely for the acting, though having a say in matters which closely affect the actors, such as lighting, make-up and costume. Where the programme refers only to the director with apparently no producer it can be assumed that this person is in fact the producer. The other designations listed on most programmes (box-office manager, publicity manager, wardrobe mistress, etc.) are self-explanatory.

Grouping of characters is a production matter. The scene on the stage should be 'composed', as the audience sees it, in the same way as a painting, i.e. so that it is balanced properly. Interpretations of this can vary according to taste, or the balance can be deliberately upset at a given moment to give emphasis to a special point, but the run-of-the-mill scenes should have this balance.

A line of players in general ought to point towards the main character of the moment; a bunch of them are most effective if they are in a triangle with the point towards the main character. This is not merely a matter of keeping things tidy but the best way to give visual emphasis. Disorganized grouping tends to distract the audience's eye.

The communal eye tends to be attracted by movement and therefore the producer has to be sure that any movement made on the stage has a purpose to it, usually to call attention to the moving actor who may be about to say an important line. By the time he or she says it the audience's eye is already trained.

One of the surest ways of 'stealing' a scene is for a supporting character to keep fidgeting about while the main character is speaking.

The producer also has to plan when and where the characters should sit or stand; you cannot have people bobbing up and down at will. An amateur actor may feel he has sat down long enough and he gets up again. The audience, less on edge, may note he has been seated only a few seconds and has risen needlessly, and perhaps find it funny in the wrong place. Main speeches are usually delivered standing: imagine someone declaiming 'Friends! Romans! Countrymen!' sitting down. Watch what the supporting characters are doing during a speech; it can be a good indication of the quality of the producer's work.

'Business' – busy-ness, activity, dumb-show – is especially important in comedy and farce where the producer has a very free rein, and its range and inventiveness here should be commented upon in the review. It should be said that there is some difference between comedy and farce and the programme does not always obligingly state 'A farce in three acts by...' The dictionary definitions are: *comedy* – stage play of light, amusing and often satirical character, chiefly representing everyday life, and with a happy ending... branch of drama concerned with ordinary persons and employing familiar language; *farce* – dramatic work merely to excite laughter... absurdly futile proceedings, pretence, mockery.

Walking about on the stage is also, or should be, carefully controlled by the producer. Imagine that in a serious scene two characters start to walk across the stage from opposite sides. In the centre of the stage they meet and dither about to pass one another as you may sometimes do when walking on a crowded pavement. The whole seriousness of the scene collapses. It is an elementary fault. This particular blunder is called a scissors cross and is about as welcome on the stage as are transposed lines in a newspaper. Stage furniture has to be carefully placed to prevent it.

Exits and entrances have to be timed carefully for best effects. To quote an extreme example, characters inside a room should not normally finish speaking and then endure a long, awkward pause before someone bounces through the French windows asking 'Anyone for tennis?'

Oddly enough, kissing, a perfectly natural action, is one of the most difficult for the amateur producer to stage, especially in a serious love scene. The players will either tend to make the kiss too short, a peck, which looks comical; or they prolong it passionately until the audience tires of it and possibly starts to titter.

Musicals present a more difficult problem because a producer has a chorus to contend with as well as actors or singers. Poor handling of the chorus on stage is a hallmark of the bad producer. Either the singers stand immobile like gravestones or they fidget and fumble and grin and move around individually, distracting the audience from the soloists. They must also move naturally as a group, neither like an army squad at the double nor a flock of sheep cascading along after a leader. Their expressions have to be appropriate, not looking surreptitiously out at the audience but at the main singer. Group movements and individual movements in a chorus have to be planned in advance and adhered to.

The producer also has to have a controlling say in the acting itself, to decide on the relative stress to be given to each role. You cannot, for instance, have a butler giving such stress and moment to his lines that he distracts from the heroine. The producer also decides the pace of the acting, which will vary from scene to scene, though predominantly it ranges from fast for farce to slow for tragedy. Slow farce is one of the curses of amateur drama. In fact, with its elaborate stage conventions, farce is best left alone by amateurs.

The stage manager is responsible to the producer for the general appearance of the set, scene changing, etc. and for seeing that doors on sets open and close properly. When there is a time change in the play, e.g. if Act 2 is stated to be 'One year later', the stage manager must make sure the scene is properly changed and not leave the same vase of flowers on the mantelpiece. Clock times must be appropriately altered.

Lighting should have the most-used parts of the set the best lit. Generally, comedy or farce need bright lighting, tragedy less bright. Original effects in lighting, even if they are praiseworthy attempts, should not be obtrusive in themselves.

The same applies to background **music**, which should be effective but not particularly noticeable. In musicals it is a common fault for the accompanying music to be too loud, forcing the singers to assert their voices and possibly spoil their tone. If this happens you can blame the musical director; musicals are the one sphere where the word 'director' is almost invariably used and the musical director is an important member of the company.

Offstage noises present problems though the tape recorder helps. The noises themselves must be reasonably convincing and their synchronization or timing needs great attention, or else you get the embarrassed pause before, say, a telephone bell rings, guns that won't fire, lighters that won't light, clocks that don't chime on time.

Prompting is normally done from the right-hand side of the stage (as the audience sees it). The prompter has to make the prompt audible to the players but not to the audience. Some amateur groups are frightened of the latter possibility and have to prompt several times on one line.

The actor's capability is affected before the play opens by the **casting**, and amateur groups with small memberships may be forced to cast inappropriately. No amount of good acting can overcome the unreality this creates.

Assuming the casting has been appropriate, one can consider the confidence and assurance of the player. Is the actor dominating the part or the part the actor? Is the actor over-acting – giving too much emphasis to indifferent lines, speaking too loudly, using too much facial expression, too much gesture?

Or is the actor under-acting – wooden in facial expression, gesture and movements? Speaking too softly, throwing away good lines? Watch, too, the understanding an actor puts into a part, how a young man can think himself into being an old man on the stage, or how a brisk young woman can think herself into Elizabeth Barrett Browning.

If you cannot hear properly what is going on on-stage, diction is at fault – players dropping their **voices** at the ends of words or not stressing consonants more than in ordinary speech. Monotony of tone is also annoying.

Foreign accents or local dialects should have received some study and should be consistent throughout the play. The speed of speech also affects its clarity: gabbling should produce a black mark on the reviewer's programme along with shouting or mumbling. This applies especially to Shakespeare, where the words are the beauty of the play.

A player's acting also has to be looked at as a whole as well as in detail. Does an actor convey the characteristics of the role: a bluff hunting gentleman, a meek little clerk, a CID officer? Does he make it a fairly standard portrait or does he permit his character to have some deviations from the obvious? Does she convey effectively the emotions of the role: anger, affection, disgust, envy, etc.?

Drama festivals

In many areas, drama groups get together periodically to produce a festival of plays or excerpts with an expert adjudicator giving an opinion on each entry. Covering such festivals is principally a straightforward report-ing job. Your main task is to record what the adjudicator says at the end of each evening, not forgetting to report any news stories which might come out of the festival. It would be discourteous to put forward your own opinions over those of the adjudicators.

Although covering such a festival differs considerably from reviewing plays, listening to these expert judges can be instructive for the young reviewer. The adjudicators provide a detailed example of what a reviewer should be looking for and the criteria to use in assessing a performance.

Music

'I like music but I don't know a lot about it.' This is a common reply from young journalists when asked if they can cover a concert or music recital.

If you can say this there is no reason why you should not produce an adequate notice of, say, 300 to 400 words. They will probably not be the same sort of words that an experienced music critic might write but the notice should capture something of the feel of the concert and express a point of view which those people who attended will find valid and those who did not will find interesting.

In passing, here is a point of vocabulary: a musical evening by an orches-tra or choir is usually called a **concert**; one by a soloist or small group of musicians is a **recital**.

Before you go to the concert or a recital learn what pieces are to be played and find out what you can about them. There are dictionaries of music and your office may have a copy; the public library will have several. The organizer of the concert or recital will probably be willing to answer questions if you ring up; such as whether the programme includes pieces of special interest or that are seldom played.

At the concert consider the music and the performance. Listen carefully to each piece – the quieter and more subtle as well as the loud and brilliant – and ask yourself 'What impressed me the most?' Then 'Why did this piece or this performance impress me?'

Sometimes a programme is built round one work. If an orchestra introduces a soloist to play a concerto or if all (or almost all) the second half of a recital is taken up with a single piece, this work must be a major item in your review. On the other hand, there might be no single major offering in the recital or concert and your best course will be to single out for your main discussion the pieces which impressed you most.

Try to capture as accurately as you can the impression the music makes upon you. Is it triumphant or full of peace? Is it stately or lively or shattering? Has it the exquisite phrasing of the eighteenth century, or is it a modern piece speaking to you of your own time?

Then ask yourself how far the orchestra or soloist has contributed to the impression you have received. The chances are that the performance you heard was middling to good. Even amateur and school orchestras rehearse much more seriously than they used to. On the other hand, you suddenly realize perhaps that the wave-like phrases of a Sibelius symphony are sweeping majestically across the orchestra. Or perhaps the violin tone in the Mozart has just that extra accuracy which brings out the music's full beauty. Now you have something to write about.

You should, of course, make yourself familiar with the **orchestra** instruments and watch to make sure you know which are playing.

A symphony orchestra has four main groupings: the 'strings', that is, the instruments of the violin family on which orchestral music is usually based; the 'woodwind', which are pipe instruments of one kind or another; the brass (trumpet, trombone, tuba, horn); and percussion. A brass band consists of brass and percussion only; a military band of brass, percussion and woodwind, and perhaps saxophones. The saxophone family is rarely found in compositions for orchestra.

Writing about instrumental soloists, quartets and other groupings is a task very similar in character to that of writing about orchestras. The groupings you will meet most frequently are the string quartet (two violins, viola and cello) and the piano trio (violin, cello and piano.)

Singing

Writing about singing presents problems of its own. Choirs need to be regarded rather like amateur drama groups and, indeed, choristers and amateur actors come together in operatic societies.

Some choirs aim at nothing more than the entertainment of themselves and of small, private meetings. The more ambitious choirs are usually conscientiously rehearsed so that it is unwise to criticize them severely unless you can say with exactness what you think is wrong. One common fault is a lack of natural feeling for musical rhythm. If a choir gives a leaden-voiced performance of a Negro spiritual, say so.

Choirs normally sing in four parts: that is, they are divided into four groups, each of which sings a different line of music. In a mixed choir the four groups, from high to low, are sopranos, contraltos, tenors and basses. If the two upper groups were composed of boys rather than women, they would probably be known as trebles and altos.

In a men's or **male-voice choir** the groups are top tenor or counter tenor; second tenor; first bass or baritone; second bass. In listening to a male-voice choir, listen for the quality of the top-tenor tone and the clarity of the two 'inside' parts (second tenor and first bass). Few men can sing top tenor and a male-voice choir needs four men who can reach the top notes without quavering. The second tenor and first bass parts can be difficult for a singer to follow as other people are singing both above and below, but if these parts are not sung with confidence the result can be fuzzy.

One of the strengths of male-voice choirs is their sense of drama. They should be praised for it when it is achieved.

Much of the difficulty of writing about singing stems not from choirs but from soloists. What on earth are you to say about a man who sings 15 or 16 middling-to-good songs in a competent but unremarkable way? **Amateur operatic productions** are frequently and, for the critic, embarrassingly let down by the vocal inadequacies of their principals. Again, you have to say so but be generous in praise for someone who sings really well.

It is worth noting that there are two schools of thought as to what constitutes good singing. In the past, singers aimed primarily for power and for quality of tone and diction, and these are still the standards by which most people judge them. One modern view, however, is that quality of tone is less important than putting across the meaning of the words: if the words are harsh, then the tone should be harsh. With a tape recorder singers can listen to and study their own performance in detail and work out the best way to sing or say each phrase for maximum effect.

One way to ensure that you are never stumped for something to write about at a concert or recital is to keep your eyes open. Music is primarily of the ear but the audience see a concert; they do not just listen to it. The reason why that rather buxom wench has got such resounding applause for singing Puccini and Verdi is not just that she has sung well. It is that her stage presence is so commanding. And that man who is playing the violin: is he young or elderly, tall or short, matter-of-fact or demonstrative? Does the orchestra look as if it enjoyed playing this piece rather than that one? At a performance you cannot tell much about the value of a **conductor's work**; a conductor's real impact is in rehearsal. But many are born showmen. This one sways happily to the rhythm of a waltz, that one looks as though he is about to fling himself full length across the grand piano and into the violas. Impressions of this sort will cheer up your report.

If at all possible, always have a word in the interval with the organizers and soloists. You can see from your seat whether the concert is well attended. If the hall is full, that is news. But it is also news that the clarinet soloist in the lounge suit lost his luggage on the train. You hear about this only by making use of the interval.

You can ask about the programme too. Why were these particular pieces chosen? Did some present special difficulty? Perhaps one soloist who came as a replacement had never seen some of the music before she arrived. You can ask soloists if they have links with your neighbourhood or whether they have visited it before.

Some music has an immediate appeal. You may be more likely to appreciate other music if you know what to expect. It is well worthwhile, and not very difficult, to get clear in your mind the first movement – slow movement – dance movement – quick finale construction of the typical symphony, and also a general picture of the development of music from Bach and Handel to the more courtly Mozart, the fire of Beethoven, the expanding orchestras of the Romantics, the dreaminess and impressionism of Debussy, the search of modern composers for new styles.

A concerto is a symphony in dialogue between soloist and orchestra. A sinfonia concertante is a concerto with more than one soloist. In a fugue the music is divided into parts, a theme being stated in one part and then repeated in the others so as to form with variants an interwoven texture of sound.

Pop, folk and jazz

Popular music – the sort you do not expect to be whistling or even to remember in a couple of years' time – is best treated as you would a stage performance. It is not always so much the music that counts as the quality of the performer.

Folk songs have grown increasingly popular and jazz has its festivals. You may have to attend a jazz or folk-music concert and write about it as music, not just as entertainment.

In many folk songs the words are as important as the singing, so you need to look for clear enunciation and good evocation of atmosphere. Basically, like any singing, it is a matter of a good voice put to good use, with a feeling for words and for the rhythm and lilt of music.

With jazz you are looking for musical feeling and originality. Resist the temptation to write round the concert – for example, all about the player and when he or she first played these pieces. Resist the temptation also to get lost in a technical language the readers will not understand.

Jazz, originally and essentially, is informal music with little or nothing written down. In traditional jazz, a musical theme is played, then the soloists either together or separately work out a series of variations on the theme as the mood takes them.

The 'traditional' jazz band of the 1920s might, for instance, have clarinet, trumpet and trombone soloists, with drums, banjo, piano and five-string bass to provide an accompaniment. The five-string bass, played with the fingers, not with a bow, is a double bass with a fifth, deeper string added. It replaced the big brass sousaphone of earlier jazz bands.

Over the years, most instruments have had their run in jazz, which has become increasingly intellectual and has moved beyond the simple chord progressions around which the trumpeters and clarinet players used to weave their way. Modern jazz draws on Bartok and other serious composers and may have no theme: the musicians start playing and rely on their sympathy with each other's playing to keep together.

A distinctive feature of jazz is its arrangement of notes in irregular patterns; accents do not come where the ear expects them. The pitfall of jazz is that its very irregularity should become a set pattern. It takes a good musician to prevent the music forming into a dull, repetitive mould.

Do not be over-enthusiastic about the tenor-saxophonist who hoots a repetitive torrent of notes into a microphone for a solid five minutes. A common failing of jazz musicians is to go on and on and on. Freshness, crispness and conviction – these are the qualities to look for.

Films

In film reviewing the reviewer has to pay attention to what his or her newspaper wants. Is the reviewer writing for a newspaper's entertainment guide which merely indicates the sort of film it is and may only rarely give an opinion? If so, publication is usually timed to precede the local showing of the film.

Or is the reviewer writing a considered judgement of a film which has just had its national premiere and will not be showing locally for some time? Is the reviewer producing a judgement of a film premiered some time ago which is showing locally or will shortly be shown so that the review becomes a guide?

Papers publishing the 'entertainment guide' type of review do not have to send reviewers to the premiere or press show because all they require is a reminder of what the film is about. In practice, this will be a short résumé of the story, which should not betray the ending or any surprise twists. It can be obtained from a variety of sources. One of these is the publicity material sent out by the film company, most of which contains a straightforward story summary. There are also books giving film synopses.

Reviewing gets more difficult when a famous actor is having a go at, say, a film version of *Hamlet*. The principal interest here is not the story-line ('A young prince in Denmark who suspects that his father was murdered by his uncle...') but the success or failure of the actor. If he has made a success of it you can hardly fail to mention the quality of the acting, perhaps of the direction and photography too, and you are thereby forced to express an opinion as opposed to merely recounting the facts about the story.

It is up to you, as a reviewer, to see that your office is taking reputable magazines and publications dealing with the cinema in order that you may gauge what sort of reception the film has had. Life is much less dull if you are allowed to go to see the press show at the local cinema when you can write a review based on your own reactions.

The principal questions in film reviewing are: is the story credible in its context? Would people really behave like that? This applies equally to heavy drama or farce, though in the latter you have to allow that the characters may be extraordinary people. Are coincidences stretched too far? Are unlikely developments dragged in to keep the story moving? Is the story dull because it is predictable, or is it inventive and surprising? Does the story go over ground that has been covered before, or does it pioneer the examination of a new type of subject in a new way? If it does go over the same ground – and many Westerns do – does it find anything new there?

The star system does not have the grip it used to when major films were merely vehicles for a particular much-publicized actor or actress, but nevertheless they remain important. Some stars have an inherent box-office attraction, drawing good crowds to any film in which they appear. The review must pay some attention to this, comparing the star's present performance with past ones, commenting on whether the part is right for the star (or not), whether he or she makes a success of it.

The star's **acting** demands the same sort of detailed examination you would give to acting on the stage. However, the cinema differs from the theatre in that the close-up eye of the camera means that the slightest tightening of the lips can be seen clearly perhaps 200 feet from the screen, whereas it would be quite lost on the stage. Where stage actors have to emphasize voice, expression and gesture, film actors have to under-play by stage standards because everything is going to be amplified and magnified.

Acting alone can also be a little misleading since not all of it can honestly be attributed to the actor's inspiration. For one thing, films are not shot in sequence – the last clinch on the screen may have been the first scene filmed on the set. Great dramatic scenes occupying perhaps ten continuous minutes may have been pieced together from two-minute takes shot at odd times. Nevertheless, Kim Novak, for example, has disclosed that she felt real vertigo in James Stewart's arms in the film *Vertigo*.

Films also have a ubiquitous person who is called a **director** whose job is to direct the actors. The director will have studied the script closely and decided in advance how each scene should be played and how it should appear on the screen as regards movements, pace, gestures, characterization, lighting, setting, camera angles, etc.

The director can also influence the editing – the sequences in which separate shots are shown on the screen and which of many takes should be used; deciding the visual treatment and the length of time each shot is allowed to run; what to leave out to make a satisfactory running length. Many directors have names better known than those of their actors. In their films the standard of direction may be of more interest than the acting but, in any case, a film's direction should be commented upon. In a film by a really famous director the same comparisons between this and past work should also be made.

Photography goes hand in hand with direction and in some films may be good enough to warrant comment, not on technicalities but on how much it adds to the atmosphere of the film by its choice of lighting and selection of shooting angles.

Lastly, is the film good of its kind? If you attend press shows you will inevitably have to sit through films which you might find quite unentertaining but which will nevertheless have a wide general appeal. Everyone has preferences and the film you are not keen on may not be a bad film. The temptation is to be scathing or scornful, but this would hardly be fair to those of your readers who would be interested in seeing this sort of film.

Television

Television reviews, unlike those of films, theatre and books, cannot normally help the potential viewer/buyer/audience, since a TV programme is a one-off event until it turns up as a repeat. It is true that many classical music, jazz and pop concerts have the same status although, where they form part of a tour, a review of the opening performance can influence the potential audience at the next venue if the review publication reaches that far.

Despite this apparent handicap, there is no doubt that some newspapers and magazines consider that their readers enjoy reading programme reviews, perhaps to see how far the reviewer's opinions support their own, since they continue to read them. Others are content to settle for printing programme summaries for the day, and including information about forthcoming programmes and those taking part within a general show-business column. Sometimes, especially in the popular tabloids, the topicality of a much-watched TV programme is used as a peg for news stories about the cast or for personality interviews. This area of show-business, whether on news or features pages, strictly, however, has nothing to do with reviewing, with which this chapter is concerned.

There is no doubt that some readers like to know what the critics have to say about the programme they watched the night before. There is equally no doubt that television programmes require and justify value judgements by reviewers to help establish standards. In making such judgements the writer can call, to some extent, upon the parameters used in reviewing films. The success or failure of the programme's aims, the use of special production techniques, the acting, the film editing, camera work, use of outside settings, music – all these are components of a programme's success. But in the intimate world of a screen which sits in one's own home the actual words, the script, assume greater importance. What the words say – what the programme has to say – to its captive family audience is vital in assessing its success, and also its suitability.

It is thus that a number of TV programmes have been the subject of the sort of controversy that seldom occurs with other art forms where audiences choose more selectively, and this is a factor of which the critic must take note. Even the timing of programmes for viewing needs to be considered.

There are also substantial differences of technique in presentation, camera work and the sorts of visual material used which make TV a different world from the cinema. To project some television programmes on to a cinema screen would rob them of their effectiveness just as the true impact of some wide-screen films is lost in the living room.

The one cannot be judged by the standards of the other. The true gauge is to what extent the two camera-based art forms succeed each within the confines of its own medium.

Books

Newspapers review books for two widely different purposes. One is to use material from the book to write an interesting article, the other to review it as a book. Unless you are writing for one of the more serious newspapers the first purpose is the one with which you will mainly be concerned.

Whatever sort of review you write, there is no substitute for reading the book, though there is no need to prove you have done so by pointing out that on page 167 'their' should read 'there'.

As you read, make a note or insert a marker when you come to a specially interesting passage. Look out for lively incidents and lively people. If yours is a local paper, watch for any references to places within your circulation area: any incidents that took place in your area might be worth retelling in full. If the book concerns some modern problem, what light does it throw upon it?

Many books are mines of information for feature articles, and writing a review of them is a task similar to that of writing a feature (see Chapter 15). You start with the most important fact or liveliest incident which the book contains and, having announced the name of the book, with its author, publisher and price, you set out the other interesting facts and passages you have gleaned from it in a thread of argument. If the book tells a story, you will have to summarize it at some stage even if you concentrate on particular parts.

Sometimes a review of this factual kind will in itself make clear whether you found the book well and clearly written. If this does not go without saying, you should try to work in two or three sentences stating what you thought of the book's quality. Was it exciting? Simply written? Obscure? Did it get bogged down in dull detail? Was it inaccurate in any way? Did it have life and originality?

When you are writing about a **novel** or one which aspires to literary stature rather than merely imparting information, the question of quality becomes paramount. 'How good and interesting is this work as a book?'

If it is a detective story or a romantic novel or some book of no great pretensions, the test will be 'How entertaining will readers find this?' You will need to write a sentence or two about the situation or the plot so that your readers can know the kind of book it is. They may wish to buy it. You should ask yourself also whether the characters seem true to life. Would people act the way they did and say the things they did? Were the characters dull or colourful? Was the plot ingenious or merely contrived? Were suspense and tension well built up? Was there a touch of humour to make it more entertaining? Was it easy to read? Did the author evoke with skill the scene where his action was supposed to take place? If the scene was intentionally vague and frightening, was this effect well achieved? What is the author's outlook? Is the author pessimistic about people and their motives?

The author's outlook gives many books their tension. A writer can also diminish the effect of a book by being too concerned with what he or she is trying to say. Characters can become marionettes acting not out of their own humanity but out of the ideas of their creator. Other authors have a gift for making their characters vibrate with life.

If the book you are reviewing is by an author who has written others, it is useful to say how it compares with them in style, subject and treatment, perhaps in attainment too. Some people will have read the earlier ones and will be wondering whether to buy or read this one.

The author may be a local person or have **local connections**. Find out about them and tell the readers. Alternatively, if you – and probably the readers – have never heard of the author before, do not just give the author as a name. Try to say in a few words who they are, how they came to write the book, what is particular about their style, their background, their world.

17 NEWSPAPER STRUCTURE

The circulation and staffing of a national daily is obviously much greater than that of a town evening paper or country weekly but the basic functions are the same, differing only in scale. They are: to collect, check and typeset the news, features and advertising; to take and process the pictures, to put them all together to produce a newspaper that answers the needs of the readers and reaches the sellers on time, and to account for the money transactions involved. One might add that in order to continue these functions it is also necessary to make some profit for the shareholders.

Who does what

So who does what? The chart on page 212 shows a specimen average-sized newspaper set-up. Bigger organizations will add further sections and people with special responsibilities, and their executives will be provided with deputies, assistants and other staff not shown here. The relative status of sections and departments may vary, though not substantially. Smaller organizations will not need all sections and titles shown; some functions might be amalgamated into one person.

For instance, organizations with several newspapers might have an editorial director concerned with policy and budgeting who is senior to each editor. On the other hand, on a smaller paper the editor might sit on the board and have quite considerable powers. On a provincial evening paper the assistant editor might also take charge of features and work with the chief sub-editor on layout; there would be no separate features editor or layout person. National papers often have several assistant editors and a complete art department for drawing layouts.

At management level functions might be similarly amalgamated, the managing director doubling as the general manager, and the circulation

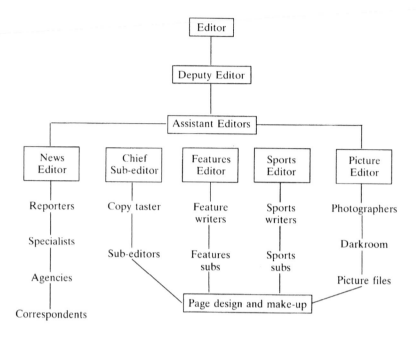

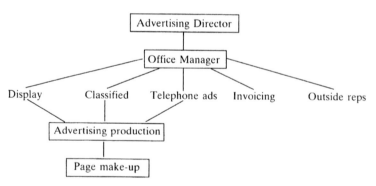

Figure 17.1 *Who does what? This chain-of-command diagram shows the set-up in the editorial and advertising departments of an average sized newspaper*

manager being in charge of transport and distribution and perhaps special promotions.

On small weeklies the titles might be different, the chief reporter being the news editor, the deputy editor being the chief sub-editor, with the chief photographer performing the role assigned on a big national paper to the picture editor or art editor.

In view of the great number of titles containing the word 'editor' it should be explained that the descending order of seniority is usually: editor, deputy editor, assistant editor, news editor/features editor/sports editor, chief sub-editor, sub-editor. On bigger papers there can be other middle-rank 'editors' such as art editor, picture editor, foreign editor, political editor and so on, all with roughly the same place in the pecking order as the news editor/features editor/sports editor. On some newspapers you might get intrusive titles such as managing editor (who is often concerned with managerial aspects of the department but can be above the editor) and associate 'editors' whose importance can vary.

The actual editing is done by sub-editors (either news, features or sport) of whom there might be four or five on a small weekly up to as many as thirty or more on a national quality daily. They work under their departmental chief sub-editor, or perhaps under a features editor or assistant editor responsible for choosing the stories and pictures for the pages.

Among reporters and feature writers (the news room and features department) there can also be a great variety of titles such as chief crime reporter, show-business reporter, fashion editor, education correspondent, City correspondent and so on. You could say that there are as many titles on a newspaper as there are special functions allocated to specific people.

Copy input

Staff reporters are the main source of copy input for most newspapers, but there are other sources. For example, we have seen that village correspondents and organization secretaries send reports of meetings and sports results to many weeklies and some evening papers. In some cases these go to reporters first; in others they are given straight to sub-editors for checking and perhaps rewriting.

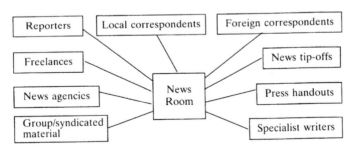

Figure 17.2 *Where the stories come from – the news room as the heart of the news-gathering operation*

A much bigger source of copy is the news agencies, and in particular the Press Association, which handles national news in the UK, and Reuters, whose service of world news is taken by most offices. Such agency stories might be used as they arrive, perhaps at reduced length, if they are of interest to the paper's area, or be incorporated into a story to which a staff reporter has contributed part, or is collating. Newspapers pay a rent to news agencies to use their various services as and when needed.

Most papers also take copy from accredited local journalists who operate in their area on a retainer and lineage basis, and they might also use the services of self-employed freelance journalists, sometimes by regular contract arrangements, or at other times because a staff journalist is sick or on holiday, or because the freelance has a special story they want to buy.

While reporters might provide some of the paper's features there are usually specialist feature writers also filing copy, perhaps a staff leader writer, and again the use of freelances for specific features assignments. In addition, nearly every paper has its part-time specialists writing such pieces as the gardening or good-food column or the weekly chess problem.

What happens to your story

Once you have keyboarded your story into the computer, checked it through and written 'end' on it (or the copy taker has keyboarded it for you) it enters the production system, going first to the news editor's or chief reporter's 'queue' to be read and checked again. Then it goes to the copy taster, who is sometimes also the deputy chief sub-editor. The copy taster is a senior journalist with a well-developed news sense whose job is to discard what is unsuitable or unwanted for the editions and to shortlist and put in order the remainder. Sometimes a copy taster will raise queries in copy with the reporter.

Under the old hot metal system, in which the lines of type on the page and even the pages themselves were cast in metal, the copy taster's day started with a mountain of typewritten sheets which had to be read and either spiked or prepared in neat piles for the chief sub-editor's attention. Throughout the day more stories from reporters and news agencies would land on the copy taster's desk to be read and sorted.

As a result of the almost universal adoption of direct computer input the copy taster now reads his or her way through the various queues of stories emanating from the newsroom, the features department and the agencies. The directory of files (stories) that have been written is consulted and each file called up in turn and read on-screen. The ones

Figure 17.3 *A sub-editor calls up a story – note the extra row of command and function keys at the top of this editing keyboard*

selected are then put into a working 'queue' to await use on the various pages, and the remainder set aside on the electronic 'spike' from which they can be recovered should a query arise. A good copy taster might still keep a brief pencil note of stories, however, to furnish quick answers to queries or as a reminder of what has been received and what is still awaited for the various pages.

As the pages are planned and production unrolls, the chief sub-editor calls up the stories on-screen, reads them, allocates them their place on a page, their length and headline type, and 'sends' them to a sub-editor with any special instructions for editing on-screen.

The editing process might involve checking names and details, cutting the story to fit, perhaps blending two or more copy sources together (called up by means of a split screen), in some cases rewriting parts of the story, and writing a headline and cross-heads. It might also be necessary for the sub-editor to check back part of the story with the writer, or to refer to the cuttings library for previous references to it.

The sub-editor's keyboard is bigger than a writer's, since it has additional command and function keys to enable the required type and type size to be chosen, the headline to be examined for fit, a line count to be made and the whole hyphenated and justified (i.e. squared off as on the page) and sent to the electronic typesetter.

It should be noted that the story as it exists in the computer is still as keystroked by the writer, subject to any changes in text made by the sub-editor. There can also be legal changes made on-screen by the office lawyer or a revise sub-editor with a legal brief. Since proof readers as such are no longer part of most editorial systems there is often a fail-safe revise sub-editor who reads all edited material just before it enters the pages to check for spelling lapses, miskeying and other late clangers. On passing all these hurdles the story, as revised, continues on to the typesetting stage, becoming finally the words that greet the reader upon opening the page.

Page production

The pages of a newspaper start life as drawings, made either by the journalist in charge of the page – perhaps the assistant editor or the chief sub-editor – or, in the case of most big newspapers, by the art desk under the guidance of the art editor, working with the page executive. Whatever the means, what goes on a page, the pictures that are chosen, and how the contents are presented are editorial decisions.

On national dailies the executives who plan pages are referred to collectively as the 'back bench' and the senior executive in charge of the back bench is the 'night editor' whose job is to plan the production of the paper in accordance with the decisions of the daily or twice-weekly editor's conference. On small evening papers and country weeklies there is a more modest executive presence consisting perhaps of only the editor and the chief sub-editor.

Copies of all page plans (layouts), once they are approved by the editor, are supplied to the chief sub-editor for sub-editors to check their stories against their position on the page. The actual making up of the pages (which, under the hot metal system, was done by putting together lines of metal type and metal blocks of illustrations inside a frame) is now carried out photographically by one of two methods: cut-and-paste and full-page composition.

Cut-and-paste

This method, which is still widely used, involves printing out all the stories and headlines by means of photo typesetters, and the pictures and adverts by means of a laser printer. The resulting bromides are then cut up and pasted

Figure 17.4 *The cut-and-paste method – a compositor makes up a page using typeset bromides of stories. Note the page layout and rolls of stick-on tape rules*

on to a page card by the make-up compositor by reference to the page layout. Any adjustments or updates or changes of layout are carried out by the compositor using paste and scalpel, under the guidance of a sub-editor.

Once everything fits and the page has been photocopied for checking by the editor and other executives, it is photographed and fed as a negative into a plate-maker. This produces a printing plate for printing usually by the web-offset method, although it is possible to produce an impression plate for use with letterpress printing.

Full-page composition

Here the paste-up stage is dispensed with and the stories, headlines, pictures and adverts are all processed inside the computer and fed straight on to a page grid prepared on a special screen. The make-up journalist, using a 'mouse' control or command keys, manipulates the various elements of the page on-screen until they occupy the positions on the grid specified by the page layout. When adjustments have been made (electronically) and everything is fitting and has been checked, the page is printed out and fed straight into a plate-maker which produces a plate ready for printing.

Difficulties with graphics – particularly with half-tone pictures and with colour – at one time delayed the take-up of full-page composition by many papers, but developments by systems builders and the ever-increasing speed and capacity of computers is beginning to make full-page composition the norm. Its cost-saving has important implications for newspaper companies looking to launch new products.

Press and post-press

The system of page production described above interfaces most naturally and economically with the new generation of web-offset presses which print from a smooth printing plate by a method in which the ink is offset by a 'blanket' on to the rolls of newsprint. The advantage of web-offset presses is that they are suited to colour printing, which is used nowadays in all manner of newspapers. Nevertheless, the page image can be transferred to low-relief polymer plates which can be used if a company wishes to continue with its rotary presses printing by direct (ink) impression under the letterpress method, although this is becoming rare.

By either method, each plate prints one text-size or two tabloid-size pages. These are gathered together in correct page order as they flow off the press and pass through a folder which shoots out the completed newspapers for stacking and baling. Copies come off the press in quires, a unit with variable interpretations, of which the most common is twenty-six copies, though sometimes twenty copies. They are delivered to the wholesalers, and thence to the retailers, by the number of quires.

Conclusion

If the emphasis in this chapter has been rather technical, young reporters should remember that computerized technology, which has caused a revolution in newspaper production and put an end to old printing skills, has not changed the basic skills and standards required in reporting. News has still to be identified, gathered and checked; knowing how to handle people and organize sources are as vital as ever, as are the mechanics of shorthand and a knowledge of the law; the criteria of good news writing remains the same.

The big plus is that the advent of the VDU has given writers a tool far superior to the old-fashioned typewriter and has made word accuracy and good presentation easier to attain, and revisions of stories simpler and faster. But it remains just a tool. The content of a newspaper still depends on the skill of its reporters and feature writers.

18 LOOKING THINGS UP

The main thing about works of reference is to know what books your office has and what information they contain. The chances are you will not find the vast, up-to-date selection which books on journalism usually prescribe.

Your office will probably have several dictionaries and a British and maybe a world gazetteer of place names; an atlas, a *Who's Who*, a thesaurus, perhaps a copy of *Burke's Peerage* and *Crockford's Clerical Directory*.

Do make yourself familiar with the books that there are, including those pushed to the back of the cupboard. You can save yourself a lot of time digging up information if you happen to know a book contains it. Make yourself especially familiar with *Whitaker's Almanack*, though you will not score high in the journalists' National Certificate by putting *Whitaker* against every question asking 'In what book would you look for. . .?' The fact remains that you can look up a surprising number of things in *Whitaker*, not just about government and parliament but even about sport, building societies and insurance.

If you have space on a shelf or in a cupboard, hold on to local pamphlets and reports which may be useful for future reference. It is no use piling them in a heap as you will forget what you have got and will not be able to find a reference even if you remember it. Stand your pamphlets up in some rational order, by place names or subject.

Minutes of councils and other official bodies should always be kept. So should research reports to which people are going to make references in speeches and policy statements. When your space for pamphlets is full, be ruthless in throwing out those you did not need to consult. It is easy to have too many books of the wrong kind with the useful ones hidden among them.

Keep cuttings of your own major stories; you will find them useful if the subject recurs. Your office library of cuttings should, however, be a main source of reference. It can give you biographical detail about someone in the news, or an earlier cutting on a story you have not previously covered, or save you asking a lot of unnecessary questions about facts your newspaper has already been told. Bear in mind that cuttings can be inaccurate. If you discover four in which information has clearly been copied one from another, check the information just in case the first reference was wrong.

However well supplied with books or cuttings your office may be, you will quite often need to go to your newspaper's own reference library or to the reference department of your town's public library. This will have a comprehensive collection of reference books and also of material on local history if the library is of any size.

Below is a selection of useful books which you might find in your newspaper office or at the public reference library.

The arts

Who's Who in the Theatre; Who's Who in Music; Oxford Dictionary of Music (one volume); *New Grove's Dictionary of Music and Musicians* (twelve volumes, also in one volume); *Oxford Companion to English Literature; Oxford Dictionary of Quotations; Buildings of England; a study county by county of buildings and towns,* (Dr Nikolaus Pevsner, Penguin Books); *Encyclopaedia Britannica* (you can check on great artists, writers and musicians and their works); *Arts Council Annual Report* (lists grants to local societies); *Spotlight* lists actors, actresses and their agents.

Aviation

Jane's All the World's Aircraft.

The Bible

A concordance; this enables you to locate any biblical phrase by looking up one of the words which it contains.

The churches

See pages 155 to 164.

English language

Roget's Thesaurus (good if you are searching for the right word); *The New Fowler's Modern English Usage* edited by R. W. Burchfield; and *Usage and Abusage* by Eric Partridge (Penguin Reference Books). See also page 91.

Geography

Atlas of Britain; The Times Atlas (worldwide); *Encyclopaedia Britannica* (atlas and index volume); a gazetteer (for example, *Bartholomew's*), i.e. a dictionary of place names with their position; *Automobile Association Handbook* (road maps and distances).

History

Cambridge Modern History (detailed account in many volumes of the history of Europe since the Renaissance); *Encyclopaedia Britannica* (biographies, battles, etc.); *Dictionary of National Biography* (many volumes full of people who made their mark in their own time, also a concise one-volume version); *Who Was Who* (notes on people who have died in the recent past); local histories.

Industry and companies

Stock Exchange Year Book (many offices have this; it gives details of companies quoted on the Stock Exchange); *Whitaker's Almanack* (lists employers' associations, research associations, trade unions); *Directory of Directors*.

Local government

Municipal Year Book (gives members of councils with their addresses; also names chief officers and includes development corporations, health authorities and trusts); handbook or yearbook of your local council (gives council information in some detail); *Abstract of Accounts* (shows how a council has been spending its money in previous years); *Report on the Census* (gives facts town by town and parish by parish on people and their homes). The *IHSM Health Services' Year Book*.

Local information

Local directory (probably Kelly's; gives names of householders, lists of associations, tradespeople, etc.); *Buildings of England* (Pevsner; county volume will give information on local buildings); town guide or brochure; voters' lists (up-to-date list of householders); town or county histories; railway histories (for example, *Tomlinson's North-Eastern Railway*); university calendar (gives staff, etc. of your local university); universities' lists of experts, *Report on the Census* (people and their homes).

National affairs and information

Britain, An Official Handbook (this handbook is indexed and is published annually; a mine of information); *Civil Service List; Foreign Office List; Whitaker's Almanack* (has something about nearly everything); *Keesing's UK Record* (useful); *Annual Abstract of Statistics* (yearly figures of population, production, trade, finance, transport, road accidents); *Monthly Digest of Statistics* (monthly statistical tables; not so wide ranging as the *Annual Abstract); Statistics of Education* (published annually; tells you how many children are at school); telephone directories (if you want an address outside your area, you will find your local library and head post office has a full set of directories – useful for tracing and checking names of organizations. See also *Yellow Pages*). CBD Research publishes lists of associations and committees.

Parliament

Whitaker's Almanack (lists MPs and election results); *Vacher's Parliamentary Companion* (published every two months and therefore more up to date than *Whitaker's); Dod's Parliamentary Companion; Hansard* (verbatim account of speeches, published daily); Acts of Parliament (public libraries usually have them in annual volumes).

People

Who's Who (it is easy to forget when you have to find out something about a person that they may be in *Who's Who*. This book includes, for instance, university professors and Members of Parliament); *Burke's Peerage* (if someone has a title you can find all about them in here); *Commonwealth Survey* (includes some biographies of people in the news); *Medical*

Directory (reference book for doctors). Public libraries also have reference books for engineers, accountants and other professional people.

Press and radio

BBC Year Book; Radio & TV Who's Who; Benn's Media Directory (lists newspapers, editors, etc.); *Willing's Press Guide; McNae's Essential Law for Journalists* (Butterworths).

The services

Navy List (of officers, etc.); *Army List; Air Force List; Jane's Fighting Ships; Jane's All the World's Aircraft.*

Sport

See pages 175–6.

World affairs

Keesing's Record of World Events: This is a record in detail of important events round the world, published in frequent short sections. Its index enables you to look up events of the recent past whose detail or date you have forgotten. It does need a bit of patience to find what you want in the index. Look up the country concerned, and then look through the subheadings. Britain appears as 'United Kingdom'. *International Who's Who; Who's Who in America.* If your office takes the trouble to file it, the *Commonwealth Survey* can fulfil a similar purpose to *Keesing's*. It is free from the Central Office of Information's regional office. *Whitaker's Almanack* includes notes on foreign and Commonwealth countries, on European co-operation, and on the past year's events.

1 9   A NOTE ON ETHICS

This book has stressed fairness and accuracy. These give journalism honesty. They also promote the credibility and authority of newspapers and so help defend journalists against their critics. Remember that once in the library, on microfilm or on a database your writings are the stuff of history. Eminent journalists, relying on what someone once wrote somewhere, still report that the Rocket was the first locomotive on the Stockton and Darlington Railway. In fact, it ran on the Liverpool and Manchester.

Accuracy is a matter of interpretation as well as fact. Make sure that figures you quote mean what you say they mean.

As every freelance knows, reports that appear in newspapers can in some respects be inaccurate. The strapline on a prominent story in a quality paper read:

> Government aid to bombed city centre could total £1 billion over three years

The opening sentence of the report read:

> Manchester won £43 million of Government funding yesterday to underpin an ambitious reconstruction package which is likely to attract up to £1 billion of investment over the next three years.

The strapline was based on a false assumption that the £1 billion, not just the £43 million, was coming from the Government. The reporter probably did not realize he had been even faintly ambiguous but the slight ambiguity led to error by the headline writer.

A former BBC man, John Wilson, points out in *Understanding Journalism* that news travels badly. He plots the path of a story 'picked up first by a seasoned freelance from a whisper, adapted knowingly after a call to police headquarters miles away, further embellished when rendered into journalese as the report is filed to an agency, snappily rewritten before it gets on the agency wires, remodelled once more by a newsroom sub-editor, and then improved by a judicious word massage here and there from a more senior editor before it reaches the trusting public as a true record of what happened. By then the merchants of truth have delivered a reasonable approximation or, for all they know, a gross distortion.'

The problem is that the people who put news into newspapers weren't there when it happened. They know only what the reporter has written down. Some sub-editors pursue every query and imprecision, thereby leading reporters to illuminate points they never thought of or inquired into. Sub-editors may improve a report by introducing relevant material which the reporter did not know about. They see more stories than reporters and acquire a better idea of what makes a story compelling. But they also struggle with copy about places they never visited and on subjects in which they do not have much knowledge. Changes made by a sub-editor can introduce inaccuracy.

The best way for reporters to ensure their stories are accurate when published is to write them in a form which, as far as possible, does not need to be changed. Interviews should nail down the facts precisely. If you are in no doubt, the sub-editor should be in no doubt either. Don't accept other reporters' facts without checking them. You will sometimes need to check what you think you are sure of: remember the Rocket.

Begin with a striking news point and let the story unfold from there in a clear, unbroken flow of thought which sub-editors, and readers after them, can easily follow. Find out if possible the space available and write only the number of words required for the space. Explain technicalities simply. Be sure you understand precisely what the technicalities are.

Don't allow what you write to be influenced by any outside interests you may have.

Re-read your copy. Rewrite anything that is even slightly ambiguous. Ambiguities turn into falsehoods if rewritten by someone else. If at all possible, read the version of your story which is to be printed. (This also ensures that any late changes you or an editor have made actually reach the paper.)

But don't be in high dudgeon because your story has been changed. Sub-editors are more often right than wrong.

Press complaints

In 1989/1990 two Private Members' Bills on protection of privacy and the right of reply completed their committee stages in the House of Commons. In 1989, the Government appointed the Calcutt committee to look at how the privacy of individuals should be protected against press intrusion. The Calcutt Report suggested new legal curbs if the press did not behave. It led to the creation of a new Press Complaints Commission to secure compliance with a Code of Practice produced by a committee of editors.

This code calls for accuracy, the correction of errors, a chance to reply to published inaccuracies, and a clear distinction between comment, conjecture and fact. This last requirement is somewhat unrealistic, given the manner in which many leading journalists blend fact, explanation and comment. But wrapping up bias as fact is plainly wrong. The code outlaws harassment and declares intrusions into private lives without consent to be unacceptable unless justified in the public interest. In particular, journalists should obtain permission before entering non-public areas of hospitals. In inquiries involving personal grief or shock, they should be sympathetic and discreet.

They should not use subterfuge unless, in the public interest, they need information they cannot otherwise obtain. Unless in the public interest, they should not take away documents or photographs without the owner's consent. They should not interview children on subjects involving their welfare without a parent's consent. They should not approach children at school without the school's permission. They should protect confidential sources of information.

They should not make prejudicial references to someone's race, colour, religion, sex or sexual orientation, or give details of these unless they are directly relevant to a story. The code also includes provisions on court and crime reporting, set out in Chapter 8 of this book.

Complaints considered by the Commission raise some important points:

- **Addresses**. Normally, publishing the street where someone lives avoids confusion with other people of the same name. But it is wrong to publish a full address or otherwise identify a house if this puts people in danger or attracts unwelcome attention, unless the public interest is involved. Similarly, to avoid attracting the attention of burglars, do not give full addresses of well-known people or of those away on holiday or frequently travelling abroad.
- **Impartiality**. The Commission makes it clear that newspapers are not required to be impartial. It also states, however, that it is wrong to present only one side of a legal dispute. You can also cause offence by giving only one side of a local controversy.
- **Illustrations**. If you want to illustrate a critical report or one on some problem, get a relevant and up-to-date picture. Don't select a library photograph taken somewhere else or on some other occasion or for some other purpose. Don't use a smiling picture of a father with a report on an inquest into the death of his child.

- **Unwarranted assumptions**. Never make assumptions from the known facts. A man who advertises bluebell bulbs has not necessarily dug them up in the wood. He could have grown them.
- **Cuttings**. If using cuttings be careful they are not outdated or actionable. Try to ensure that a story in a cutting was not subsequently the subject of a correction or legal action.
- **Promises**. Do not give promises you are not in a position to fulfil. If you promise confidentiality, stick by what you say.
- **Notes**. Keep notes. You may need them if your story is challenged. Many newspapers require notebooks to be filed for a set period, such as three or six months, in case of legal action which questions accuracy. Libel actions can be started up to and sometimes more than a year after publication.
- **Plagiarism**. It is wrong to copy another writer's work. If you quote it, acknowledge the author.
- **Follow-ups**. If you follow up a story in another newspaper, check the facts and quotes it gives and make sure your own piece genuinely takes the story further.
- **Evidence**. Don't make allegations you cannot back up with facts.
- **Children**. Don't identify a child under 16 in a sex case even if the police have decided not to prosecute.
- **Names**. Don't publish the name of a sick person without permission.

Accountability

Fairness and accuracy are not everything. Newcomers to journalism might imagine that all they have to do is to get it right. There are other problems.

Several concern accountability. Except in rare circumstances, British journalists are not publicly accountable for what they write about and how they write about it, provided they stay within the law. Yet they perform public functions. They provide the public with news. They also provide a means by which public figures are called to account, dissenting opinions expressed, and society's assumptions challenged. Journalists' lack of accountability enables them to do this.

But lack of accountability also allows journalists to be sensational, damaging and unfair. Some critics complain that their attitudes and choice of subjects are too influenced by their bourgeois or Europeanized culture. Others complain they are not sensitive enough to women, to ethnic minorities and the disabled.

In Africa, where the bulk of journalism was until recently controlled by governing political parties, governments have tried to curb both the sensationalism and the criticism of the private press by appointing councils and restricting journalism to registered or well-qualified practitioners.

In much of the world (and in Britain in war situations), journalists are under pressure to heed the 'national interest' as defined by their government. In many countries this pressure is reinforced by wide-ranging laws on sedition and national security. But real national interest is usually better served by disclosure (by governments and journalists alike) than by self-censorship and suppression.

Informants

The duties which journalists owe to informants are to be fair and accurate in reporting and to respect their confidences. They are not obliged to omit what informants want omitted, nor to include what they want included.

The phrase 'off the record' presents a problem. If it means that a disclosure is not to be reported at all, it raises the question: what is the point of the disclosure? If speakers go 'off the record', it is as well to check what they mean. Some journalists publish anyway and leave the arguments for afterwards. If important people get carried away over lunch with a journalist, it is lame for them to claim afterwards that it was off the record. After all, they know who they were lunching with.

Confidential sources must be protected but informants might have their own reasons for giving you an exclusive story. If you realize you are being used, what do you do? The normal course must be to publish because self-censorship is pernicious and interferes with the readers' right to the information they are paying for. But bear in mind that the story is probably bigger than one informant's slanted version of it.

Many informants feel they have bought favourable reporting with a free lunch or free ticket. Often they have. There is a good story to tell and the well-lunched reporter tells it. However, reporters have to realize that there may be other points of view and that, if they get away from the official press party, they may hear different stories.

Serious ethical dilemmas do arise. Is it right, for instance, to accept a free trip and write glowingly of holidays in a country with an oppressive government which basks in favourable holiday publicity? Or, if the holiday piece is written, is there an obligation also to tell the other side of the story?

People in the news

People's lives are affected by what is published about them. Publicity can bring people new opportunities. It can also cause them to leave for another town or even another country.

Concern about abuse of children has brought a wave of publicity about past offenders which is understandable but also disturbing. The

Rehabilitation of Offenders Act protects people, sentenced to two and a half years or less, who have been going straight for some years. But hounding seems to have become almost respectable. Should journalists inflame the anger and fearfulness of the times?

A consensus is forming that people in the public eye should be prepared to accept publicity but that those out of it should be more kindly dealt with. However, some people in the public eye have been badly treated by intrusive journalists. At the same time, sparing the not so well known has a cost if important news of crime or disaster is involved.

It is unfair to report allegations about people unless there is evidence to support them. Serious allegations need to be backed by assiduously collected evidence, written if possible, because people who have provided spoken evidence may not back you up. Allegations against police officers, even unnamed, need careful handling. If they are not, the Police Federation may back a suit for libel. It won a string of cases before losing one to *The Guardian* in early 1997.

Journalists and their readers

Journalists are accountable to their editors who bear the legal responsibility for what is published. They also have an accountability to their readers for the accuracy of their reporting and the fairness of their conduct. Readers are a restraining influence on journalistic excesses. They also offer support.

Readers enjoy making comments and do not shrink from making complaints. Always listen to a complaint with courtesy and discuss a correction, if one seems appropriate, with your editor or news editor. In some cases the matter can be resolved by a published letter.

Some people advocate formal right of reply to opinions expressed in a newspaper. It is hard to see how this can be granted without cutting the space for news content. Editors may agree, however, to publish a reply.

There comes a point, however, where worrying about what other people think ceases to improve newspapers and impedes their work. Broadcasting executive John Wilson writes in *Understanding Journalism*: 'There is every reason to believe that in the media being more answerable means being less valuable.'

Further reading

Understanding Journalism (Routledge) by John Wilson, former editorial policy controller at the BBC, is primarily about broadcasting but gives much space to newspapers. Apart from ethics, it discusses libel, gagging injunctions and the case of freer access to official information.

20 CAREERS IN JOURNALISM

Newspaper reporting, as these chapters have shown, is a craft with rules and procedures, with techniques and deadlines. But it is not a job for anyone. Unlike practitioners in other professions, the reporter, even before formal training begins, has to have a flair with words and the urge to communicate in words.

There has to be a curiosity about the world around and a sympathy – an empathy even – with people and their situation and activities. It is a job big in human terms and human contact; a job that cannot exist merely at a desk or at the end of a telephone. If you're looking for a nine-to-five routine with a useful salary cheque at the end of the month it would be better to take up dentistry or the civil service.

An awareness of these things must be shown right from the very first job interview. Your hardest task will be to convince editors that you are the person they are looking for. For entry into journalism remains, as it ever was, a matter of personal approach between the aspirant and the editor whether the job has been advertised or you are writing on spec.

Your education must be right, of course. It is possible to get by on a clutch of high-grade GCSEs, but generally two A-levels, preferably in English with perhaps economics or a modern language, will be asked for. A degree in English or a media-related subject will count with some editors; today about half the entrants into newspaper training will have already taken degrees. Even more important will be any file of written articles you can present, published or unpublished, from school magazines or whatever – any indication that writing is in your blood.

Once you have been taken on by your first newspaper you become a trainee reporter, and your training starts immediately.

The NCTJ

British universities have now recognized journalism as a viable degree subject and are offering BA degrees in it. These will provide a useful grounding to students wishing to graduate before starting their career. Entry into the profession, however, whether for those with degrees or with A-levels, is subject as in other professions to a period of industry-based training which includes assessment, examinations and a professional qualification at the end.

The main training body for this purpose, and the one that since 1952 has regulated training for the industry, has been the National Council for the Training of Journalists, which is funded by provincial newspaper proprietors through the Newspaper Society, and operates from the Latton Bush Centre, Southern Way, Harlow, Essex. The council runs courses, sets examinations and awards a National Certificate to candidates after an approved course of study and the successful passing of examinations.

More than 750 candidates, approximately half of them women – the main annual intake of journalists in Britain – enter the NCTJ training scheme each year. They do this through one of two ways: as direct entrants, having found themselves jobs on newspapers, or as full-time students on a one-year pre-entry course run at colleges accredited by the NCTJ. For the pre-entry course a student does not have to find a job first, although a few are sponsored on half-pay by their newspaper.

The direct entrants, whether graduates or non-graduates, are registered by their newspaper, or news agency, with the NCTJ. Their editor is then sent a distance learning pack to present to them on their first day of employment. This consists of three ring binders containing fifteen units of printed learning material with self-assessment tasks, a video tape, eight audio tapes and a newspaper style book.

The distance learning pack includes instruction on the reporter's job and keyboarding, an introduction to shorthand and law, the elements of news writing and interviewing, rewriting handouts and covering local government, together with tutor-marked assignments, and it constitutes a foundation course which student journalists are expected to complete during the six months' probationary period working for their newspaper.

At the end of this period they are sent by their newspaper on a twelve-week block release course at a college accredited by the NCTJ. During this course they are assessed on the results of their foundation work and take preliminary examinations in newspaper journalism, law, public affairs and shorthand.

When these examinations have been passed and the trainee reporter has completed two years' on-job training in full-time employment, he or she is entitled to sit the National Certificate examination. This consists of four main sections: a face-to-face interview with telephone follow-through to produce a story; speech reporting, the write-up to include follow-up ideas; a news story, using information from several sources; and newspaper practice.

Holders of the Certificate will be awarded one credit by the Open University towards a degree.

Students, graduate or non-graduate – the latter must have two A-level passes and two GCSEs including English at either – who are accepted for the NCTJ's one year pre-entry course undertake full-time study, with examinations, at one of eight accredited colleges situated at: Harlow, Belfast, Cardiff, Redruth, Darlington, Portsmouth, Preston and Sheffield (which is also the base for press photography training). A number of these colleges are also used for direct-entry block release courses.

On completion of the course they join a newspaper (the pre-entry course is usually of help in finding a job) to continue their training in-house and proceed to the National Certificate examination after which they are deemed to be fully trained. In some areas local council grants are available for students accepted for the pre-entry course.

In-house training

To the young reporter, whether a direct entrant or from the pre-entry course, the on-job facilities at their first newspaper play a vital part in their training in the first two and a half years, and there is an increasing stress being placed by companies on in-house training arrangements. Many have a training officer or manager and perhaps a seminar room and the progress of trainees is carefully guided and assessed.

Some companies have fully fledged training programmes, many of them approved by the NCTJ and run in conjunction with their examinations. Others, for which you have to have obtained a job on one of the company's newspapers, issue their own certificates on completion of training. The principal in-house schemes are:

- Trinity International, Groat Market, Newcastle upon Tyne.
- The Journalism Training Centre (independent), St Leonard's-on-Sea, East Sussex.
- United Provincial Newspapers, Leeds.
- Eastern Counties Newspapers, Rouen Road, Norwich.
- Midland News Association, Old Hill, Tettenhall, Wolverhampton.
- Trinity Newspapers (Southern), Chester.
- Southern Newspapers, 1 High Street, Christchurch, Dorset.
- Emap Group Training Scheme, Peterborough, Northants.

There is some direct entry into national newspapers in specialized fields such as leader writing and financial journalism but national papers on the whole draw their staffs ready trained from provincial papers and have no training facilities of their own.

An advantage with provincial and local papers is the great range of work and experience offered to the young reporter. It is customary for three months' sub-editing experience to be included in in-house training, thus providing a useful first step towards skilled jobs on the editing and production side of newspapers. An opportunity to do industrial and political reporting and arts reviewing can sow the seeds of specialisms to come.

NVQs

An added emphasis was given to training arrangements by the introduction in 1992 of the Government's National Vocational Qualifications, which have been accepted by newspapers as they have by other industries.

These, whatever the job or profession, specify certain necessary standards of competence and knowledge based on in-house assessment by an approved training officer. The policy of the NCTJ and the independent in-company schemes is to provide the necessary training to enable students to qualify for the NVQ certificate at the same time as they undergo their professional training during their job.

NVQs are offered alongside the NCTJ's National Certificate though the possibility exists at the time of writing that the two might become merged.

Journalism degrees

BA degrees in journalism are now available at City University, London; the College of Printing, London; the London Institute, the City of Liverpool Community College, and at the universities of Wales (Cardiff), Central Lancashire (Preston), Liverpool John Moores, Bournemouth, Luton; Teesside, and Napier (Edinburgh); and also at Falmouth School of Art and Design and Southampton Institute of Higher Education.

These new degrees combine a practical induction into journalism with an academic examination of newspaper practice and attitudes. The main journalism content is offered alongside a subsidiary subject such as sociology or a modern language.

While, as with other vocationally based degrees such as those in law, commerce and economics, a journalism degree does not qualify a person for a career, it does provide a broad base on which to build for the professional training and examinations that follow. It also offers an attractive choice to students wishing to take a degree before starting career training, and to Commonwealth or foreign students seeking to acquire a graduate qualification in journalism rooted in British newspaper practice.

For some years there have been degrees in media studies available from universities and polytechnics. While some are heavily into sociology or linguistics and can disappoint students looking for a career in the media, more and more are offering vocationally based modules in such areas as newspaper and magazine journalism, broadcasting, public relations, advertising, typography and media design.

Typography, graphics and media design are given prominence in BA courses at Reading and Portsmouth Universities and at London University's Royal Holloway and Bedford College. The course at Reading has set a number of graduates on the road to careers in newspaper and magazine design.

Other courses

For the graduate there are one-year post-graduate diploma courses in newspaper journalism or TV and radio journalism at City University, London; the University of Central Lancashire; the University of Wales, Cardiff, and one run jointly by Glasgow Polytechnic and the University of Strathclyde.

Students can take a two-year Higher National Diploma in journalism at Napier Polytechnic, Edinburgh, or at West Surrey College of Art and Design. City College at Norwich also offers an HND in journalism.

Looking ahead, for reporters who have completed their training, there is an assortment of short courses run by the NCTJ in London, Rugby, Harlow and Scotland, and open to all comers, which include such subjects as financial journalism, sub-editing, news-editing, computer graphics, design, colour for newspapers and newspaper management. Special courses by the council's tutors are available to be run in-house.

Plans are also a foot, of particular benefit students abroad for the NCTJ to run correspondence courses leading to certificates in reporting and sub-editing and other areas of career journalism.

Access courses

Access courses are available for mature students seeking entry into newspaper journalism. The NCTJ supports one-year Access courses at a number of colleges of further education. Those successfully completing a course get a certificate equivalent to A-levels which gives access to the selection procedure for the NCTJ pre-entry course. Details can be obtained from the NCTJ (see page 231).

APPENDIX 1
INVESTIGATIVE
REPORTING

Most reporting presents people, events, companies and organizations at their face value: it does not make judgements. Investigative journalism does make them. It reports what critics say, and draws attention to mistakes and abuses. It exposes what – whether for good or ill – is happening in secret behind the public image.

Peter Watson worked on Insight for the *Sunday Times* and has since made two lengthy investigations in the art world. He says that to be an investigative journalist you have to get into a situation where people leak information to you. That means you have to know what you are talking about.

Three different types of article get grouped under the investigative heading:

1   Narratives retelling in detail the news story or scandal of the week. (Rupert Murdoch once described this as reporting in width.)
2   Leak journalism. Someone, for good or bad reasons, offers a story or documents putting someone else or some organization in a bad light.
3   Real detective work, set off by a news story or a chance remark by someone in the know. A building contractor suggested to Ray Fitzwalter, then of the *Telegraph and Argus*, Bradford, that he look into a firm called Open Systems Building. This led to the unmasking of John Poulson, an architect who had wangled contracts from several public authorities in North-East England.

It is often chance that opens an opportunity for investigation. Peter Watson, who had grown tired of being a psychiatrist, joined with Ludovic Kennedy in a successful campaign to win a pardon for a man jailed for murder in Scotland.

A little later a Scot who had been in jail in what was then Rhodesia called on him. He asked for £20 and said he had a message from a cellmate called Kenneth McIntosh. The message suggested it would be worth Watson's while to visit McIntosh's brother-in-law in Aberdeen. Watson did so, and the brother-in-law proved to have documents from McIntosh outlining a scheme by which the international sanctions against Rhodesia were being circumvented. Watson checked out the story and, after it was published in two issues of the *Sunday Times*, he was invited to join the Insight team.

One of Watson's stories exposed the control units which had been secretly set up in prisons. Some prisoners were sent to them for solitary confinement for 90 days. If they misbehaved, the 90 days began again; they could be in for as much as a year. Watson got a call from a friend of the sister of Michael Williams, a black prisoner. When he said he wanted to visit Williams, the sister told him he couldn't: Williams was in a control unit. So the story of the units was out.

Insight was initiated in the 1960s by Clive Irving and got into investigative reporting with its account of the adultery and downfall of the then War Minister, John Profumo.

The name Rachman cropped up on the fringes of the Profumo scandal. Irving's colleague, Ron Hall, had a friend in the property business; and so the story emerged of Rachman winkling out low-paying tenants so he could sell property at a profit.

Another Insight journalist, Colin Simpson, formerly worked in antiques and knew about rings formed by dealers to acquire goods cheaply and re-auction them among themselves. He joined a ring. The *Sunday Times* exposed the ring by sending reporters to interview its members simultaneously.

Another celebrated Insight exposé followed the collapse of the Fire, Auto and Marine (FAM) insurance company, which was run by a Sri Lankan, Emil Savundra. An MP remarked to Harold Evans, then chief assistant to the editor of the *Sunday Times:* 'It's interesting about this Pakistani who's got away with all this money.'

Evans rang a Sri Lankan friend, who told him that Savundra had been in trouble for fraud before. Simpson obtained a list of share certificates which FAM claimed to hold. Harold Evans telephoned the chairmen of the companies listed to see if FAM's claim was genuine. It wasn't.

Several journalists worked on different aspects of the Savundra story, demonstrating the advantage of having a team. Peter Watson points out that Insight's team of four could ask the same question in four places at once and compare the answers.

Watson's later freelance investigations have concerned art. He set out to write a book about thefts; but an art detective in Florence suggested it would be more interesting to try to recover stolen paintings. Watson posed as a buyer and got on the trail of a restorer in Northern Italy whose trick was to take away old pictures hung high in churches, and return them apparently restored. What he actually returned were copies. The originals went to New York, a priest acting as courier. Customs recovered several pictures and made arrests.

The crucial point about investigative reporting was made by a *Sunday Times* lawyer, James Evans. He said that any defamatory statement must be backed by legally admissible evidence. A tape recording of other people's conversation, for example, is not legally admissible. You can, however, make an admissible recording, even with a hidden recorder, if you are yourself a party to the conversation.

The James Evans dictum requires in point of fact a higher standard of investigation than a prosecution in court. A prosecution requires a case, supported by witnesses, for the defence to answer. A journalistic investigation, if it is to be libel-proof, must establish a case that the other side cannot answer.

Witnesses' allegations are not enough, particularly as they may not turn up in court. Ray Fitzwalter, who helped unmask the Poulson scandal, says that the best evidence is an original document.

Peter Watson's 1997 book *Sothebys: Inside Story* shows the difficulties, even with three cases full of documents. The papers you have may not tell the full story. You need to know that your documents tell the truth and that signatures are genuine. Particularly for television, you need a response from your quarry to any allegations you are making. But, if the documents are stolen, you cannot simply put questions and allegations to their owner, or he can stop you using them.

Watson was able to authenticate his documents partly by attending a court case in which they were used, partly by investigating the story they told. He traced antiquities from Indian villages to dealers in Bombay and London. He found people using a mechanical digger to break into ancient tombs in Italy. He got a woman, with a camera hidden in a brooch and a recorder in a bag, to make a deal in Milan to get an old painting to London in contravention of Italian law. In fact, in the end, Watson's hard evidence for his allegations about how some items come to be in art auctions was pictorial.

This suggests one reason why big-time investigative journalism has tended to move from newspapers to the pictorial medium of television. Newspapers also seem less willing than they used to be to allow journalists to spend months on inquiries which, even if successful, make only a couple of articles.

Nevertheless, important things are happening that are not necessarily recorded day by day in orthodox news stories. To watch a television documentary on recent history is to realize how much of what is now recognized as important was little noticed or understood at the time.

There is probably much about contemporary life which ought to be questioned. Asking the searching questions is part of the reporter's trade.

Further reading

The Pearl of Days, by Harold Hobson and others (Hamish Hamilton, 1972). Philip Knightley's chapters in this history of the *Sunday Times* discuss the early years of Insight.

Web of Corruption, by Ray Fitzwalter and David Taylor (Granada, 1983). Story of the Poulson affair.

Sothebys: Inside Story, by Peter Watson (Bloomsbury, 1997).

APPENDIX 2
CODE OF PRACTICE
FOR THE PRESS

The Press Complaints Commission is charged with enforcing the following Code of Practice which was framed by the newspaper and periodical industry and ratified by the Press Complaints Commission.

All members of the press have a duty to maintain the highest professional and ethical standards. In doing so, they should have regard to the provisions of this Code of Practice and to safeguarding the public's right to know.

Editors are responsible for the actions of journalists employed by their publications. They should also satisfy themselves as far as possible that material accepted from non-staff members was obtained in accordance with the Code.

While recognizing that this involves a substantial element of self-restraint by editors and journalists, it is designed to be acceptable in the context of a system of self-regulation. The Code applies in the spirit as well as in the letter.

It is the responsibility of editors to co-operate as swiftly as possible in PCC enquiries.

Any publication which is criticized by the PCC under one of the following clauses is duty bound to print the adjudication which follows in full and with due prominence.

1 Accuracy

(i) Newspapers and periodicals should take care not to publish inaccurate, misleading or distorted material.

(ii) Whenever it is recognized that a significant inaccuracy, misleading statement or distorted report has been published, it should be corrected promptly and with due prominence.

(iii) An apology should be published whenever appropriate.

(iv) A newspaper or periodical should always report fairly and accurately the outcome of an action for defamation to which it has been a party.

2 Opportunity to reply

A fair opportunity to reply to inaccuracies should be given to individuals or organizations when reasonably called for.

3 Comment, conjecture and fact

Newspapers, while free to be partisan, should distinguish clearly between comment, conjecture and fact.

4 Privacy

(i)   Intrusions and enquiries into an individual's private life without his or her consent including the use of long-lens photography to take pictures of people on private property without their consent are only acceptable when it can be shown that these are, or are reasonably believed to be, in the public interest.

(ii) Publication of material obtained under (i) above is only justified when the facts show that the public interest in served.

Note – private property is defined as (i) any private residence, together with its garden and outbuildings, but excluding any adjacent fields or parkland and the surrounding parts of the property within the unaided view of passers-by, (ii) hotel bedrooms (but not other areas in a hotel) and (iii) those parts of a hospital or nursing home where patients are treated or accommodated.

5 Listening devices

Unless justified by public interest, journalists should not obtain or publish material obtained by using clandestine listening devices or by intercepting private telephone conversations.

6 Hospitals

(i)   Journalists or photographers making enquiries at hospitals or similar institutions should identify themselves to a responsible executive and obtain permission before entering non-public areas.

(ii) The restrictions on intruding into privacy are particularly relevant to enquiries about individuals in hospitals or similar institutions.

7 Misrepresentation

(i) Journalists should not generally obtain or seek to obtain information or pictures through misrepresentation or subterfuge.
(ii) Unless in the public interest, documents or photographs should be removed only with the express consent of the owner.
(iii) Subterfuge can be justified only in the public interest and only when material cannot be obtained by any other means.

8 Harassment

(i) Journalists should neither obtain nor seek to obtain information or pictures through intimidation or harassment.
(ii) Unless their enquiries are in the public interest, journalists should not photograph individuals on private property (as defined in the note to Clause 4) without their consent; should not persist in telephoning or questioning individuals after having been asked to desist; should not remain on their property after having been asked to leave and should not follow them.
(iii) It is the responsibility of editors to ensure that these requirements are carried out.

9 Payment for articles

(i) Payment or offers of payment for stories or information should not be made directly or through agents to witnesses or potential witnesses in current criminal proceedings except where the material concerned ought to be published in the public interest and there is an overriding need to make or promise to make a payment for this to be done. Journalists must take every possible step to ensure that no financial dealings have influence on the evidence that those witnesses may give.

(An editor authorizing such a payment must be prepared to demonstrate that there is a legitimate public interest at stake involving matters that the public has a right to know. The payment or, where accepted, the offer of payment to any witness who is actually cited to give evidence should be disclosed to the prosecution and the defence and the witness should be advised of this.)

(ii) Payment or offers of payment for stories, pictures or information, should not be made directly or through agents to convicted or confessed criminals or their associates – who may include family, friends and colleagues – except where the material concerned ought to be published in the public interest and the payment is necessary for this to be done.

10   Intrusion into grief or shock

In cases involving personal grief or shock, enquiries should be carried out and approaches made with sympathy and discretion.

11   Innocent relatives and friends

Unless it is contrary to the public's right to know, the press should avoid identifying relatives or friends of persons convicted or accused of crime.

12   Interviewing or photographing children

(i) Journalists should not normally interview or photograph children under the age of 16 on subjects involving the welfare of the child or of any other child, in the absence of or without the consent of a parent or other adult who is responsible for the children.
(ii) Children should not be approached or photographed while at school without the permission of the school authorities.

13   Children in sex cases

1   The press should not, even where the law does not prohibit it, identify children under the age of 16 who are involved in cases concerning sexual offences, whether as victims or as witnesses or defendants.
2   In any press report of a case involving a sexual offence against a child–
   (i)   The adult should be identified.
   (ii) The word 'incest' should be avoided where a child victim might be identified.
   (iii) The offence should be described as 'serious offences against young children' or similar appropriate wording.

(iv) The child should not be identified.

(v) Care should be taken that nothing in the report implies the relationship between the accused and the child.

14 Victims of crime

The press should not identify victims of sexual assault or publish material likely to contribute to such identification unless there is adequate justification and, by law, they are free to do so.

15 Discrimination

(i) The press should avoid prejudicial or pejorative reference to a person's race, colour, religion, sex or sexual orientation or to any physical or mental illness or disability.

(ii) It should avoid publishing details of a person's race, colour, religion, sex or sexual orientation, unless these are directly relevant to the story.

16 Financial journalism

(i) Even where the law does not prohibit it, journalists should not use for their own profit, financial information they receive in advance of its general publication, nor should they pass such information to others.

(ii) They should not write about shares or securities in whose performance they know that they or their close families have a significant financial interest, without disclosing the interest to the editor or financial editor.

(iii) They should not buy or sell, either directly or through nominees or agents, shares or securities about which they have written recently or about which they intend to write in the near future.

17 Confidential sources

Journalists have a moral obligation to protect confidential sources of information.

18   The public interest

Clauses 4, 5, 7, 8 and 9 create exceptions which may be covered by invoking the public interest. For the purposes of this Code that is most easily defined as:

(i)   Detecting or exposing crime or a serious misdemeanour.
(ii) Protecting public health and safety.
(iii) Preventing the public from being misled by some statement or action of an individual or organization.

In any case raising issues beyond these three definitions the Press Complaints Commission will require a full explanation by the editor of the publication involved, seeking to demonstrate how the public interest was served.

Comments or suggestions regarding the content of the Code may be sent to the Secretary, Code of Practice Committee, Merchants House Buildings, 30 George Square, Glasgow G2 1EG

INDEX

ACAS, 150
Accountability, 227
Accuracy, 224, 239–40
Advertising, 11–12, 212, 216
Allen, Dave, 49
Amateur theatre, 94–6
Angling Times, 4
Arts reviewing:
  amateur theatre, 194–6
  books, 209–10
  drama festivals, 201–2
  films, 206–8
  general, 192–210
  music, 202–3
  news angles, 196
  pop, folk and jazz, 205–6
  professional theatre, 196–8
  reviewing techniques, 193–4
  shaping your review, 193–4
  singing, 203–5
  standards, 195
  television, 208–9
  theatre: background, 198
  theatre: conventions, 198–201
  theatre: who does what, 198–201

Balance sheets, 179–82
Bankruptcy proceedings, 100
Book reviewing, 209–10
Business and industrial reporting,
  145–54
Business Link, 146
Business Times, 50

Calcutt Committee, 225–6
Calls, 9–10
Careers:
  Access courses, 234
  correspondence courses, 234
  diploma courses, 234
  general 230–4
  HNDs, 234
  in-house training, 232–3
  journalism degrees, 230, 233
  media studies degrees, 234
  NCTJ, 230–3
  NVQs, 233
Chasing the facts, 13
Catch-lines, 73
Checking facts, 89
Chief reporter, 7, 12
Chief subeditor, 1
Christmas issues, 183
Children, 227, 242–3
Churches, 32, 102, 155–60
City column, 12
Code of Conduct, 14
Code of Practice, 239–44
Colour (pictures), 25
Comment, 186, 240
Committals for trial, 113–14
Complaints, 74–5, 225–7
Computer:
  electronic spike, 214
  entering text, 71–4, 213–16
  full page composition, 217–18
  screen copy-tasting, 214

Computer – *continued*
  split screen working, 215
  subbing on screen, 213–16
Confidential sources, 228, 243
Congo, 1–2, 5
Consistory courts, 102
Consumer guides, 183
Contacts, 9–10
Contempt of Court, 114–16
Contempt of Court Act (1981), 97,
    115–16
Contractions, 82–3
Copy input, 71–4, 213–16
Copy tasting, 214
Coroner's courts, 101
Councillors, 32, 124–33
Council meetings, 10, 124–33
County court, 100–1
Court of Arches, 102
Court reporting:
  consistory courts, 102
  coroner's courts, 101
  county court, 101–2
  courts-martial, 102–3
  court structure, 97–104
  crown courts, 98–9
  feature articles, 111–13
  general, 92–123
  High Court, 99, 115
  magistrates courts, 92–8
  privilege, 113
  reporting restrictions, 113–20
  tribunals and inquiries, 103–4
  youth courts, 97, 118
Courts-martial, 103–3
Cricket coverage, 165, 169–70, 174
Crown courts, 98–9
Crown Prosecution Service, 93–4
Cut-and-paste, 216–17
Cuttings, 12, 14, 219–20, 227

Daily Express, 71, 184
Daily Mail, 4, 49, 56, 61, 115, 131, 184
Dealing with people, 14–15
Defamation Act (1952), 113
Delane, John Thaddeus, 5
Department of the Environment, 116

Development corporations, 125
Diary columns, 12
Diary jobs, 8, 11, 26, 34–6
Discrimination, 243
Distance learning, 231
District reporting, 26–36
Divorce Courts, 119
Dobson, Christopher, 48
Dress, suitability of, 13
Dundee Courier, 131
Dundee Evening Telegraph, 131
Duyile, Dayo, 191

Editor:
  duties, 211–15
  letters to, 12
Elections and electioneering,
    136–9
Electoral procedure, 139–40
Employers, 145–7, 150–2
Employment Gazette, 20
Entering text, 71–4
Enterprise agencies, 125
Ethics:
  accountability, 227
  accuracy, need for, 224, 239–4
  addresses, 226
  children, 227, 242–3
  complaints, 225–7
  confidential sources, 228
  informants, 228
  illustrations, 226
  impartiality, 226
  news embellishment, 224–5
  plagiarism, 227
  privacy, 225–6, 225–6, 240
  promises, 227
  publicity, effect of, 228
European Parliament, 144
Evans, Harold, 3
Evans, James, 237
Evening Argus, Brighton, 110
Evening Press, York, 110–11, 131,
    189

Fairness, 15
Family proceedings, 118–19

Feature writing:
  behind the facts, 186
  building the text, 188–9
  comment, 186, 240
  consumer guides, 183
  finding ideas, 184–5
  general, 183–91
  good beginnings, 186–7
  illustrations, 185
  interviews, 185–6; *see also* 37–52
  leaders (editorial opinion), 190–1
  writing tips, 190–1
Film reviewing, 206–8
Financial journalism, 243
Financial Times, The, 4, 12, 199, 130, 184
Fitzwalter, Ray, 235, 237
Follow-ups, 12
Football coverage, 165–72, 174
Foreign words, 84–5
Freebies, 228

Glasgow, Alex, 191
Good taste, 75
Guardian, The, 4, 58, 61, 65, 229

Handling quotations, 68–70
Hansard, 134, 222
Harassment, 241
Hearst, William Randolph, 5
Herald, The, Glasgow, 63–4
High Court, 99, 115
Hidden stories, 48–9
Hillsborough disaster, 104
Hull Daily Mail, 24, 168

Idioms, 82
Independent, The, 50
Independent on Sunday, 83
Industrial journalism:
  chambers of commerce, 152
  company publications, 152
  definition, 145–6
  disputes, 148–50
  employers, 150–2
  employment and industry services, 152–3

general, 145–54
knowing companies, 146–7
shop stewards, 150
TECs (trade and enterprise councils), 146, 152–3
trade councils, 147–8
trade unions, 147–50
works councils, 150
Informants, 16–20, 228
In-house training, 232–3
Inquiries, 14, 29–31
Interviewing:
  attempts to vet copy, 51–2
  backgound, 38–9
  checking back, 46
  coaxing answers, 46
  controversial interviews, 47–8
  establishing confidence, 49–50
  general, 37–52
  hidden stories, 48–9
  preparation, 37–8
  reluctant people, 40–1
  second interviews, 49–50
  talking, 42–6
  telephone interviews, 47
  using your notebook, 42
  when interviews fail, 50–1
Intros, 53–61
Intrusion, 242
Investigative journalism, 235–8

Jane's All the World's Aircraft, 16
Jazz and pop reviews, 205–6
Journalism:
  Access courses, 234
  careers in, 230–4
  degrees, and courses, 233–4
  distance learning, 231
  in-house training, 232–3
  NVQs, 233
  post-graduate courses, 234

Lancaster Guardian, 11, 131
Lewis, Stephen, 189
Listening devices, 240
Local angles, 34–5

Local government:
  council meetings, 126–8
  council officers, 129
  development corporations, 125
  education, 124
  enterprise agencies, 125
  general, 124–33
  health matters, 124
  local councillor, the, 125–6
  ombudsman, 124
  radical change, 129–32
  services, 125
  writing up council meetings, 128,
    130–3
Local party politics, 126–4, 136–40
Lockerbie air crash, 116
London Evening Standard, 190
Looking things up:
  office cuttings library, 220
  office reference, 219
  personal cuttings, 219–20
  reference books, 220–3
Lord Chancellor's Department, 99,
  119

Magistrates' Courts, 92–8
Making inquiries, 14
Manchester Evening News, 72
Misrepresentation, 241
MPs, 9, 134–5,
Music reviewing, 202–6
Murdoch, Rupert, 184, 235
Musururwa, Willie, 184

National Certificate examination,
  231–2
National Union of Journalists, 14
New Fowler's Modern English Usage,
  89
News:
  definitions, 3, 55–6
  diary jobs, 8
  gathering, 7–20
  general principles, 5–6
  good and bad, 3–4
  ideas, 5–6, 10–12
  reports, 1–3, 5

  tip-offs, 8
  unexpected events, 8
  value, 1–4
News editor, 7–9
Newsgathering, 7–20
Newspaper:
  language, 77–91
  planning, 1–3
  structure, 211–18
Newsroom, 7–9, 213
Newspaper language:
  codes, 78
  contractions, 82–3
  current English, 81–2
  double meanings, 85
  foreign words 84–5
  idioms, 82
  loaded words, 89
  numbers, 71, 87–8
  political correctness, 88–9
  right word, the, 90
  right word order, 85
  sentence length, 79–80
  slang, 82–3
  technical language, 83–4
  variety and rhythm, 87
  worn phrases, 89–90
Newspaper structure:
  chain of command, 212
  copy input, 213–14
  copy tasting, 214
  page production, 216–18
  press and post-press, 218
  subediting, 211–16
  who does what, 211–13
News writing:
  being simple and precise, 59–61
  changing subjects, 67–8
  entering text, 71–4, 213–16
  explanations, 65
  fact and figures, 70–1
  good taste, 75
  grabbing the reader, 61–2
  handling quotations, 68–70
  helping the reader, 65
  opening sentence, 57–8
  order of facts, 62–4

presentation, 73–4
short reports, 75–6
starting with a quote, 56–7
what is news?, 55–6
where to begin, 54–5
writing to length, 70
Nigerian Institute of Journalism,
191
Northern Echo, The, 8, 187
Notebooks, 13, 42, 227
NSPCC, 97, 118
NVQs, 233
NUJ Code of Conduct, 14
Numbers, 71, 87–8

Obituaries, 12
Observer, The, 82
Ofori, Henry, 188, 190
Old Bailey, 97
Ombudsman, 124
Opportunity to reply, 240
Organizations, 31–3
Oxford Mail, 131

Page production:
cut-and-paste, 216–17
full page composition, 217
planning, 215
plate making, 218
web-offset presses, 218
Panorama (BBC), 132
Payment for articles, 241–2
Pears Cyclopaedia, 166
People, dealing with, 14–5, 21, 37–50
Photographers, working with, 22
Photographing children, 242
Pictures:
colour, 25
group, 25
ideas, 21–5
photographing children, 242
what makes a good one?, 23–5
Plagiarism, 227
Police:
organization, 121–3
useful telephone numbers, 123
Political correctness, 88–9

Political journalism:
elections and electioneering, 136–9
electoral procedure, 139–40
Independents, 136
local MP as news, 134–5
party activities, 136
party agent, 135
party organization, 140
Political parties, 32, 134–44
Porter, Marjorie, 90–1
Presentation (of text), 73–4
Press Association, 64, 214
Press Complaints Commission, 75,
108, 116, 120, 226–7, 239–44
Press Council, 75
Press cuttings, 12, 14, 219–20, 227
Privacy, 25–6, 225–6, 240
Privilege, 113
Probation Service, 120–1
Public interest (definition of), 244
Publicity, effects of, 228

Queen's Bench Divisional Court, 101
Quotations, 56–7, 68–70

Rape and indecency cases, 119–20,
242–3
Readers' letters, 11–12
Readership, 4–5
Reading newspapers, 10–12
Reference books, 220–3
Rehabilitation of Offenders Act, 229
Religion as news:
Hinduism and Sikhism, 160–1
Islam, 160
Judaism, 161–3
priests and ministers, 156–60
special behaviour, 161–2
useful telephone numbers, 164
weddings, 156
Reporting:
being fair, 15
being thorough, 15–16
calls, 9–10
chasing the facts, 12
contacts, 9–10, 29–34
council meetings, 124–33

Reporting – *continued*
  dealing with people, 14–15
  diary jobs, 8, 34–6
  district, 26–36
  entering text, 71–4, 213–16
  industrial, 145–56
  local angles, 34
  local geography, 28–9
  making inquiries, 14
  religions, 155–64
  restrictions, 113–20
  taking notes, 13–14, 42
  tools of the job, 13
  what makes a reporter, 27–8
  where to look, 16–20
  who to ask, 15–20
Reporting restrictions:
  Code of Practice, 120, 239–44
  committals for trial, 113–14
  contempt of court, 114–16
  crime stories, 116–18
  divorce courts, 119
  family proceedings, 118–19
  rape and indecency, 119–20
  young offenders courts, 118
Reuters, 214
Reuters' Handbook for Journalists, 90
Rules of sport, 166

Schools, 32, 175
Scott, C. P., 58
Short reports, 75–6
Shorter Oxford Dictionary, 3
Shorthand, 13–14
Show business, 12
Slang, 82–3
Spivey, Nigel, 184
Sporting briefs, 12
Sporting reference books, 175–6
Sports Councils, 174–5
Sports reporting:
  chat columns, 174
  colour and variety, 172–3
  going to a match, 165–7
  midweek sports writing, 173–5
  reference books, 175–6
  rules of sport, 166

  school matches, 175
  sports councils, 174–5
  statistics, 169, 174
  vocabulary, 173
  words and openings, 170–2
  writing your report, 167–73
Sports vocabulary, 173
Star, The, Sheffield, 67
Steyn, Mark, 190
Stipendiary magistrate, 92
Stock Exchange Year Book, 18
Subediting, 12, 211–16
Summarizing:
  balance sheets, 179–82
  long reports, 177–9
  short reports, 177
Sunday Telegraph, 116
Sunday Times, 41, 115, 235–7

Taking notes, 13–14, 42
Technical language, 83–4
Telegraph and Argus, Bradford, 235
Telephone interviews, 47
Television reviewing, 208–9
Terminals, 7–8, 72–3, 218
Times Guide to English Style, The,
  80–9
Thompson, Daley, 49
Times, The, 4, 5, 59, 172
Tip-offs, 8, 10
Toad shares, 1–2
Trades councils, 31, 147–8
Trade unions, 12, 147–50
Training programmes, 231–4
Tribunals and inquiries, 103–4
TUC, 147–8

Unexpected events, 8
Using your notebook, 42
Unions; *see* Trade unions

VDUs, 7–8, 72–3, 218
Venables, John, 4
Vetting copy, 52–2
Victims of crime, 243

Watson, Peter, 235–7

Weddings, coverage of, 156
Western Mail, 63
Whitaker's Almanack, 17
Wilson, John, 4, 224, 229

Worn phrases, 89–90
Worthing Herald, 131

Youth Courts, 97, 118